PRIVACY IN CONTEXT

PRIVACY IN CONTEXT

*Technology, Policy, and
the Integrity of Social Life*

Helen Nissenbaum

Stanford Law Books
An Imprint of Stanford University Press
Stanford, California

Stanford University Press
Stanford, California

Printed in the United States of America on acid-free, archival-quality paper

Library of Congress Cataloging-in-Publication Data
Nissenbaum, Helen Fay.
    Privacy in context : technology, policy, and the integrity of social life / Helen
Nissenbaum.
        p.   cm.
    Includes bibliographical references and index.
    ISBN 978-0-8047-5236-7 (cloth : alk. paper)—ISBN 978-0-8047-5237-4 (pbk. :
alk. paper)
        1. Privacy, Right of—United States.   2. Information technology—Social
aspects—United States.   3. Information policy—United States.   4. Social
norms.   I. Title.
JC596.2.U5N57   2010
323.44'80973—dc22   2009026320

Typeset by Westchester Book Composition in Minion, 10/14

For my mother
and in memory of my father ל״ז

Contents

Acknowledgments

IN WRITING THIS BOOK, I HAVE CHANNELED THE WISDOM, SUPPORT, influence, and inspiration of family, friends, colleagues, and institutions, which I acknowledge with appreciation.

The final push to complete the manuscript occurred in 2008 while I was on sabbatical leave from New York University (NYU). As a visitor in the School of Social Science, I enjoyed the outstanding working conditions at the Institute for Advanced Study (IAS) at Princeton. Seven years earlier, as a Member participating in the program on Information Technology and Society, key ideas for the book gelled. I am grateful for both of these opportunities and for the interest and encouragement of IAS permanent faculty present during both of my stays—Eric Maskin, Joan Scott, and Michael Walzer, whose *Spheres of Justice* served in many ways as a model for the framework of contextual integrity.

During the mid-1980s and early 1990s, as a graduate student and postdoctoral fellow at Stanford University, one of the epicenters of the digital boom, I was captivated by the promise of computers and information technology. There, many of the questions raised in the emerging field of "computer ethics," including those concerning privacy, took on an air of urgent reality. The opportunity to co-teach a course, "Computer Ethics and Social Responsibility," with Terry Winograd, expanded my horizons. Lively debates both inside and outside the classroom, and exposure to the organization Computer Professionals for Social Responsibility, revealed the importance of adopting broader societal and political perspectives on key issues in the field.

The Center for Human Values at Princeton University, newly founded in 1991 when I assumed the associate directorship, was an ideal setting for continuing this inquiry. Interactions with Amy Gutmann, George Kateb, and Jeremy Waldron advanced my understanding of fundamental political concepts and historical sources and approaches to evaluating public policy in ethical terms. Discussions with them and with visitors to the Center, including Ruth Gavison, whose paper on privacy is seminal, suggested how one might craft an approach to privacy simultaneously as a social issue, a moral and political value, and a stimulus for law and public policy. I am grateful for these opportunities.

I owe a debt of gratitude to Rachelle Hollander and Deborah G. Johnson, who, in distinctive ways, have been guiding visionaries for the philosophical study of ethics and information technology. Promoting the field, often in the face of skepticism and neglect, they supported numerous opportunities for intellectual engagement and encouraged me to believe I had something worthwhile to contribute. Lucas Introna and Jeroen van den Hoven, friends, collaborators, and coconspirators, have been key influences on my work, particularly in revealing to me unfamiliar philosophical theories of technology and distinctively European perspectives on privacy and data protection. At various conferences and speaking opportunities, I have benefited from insights of other philosophers: Philip Brey, Terry Bynum, Judith DeCew, Fran Grodzinsky, John Kleinig, Jim Moor, Kristin Shrader-Frechette, Herman Tavani, and John Weckert, who hosted me for a fortnight at the Centre for Applied Philosophy and Public Ethics, Canberra.

Concern over privacy as a social issue has burgeoned in recent decades. Threats posed by increasingly visible information systems, and radically visible events such as 9/11, have stimulated widespread interest in what previously had attracted a specialized if dedicated following. Preoccupation with privacy as a topic of research and scholarship has followed a similar trend. No longer the limited domain of a handful of philosophers, legal scholars, and political scientists, it constitutes an active field of inquiry cutting across disciplines and methodologies, still including philosophy, politics, and law, but also computer and information sciences, media studies, sociology, psychology, business, and anthropology. In academia, interest in privacy can be attributed not only to its growing urgency as a social issue but also to its richness as an intellectual problem.

No routine matter in any of these fields, unraveling the various mysteries of privacy calls for fundamental breakthroughs in each. As a result, privacy research and scholarship has proliferated and we ignore what is happening beyond the confines of our own disciplines at peril of missing great work. But making these forays often means feeling out of one's depth, straining to decode unfamiliar methods, strange terminology, and opaque symbolic representations. Accordingly, help from colleagues—academics, practitioners, and policy advocates—who shared and interpreted the wisdom of their respective fields has enriched the book's key concepts and arguments and directed me to useful findings and cases.

One such source of enrichment has been information law, where legal scholars, preoccupied not only with what the law says in relation to information technologies but what it ought to say for the benefit of humankind, welcomed me to their discussions. I am grateful to Niva Elkin-Koren for mind-bending conversations; Yochai Benkler for creating a place for me at NYU's Information Law Institute, and thus an ongoing link to legal scholarship; and Ian Kerr for revealing philosophical depth in legal issues. My knowledge of information and privacy law has been advanced by discussions with Anita Allen, Jack Balkin, Gaia Bernstein, Julie Cohen, Michael Froomkin, Wendy Gordon, Jerry Kang, Larry Lessig, Joel Reidenberg, Daniel Solove, Peter Swire, Jon Weinberg, and Tal Zarsky.

Langdon Winner's famous claim that technical artifacts *have* politics has been a long-standing call to action for me. It has meant scrutinizing technical systems and devices for systematic connections between their design and social, ethical, and political values, including privacy, and doing something about it. I have been fortunate to extend my grasp of these ideas in collaborations with fellow adherents: Mary Flanagan, Batya Friedman, Daniel Howe, Geof Bowker, Ed Felten, Peter Kahn, and Jean Camp. Conversations with Phil Agre about values in design and contextual integrity made me see that the descriptive account of informational norms had to be augmented by a robust evaluative component or be trapped in static conservatism.

Fascination with the science and technology of computing, information, and digital media is the seed and fuel of my enduring interest in privacy. Crossing boundaries into technical realms, however, is particularly difficult, so it was a stroke of luck when Joan Feigenbaum invited me to join a multi-institutional team, proposing a five-year project to the National Science Foundation, "Sensitive Information in a Wired World," better known by its acronym, PORTIA. In this context, conversations with Joan, Cynthia Dwork (about her work on differential privacy), Rebecca Wright, and Stephanie Forrest challenged me to clarify the framework and suggested its potential in applications to technical questions. Working with Dan Boneh on privacy in relation to vehicle safety communication systems helped me understand clever ideas behind authentication without identification, and suggested the unlikely connection with privacy in Web search. PORTIA also supported collaboration with John Mitchell, Adam Barth, and Anupam Datta, which resulted in a formal language for expressing context-relative informational norms—work that continues to this day. Probing discussions leading to our initial published findings forced me to sharpen the framework with marked departures from earlier versions. Also through PORTIA, I enjoyed two brief sojourns at the Santa Fe Institute, which offered an excellent place for cross-disciplinary discussion and quiet writing.

There is less in this book than there ought to be about important work in the social sciences, but what there is has been guided by valuable interactions with Oscar Gandy, Jonathan Grudin, David Lyon, Gary Marx, James Rule, Joe Turrow, and my colleague at NYU, Rodney Benson, with a crash course in social theory.

The inspiring and frustrating world of policy making and policy advocacy has provided much "grist for the mill." I have learned about achieving change in a complex, multilayered system from Deirdre Mulligan; about health privacy from Janlori Goldman; and about one of my most important case studies, problems with online access to public and court records, from Julian Gorelli (who introduced me to this issue), Grayson Barber, Robert Gellman, and Peter Winn. Pris Regan was my earliest mentor in this area and contextual integrity is, in many ways, a direct descendant of Regan's theory of the social value of privacy developed in her book *Legislating Privacy*.

Advocacy organizations such as the Electronic Frontier Foundation, the Center for Democracy and Technology, and Privacy International are not only champions of a right to privacy, but also fertile beds of information about it. My greatest debt, however, is to the Electronic Privacy Information Center for its unceasing advocacy and a Web site that is brimful of everything anyone might want to know about privacy law and policy. What has kept Marc Rotenberg going, particularly through times more hostile to privacy than the present, I will never know, but the world and certainly this book, are better for it.

As a member of faculty of NYU's Department of Media, Culture, and Communication, I have enjoyed the stimulation of energetic colleagues and benefited from the freedom to develop and teach courses on technology and privacy. Working with talented graduate students has enriched the work and extended its scope through their discoveries: Michael Zimmer has combined a study of privacy in vehicle safety communication systems with Web search and writes an important blog on technology and privacy; Bilge Yesil has studied the watchers and watched in surveillance settings; Travis Hall seeks cultural and historical meanings of biometrics; Solon Barocas is pursuing a political and philosophical understanding of data mining and profiling; and Daniel Howe single-handedly has coded *TrackMeNot*, a tool and an embodied idea for obfuscating Web search profiles.

For steering the project in its early stages, thanks are due to Amanda Moran, editor at Stanford University Press when the book proposal was initially accepted, and to Kate Wahl, current editor, guiding it past numerous subsequent milestones and knowing when to be firm and when to be forgiving. Thoughtful comments by Ian Kerr, Daniel Solove, and an anonymous reviewer for Stanford University Press resulted in many improvements to the text. Valuable research assistance was provided by Rachel Aridor, Timothy Weber, and John Fanning. I am indebted to Alice Marwick, without whose excellent work this book would have been impossible. She located critical cases and source materials and helped to lick an unruly text into shape with grace and coolheadedness.

Research grants have supported work on this book in essential ways: allowing time away from regular duties, enabling travel to conferences to present aspects of the theory and learn from related work of others, and drawing me into conversation with diverse groups of researchers and collaborators. I am grateful to the National Science Foundation for grants—SBR-9806234, Societal Values in an Age of Information Technology; ITR-0331542, Sensitive Information in a Wired World (PORTIA); CNS-0613893, Science of Design: Values at Play-Integrating Social Factors into Design; and CNS-0831124, Cyber-Trust: Privacy, Compliance and Information Risk in Complex Organizational Processes—and to the Air Force Office of Scientific Research, ONR BAA 07-036 (MURI), Collaborative Policies and Assured Information Sharing.

Sue Castagnetto and Lucy and Gill Harman have followed and encouraged this project over the long haul. Radha Hegde, friend and colleague, steadfastly held that a book could be completed one word at a time and supported this endeavor in countless multimedia chats.

This book is dedicated in love and gratitude to my family: Peter Sarnak, Dana, Zoe, and Ann for sustaining me with love and toleration and anchoring me in what truly matters; my sisters, Lydia Polonsky and Shirley Ehrlich, for cheering me on and shouldering great responsibility so I could keep working; and my parents, Rose and Mike Nissenbaum, for backing me in every way, all the way, with unflagging interest and unstinting faith and pride. Words are not adequate.

PRIVACY IN CONTEXT

Introduction

NFORMATION TECHNOLOGY IS CONSIDERED A MAJOR THREAT TO privacy because it enables pervasive surveillance, massive databases, and lightning-speed distribution of information across the globe. In fact, privacy has been one of the most enduring social issues associated with digital electronic information technologies. A fixture in public discourse at least since the 1960s, when the dominant concern was massive databases of government and other large institutions housed in large stand-alone computers, concerns have multiplied in type and extent as radical transformations of the technology have yielded the remarkable range of present-day systems, including distributed networking; the World Wide Web; mobile devices; video, audio, and biometric surveillance; global positioning; ubiquitous computing; social networks; sensor networks; databases of compiled information; data mining; and more. Associated with each of these developments is a set of worries about privacy. Whether expressed in the resigned grumbles of individuals, the vocal protests of advocacy groups and eloquent politicians, or the pages of scholarly publications and popular media, the common worry time and again is that an important value is a casualty of progress driven by technologies of information.

Countless books, articles, and commentaries call for reform in law and policy to shore up defenses against the erosion of privacy due to swelling ranks of technology-based systems practices. Many of them argue that protecting privacy means strictly limiting access to personal information or assuring people's right to control information about themselves. I disagree. What people care most about is not simply *restricting* the flow of information but ensuring that it flows *appropriately*, and an account of appropriate flow is given here through the framework of contextual integrity. The framework of contextual integrity provides a rigorous, substantive account of factors determining when people will perceive new information technologies and systems as threats to privacy; it not only predicts how people will react to such systems but also formulates an approach to evaluating these systems and prescribing legitimate responses to them.

Almost as many who have taken up the subject of privacy in relation to information technology have declared it deeply problematic, referring not only to questions and disagreements about its value, benefits, and harms but to its conceptual morass. Attempts to define it have been notoriously controversial and have been accused of vagueness and internal inconsistency—of being overly inclusive, excessively narrow, or insufficiently distinct from other value concepts. Believing conceptual murkiness to be a key obstacle to resolving problems, many have embarked on the treacherous path of defining privacy. As a prelude to addressing crucial substantive questions, they have sought to establish whether privacy is a claim, a right, an interest, a value, a preference, or merely a state of existence. They have defended accounts of privacy as a descriptive concept, a normative concept, a legal concept, or all three. They have taken positions on whether privacy applies only to information, to actions and decisions (the so-called constitutional rights to privacy), to special seclusion, or to all three. They have declared privacy relevant to all information, or only to a rarefied subset of personal, sensitive, or intimate information, and they have disagreed over whether it is a right to control and limit access or merely a measure of the degree of access others have to us and to information about us. They have posited links between privacy and anonymity, privacy and secrecy, privacy and confidentiality, and privacy and solitude.

Believing that one must define or provide an account of privacy before one can systematically address critical challenges can thwart further progress. Those who hold that a credible account is one that maps natural usage are confronted with a fractured, ambiguous, perhaps even incoherent concept and are understandably hard-pressed to unify the disparate strands of meaning. Maintaining all these meanings while delineating a concept to support policy, moral judgment, and technical design seems a hopeless ambition.[1]

Those who recognize the perils of inclusiveness attempt to purify the concept by trimming away some of the inconsistency and ambiguity, declaring certain uses wrong or confused. This has meant disputing the proper application of privacy to so-called constitutional cases, or it has meant rejecting control over information as part of the meaning of privacy in favor of degree of access, or vice versa.[2] A third strategy is to stipulate a precise definition necessary for a specific application without necessarily connecting this with natural etymology or a full natural meaning of the term; this is common in the works of computer scientists and engineers and necessary in relation to the purposes they clearly specify.[3]

In contrast, this book does not mediate its investigation of the unsettling stream of systems and practices through the concept of privacy. It does not carve a pathway through the conceptual quagmire to claim a definition—its definition—of privacy. Nevertheless, it is a book about privacy because it explains why the huge and growing set of technical systems and technology-based practices have provoked and continue to provoke anxiety, protest, and resistance in the name of privacy.

The framework of contextual integrity identifies the roots of bewilderment, resistance, and sometimes resignation expressed by experts and non-experts alike. According to the framework, finely calibrated systems of social norms, or rules, govern the flow of personal information in distinct social contexts (e.g., education, health care, and politics). These norms, which I call context-relative informational norms, define and sustain essential activities and key relationships and interests, protect people and groups against harm, and balance the distribution of power. Responsive to historical, cultural, and even geographic contingencies, informational norms evolve over time in distinct patterns from society to society. Information technologies alarm us when they flout these informational norms—when, in the words of the framework, they violate contextual integrity.

As troubled as we might be by technologies that diminish control over information about ourselves, even more deeply troubling are those that disregard entrenched norms because, as such, they threaten disruption to the very fabric of social life. To be sure, not all systems that alter the flow of information are cause for alarm, for there are clear cases of new information devices and systems that serve societal as well as context-based values, ends, and purposes better than those we already have in place (e.g., promoting intellectual development, health and well-being, and vibrant democracy). In such cases, the systems in question generally are and should be accepted, even celebrated.

Privacy and Personal Information Flow

Privacy is the initial organizing principle defining the scope of this book because, historically, it has been the term in which concerns, anxieties, and protests have been expressed. As the book proceeds, however, it frames its claims in terms of personal information flows, not only less encumbered with normative assumptions but useful for characterizing fundamental similarities at the heart of an otherwise disparate array of systems and devices. Because the book also seeks to provide an evaluation of these systems and devices in moral and political terms, the language of information flow allows us to sidestep certain of the disagreements and confusion associated with the concept of privacy and avoid potential question begging without sacrificing precision.

A related point about terminology: there is great ambiguity in the way "personal information" is used. Colloquially and in contexts of privacy law and policy, as well as academic research, it can mean sensitive or intimate information, any information about a person, or only personally identifying information. Here and throughout the book, following usage practices in the policy community, I use it to mean information about an identifiable person—for example, as defined in the European Union Directive, "personal data shall mean any information relating to an identified or identifiable natural person ('data subject'); an identifiable person is one who can be identified, directly or indirectly, in particular by reference to an identification number or to one or more factors specific to his physical, physiological, mental, economic, cultural or social identity."[4]

Technology and the Socio-technical

In the study of technology as a social and political phenomenon, many works acknowledge its diverse meanings but seek to build on those that ring true and are theoretically useful. In this book, too, it is important to explain, briefly, what I mean by technology as well as the related notion of a socio-technical system. To begin, consider the familiar telephone sitting on your desk. Upon initial reckoning you could see it as a self-standing technical device (think of the phone in the box when you purchased it), but its capacity to function as a telephone, enabling communication at a distance, requires that it be connected to a complex telecommunications system including all necessary hardware and software. Beyond these, a proper functioning telecommunications system depends on a host of social, political, and economic arrangements. Because complex interdependencies such as these are integral to the functioning of almost all of the technologies of contemporary societies, it is misleading to think of the study of technology's impacts on people and societies as an investigation of a stand-alone physical device—wires, hardware, and software. Rather, the object of study is the device construed in terms of key social interdependencies, as responsible for its features, function, and impact as for its physical characteristics.

In the case of the telephone, its observable characteristics in the box but disconnected from broader technical and social systems might include, say, the sound tones it makes when keys are pressed, its capacity to cause a gash on someone's head if dropped from a certain height, or its aesthetic and ergonomic qualities. But many of the most interesting features of "the telephone," including past and predicted societal impacts, are due to its properties as an embedded device. When observing, say, its effects on workplace hierarchy, on the home, on friendship, on the aged, on law enforcement, on urban development, and so forth, we do not mean the telephone in the box but the telephone connected to a telecommunications system, regulated by a host of technical standards, public policies, and even social and cultural norms. These dependencies are more evident in systems and devices that require customization, such as a closed-circuit television (CCTV) security system requiring knowledge of movement patterns in the area targeted for surveillance, but they are evident in many others, such as the automobile, and even in those we consider "plug and play," such as dishwashers and televisions.

Conscious of these complex interdependencies when referring to "the telephone," "the automobile," "the computer," and "the Internet," and wishing to highlight them, scholars of the social and humanistic study of technology refer to them as socio-technical devices and systems. Likewise, it is important to bear in mind that the devices and systems—technologies—of concern in this book, namely, those altering the flow of personal information in radical and radically worrying ways, are socio-technical. For example, radio frequency identification (RFID) technology or vehicle safety communications systems (VSCS) (discussed in Chapter 1), which might at first glance appear to be *pure* technologies, cannot be properly understood without grasping their definitional components, "identification," "safety," and "communication," all thoroughly social. Thus, when investigating why and how technological devices and systems, including RFID technologies, provoke anxiety, protest, concern, and resistance in the name of privacy, I am thinking of them as *socio-technical*; they affect us not purely by dint of physical or material properties but by properties they acquire as systems and devices embedded in larger material and social networks and webs of meaning. Accordingly, the terms "socio-technical systems and devices" and "technology-based systems and practices" are used throughout the book, but even when "technology" is used alone it should be read with awareness of the larger picture.

Contextual Integrity as a Justificatory Framework

The starting place of this book is the myriad socio-technical systems, devices, and associated practices that control, manage, and steer the flow of personal information, particularly those that have precipitated radical changes, aroused suspicion, caused anxiety, and drawn protest and resistance. They are experienced and registered as threats to and violations of privacy not only individually, case by case, but in aggregate amounting to a social crisis, a watershed: privacy itself is in jeopardy not merely in one or another instance but under attack as a general, societal value. The primary mission of this book is to confront and give a moral and political account of this pileup of technologies and practices, to pinpoint and understand sources of concern, and to provide a framework for expressing and justifying constraints expressed as social norms, policies, law, and technical design.

It is important to recognize, however, that reactions to these systems are not uniform. Nor is it the case that all systems affecting the flows of information are resisted; some are not only ignored and tolerated but are even welcomed and celebrated. In healthcare environments such as hospitals and nursing homes, for example, a plethora of devices such as blood-pressure monitors, pulse oximeters, ECGs, and EEGs complement attentive, responsive caregivers and enhance the close monitoring and recording of patients' condition that is one of the hallmarks of high-quality care. By contrast, video surveillance of public parks, frequent shoppers' card store loyalty programs, government wiretapping of telephone calls, and monitoring online transactions, also resulting in alterations of information flow, are greeted with suspicion and resentment. A satisfactory moral and political account needs to explore and explain these contrasts, to understand the sources of disagreement and conflict, and to offer approaches to resolving or at least meliorating them.

As the privacy conundrum has grown in public awareness it has attracted the attention of leaders in all social sectors, including business, government, and education, as well as scholars and researchers across the disciplines. Respondents have taken on its challenges in various ways, advocating certain public policies or promulgating guidelines within business, financial, and healthcare organizations. Legal scholars have developed and championed approaches to privacy law, both advocating for certain regulations as well as recommending to courts how to interpret existing law and past cases to afford adequate protection of privacy rights in conflicts and disagreements over the flows of personal information. Concern over privacy has also reached the scientific world of technical development and deployment, not only yielding a dedicated array of privacy preserving technologies but also leading to the adoption of hardware and software design standards by companies and consortia.

The framework of contextual integrity developed in this book does not lie fully within any one of these efforts, though it complements them (and vice versa). Like them, it attends to policy and regulation, court decisions and law, and technology design and implementation, and it prescribes or expresses support for certain directions over others. Its primary mission, however, is to articulate a foundation for these directions so we may answer questions not only of the form: *what* policies, *what* court decisions, *what* technical standards and design features, but *why* these, with answers rooted in humanistic moral and political traditions of contemporary liberal democracies. The framework provides a way to characterize systems and practices dramatically affecting the flows of information. It provides a language, a form of expression, for explaining when and why they are troubling, whether the balance of reasons favors one side or another, and (in cases of conflict) serves as the basis for prescribing courses of action, decisions, policies, and designs. In relation to perennially hard cases, the framework of contextual integrity enriches our expressive capacity for adjudication.

Comparing Contextual Integrity with Other "Justificatory Approaches"

There is, by now, a huge body of work on privacy threats of technologies developed by academic researchers, public interest advocates, legal practitioners and theorists, technology designers, and policy makers. Their purposes are not only to describe and prescribe but, like mine, to articulate systems of reasoning, to articulate justificatory frameworks—though not necessarily described in these terms by their authors.

One such approach, frequently adopted in policy-making, legal, and advocacy arenas, highlights the interest politics inherent in controversial systems and practices. Interested parties and their advocates scrutinize these systems for potential impacts on respective rights, interests, benefits, and harms. In general, controversial systems are ones found to be unbalanced in the interests they serve. Uncontroversial acceptance of healthcare monitoring systems can be explained by pointing to the roughly even service to the interests of patients, hospitals, healthcare professionals, and so on, while video surveillance in public parks is perceived to serve the interests of the watchers (e.g., law enforcement personnel) while diminishing the liberties of parkgoers, and online logging and surveillance is seen as promoting the interests of advertisers and marketers but diminishing consumer bargaining power and autonomy.

It is not uncommon for the resolution of such conflicts to involve hard-fought interest brawls, each side campaigning on behalf of privacy or against it, in favor of regulation of practice or the opposite (so-called self-regulation), for more invasive monitoring or less, and so on. Business and government interests in accumulating and using personal information have often prevailed in the face of public complaints, with a few well-known exceptions. One such exception, Lotus Marketplace: Households, a consumer data aggregation on millions of American households that was to have been distributed and sold in CD-ROM format, was quashed by its corporate backers in 1991 as a consequence of public outcry and well-orchestrated resistance by privacy advocacy organizations. In another, also following public, media, and internal criticism, Congress cut funding for the Defense Advanced Research Projects Agency's Office of Information, which would have administered a counterterrorism program proposed by Admiral John Pointdexter (formerly a U.S. National Security Advisor to Ronald Reagan) using "total information awareness" to pre-empt future attacks.

The trouble with settling conflicts through brute clashes among interest holders is the advantage it gives to those possessing advantages of power, resources, and the capacity for unremitting persistence, favoring corporate and governmental actors over the public interest in the long run. In retrospect, it is clear that the victories of Lotus Marketplace: Households and Total Information Awareness (TIA, later dubbed "Terrorist Information Awareness") have been short-lived as they have been resurrected in other more potent, more insidious forms, namely, private sector information service providers such as ChoicePoint (discussed in Chapter 2) as well as fusion centers, creations of state and city government for sharing information among agencies, and data aggregates developed by national security agencies. Although there may be several reasons why Lotus Marketplace: Households and TIA failed and fusion centers and contemporary information brokers continue to flourish, still sorely lacking from public discussions of these systems and programs is a clear understanding of what makes one acceptable and another unacceptable. Still missing, in other words, is a justificatory platform or framework to reason in moral terms about them. A brute competition among interests might win the day, but for a particular case to serve as a precedent that carries forward into the future, advocates need to be able to show that a framework of widely accepted principles supporting the first case can also apply to cases in question. When corporate backers of Lotus Marketplace: Households capitulated, they acknowledged no moral (or legal) wrongdoing, saying simply that it had become a public relations nightmare. In bowing to public outcry but conceding no ground, in principle they denied their critics the power of precedence and entrenched the interest brawl as a salient form of settling privacy disputes.

Although interest politics may be disguised in sophisticated rhetoric when concerned parties attempt to link the interests of others, even those of the public, with their own, other approaches make the case for privacy explicitly in terms of universal human principles and values. Countless works, many of them brilliant, have defended privacy as a fundamental human right (not merely a preference or an interest) by linking it to other values with long-standing moral, political, and legal pedigrees. These works have shown privacy to be a form and expression of self-ownership, an aspect of the right to be let alone, a cornerstone of liberty and autonomy, or a necessary condition for trust, friendship, creativity, and moral autonomy. The shortcoming of these works, and this approach, is not that it gets things wrong, generally speaking, but that it leaves a gap. This gap is acutely felt for those who are interested in analyzing controversial systems and in the practical mission of prescribing sound decisions in relation to them.

So, where does the framework of contextual integrity fit? A spatial metaphor may help answer this question. Consider a few of the controversial questions confronting us at the time of writing this book: whether it is morally wrong for Google Maps' Street View to include images of identifiable individuals (or their possessions) without permission, whether the FBI should be allowed to coerce librarians to divulge a library's lending logs, whether Internet service providers are entitled to track customers' clickstreams and sell them at will, whether one may post a tagged group photograph of others on one's Facebook page, whether insurance companies violate client privacy when they generate massive databases pooled from information about their clients, whether the police should be permitted to erect covert license plate recognition systems at public intersections, and so on.

Drawing on the spatial metaphor, let us place interest politics on the bottom, on the hard ground of concrete, gritty, detail. Whether the interest-brawls, as I have called them, are won and lost through force of rhetoric, brute resources, or the give-and-take of compromise and accommodation, reached by parties themselves or imposed by third-party mediators such as the courts or the marketplace, they involve concrete detail specific to respective cases in question.

If interest-brawls are conceived as taking place at ground level, appeals to universal human values and moral and political principles take place in the stratospheres of abstraction because resolutions for real-world disputes are sought in the realms of general values and principles. In the case of Street View, one may argue that it violates self-ownership; the FBI may be accused of overstepping principles of liberal democracy constituting the relationship between citizens and government actors; insurance companies might be accused of undermining personal autonomy. Although insight can be gained in identifying connections to higher-order values and principles, a common challenge to such reasoning is conflict, not only at the ground level of interests but at vaunted levels of abstraction—for example, in noting that individual liberty conflicts with national security, personal autonomy with freedoms of business institutions implicit in a free-market economy, and moral autonomy with social order.

Between the ground and the heavens, according to the picture I am imagining, is the realm of the social, and it is in this realm that contextual integrity fits. This middle realm holds a key to explaining why people react to real-world disputes in the ways they do and why they frequently express their alarm in terms of the erosion of privacy. Although it remains crucial to the understanding of these disputes that we grasp the configurations of interests, values, and principles present in them, our capacity to explain them is diminished if we attend to these elements alone, blind to the sway of social structures and norms. Tethered to fundamental moral and political principles, enriched by key social elements, the framework of contextual integrity is sufficiently expressive to model peoples' reactions to troubling technology-based systems and practices as well as to formulate normative guidelines for policy, action, and design.

Book Outline

The book comprises three parts, each comprising three chapters. Part I is devoted to technology, Part II to predominant approaches to privacy that have influenced and informed contextual integrity. Part III develops the framework of contextual integrity, circling back to technologies discussed in Part I and illustrating its application to these and others.

Part I

Part I is a contemporary snapshot of the landscape of technologies and sociotechnical systems, including a few detailed close-ups. One at a time, it is not difficult to recognize a technical system or technology-based practice as one that threatens privacy. But when considered together in a single class, they present an array of bewildering variety and the task of classifying them according to common features proves to be daunting. Yes, they affect the flows of personal information and threaten privacy, but that is not a terribly illuminating observation. Given its importance to the project as a whole, finding a satisfactory way of characterizing these technology-based systems and practices was, however, a challenge that could not be finessed.

The structure on which I settled is described in the three chapters, each mapping onto one of three capacities: (1) tracking and monitoring, (2) aggregation and analysis, and (3) dissemination and publication. It is important to note that systems and practices do not fit uniquely into only one of these categories but may incorporate more than one of the capacities and possibly even all three.

Chapter 1 surveys the vast array of technology-based systems and practices whose capacity to track and monitor people lies at the root of privacy worries, protests, and resistance. Expansion of this array is due not to any single technological breakthrough but rather to many breakthroughs, amplified by incremental advances in supporting technologies, such as input or information capture devices (such as digital photography and sound recording), digital encoding algorithms, network transmission mechanisms, information storage capacity, and general software controls. These, in various combinations and permutations, constitute the substrate for monitoring and tracking. Although attention has focused primarily on highly visible applications such as video surveillance, wiretapping, and online monitoring of Web transactions, this category includes a slew of less obtrusive, more specialized systems, some already in operation and many others under development and poised to enter the mainstream. From the mundane frequent shoppers' card to the myriad services cropping up in all walks of life, such as the one offered by wireless telephone providers to parents to track their children's movements (e.g., Verizon's "Chaperone"), to the well-meaning "intelligent homes" equipped with sundry embedded sensors enabling the elderly to live independently, to the somewhat more sinister watchfulness of workplace e-mail surveillance, these systems keep track episodically or continuously of people's whereabouts, activities, and attributes. The chapter offers a selective survey of this class of systems, with an in-depth focus on radio frequency identification technology.

Systems for monitoring and tracking are often highly visible, but the legendary powers of computing and information technologies to store and manipulate information have, arguably, contributed far more to technology-based privacy challenges. Chapter 2 presents a small sample of the breathtaking array of systems facilitated by these capacities, such as "back-end" storage capacities that are essential for almost all tracking and monitoring systems. Increasingly effective scientific approaches to organizing, analyzing, manipulating, storing, retrieving, and transmitting information make the information stored in stand-alone and distributed databases increasingly useful. Furthermore, these competencies, once affordable only to government and large financial institutions, are now widely dispersed, with the result that information is lodged not only in obvious and familiar places but in places we cannot even begin to guess. Drawing on media reports and scholarship, Chapter 2 surveys some of these, focusing on the emergent niche of corporate information brokers, such as ChoicePoint, providing a wide range of information services in the private and public sectors.

A third general capacity afforded by computing and information sciences and technologies is the capacity to disseminate, transmit, communicate, broadcast, or publish and publicize information. As with the other two, this capacity was initially exploited by a few large institutional actors such as news and other centralized broadcast media but rapidly has promulgated throughout society, due mostly to progress in and wide adoption of digital communications networks, predominantly the Internet and the World Wide Web. Chapter 3 discusses hard privacy issues raised by these remarkable technology-based changes, with extended attention devoted to two cases: (1) the placement of public records, including court records, on the Web and (2) the intriguing challenges posed by so-called Web 2.0 applications, including social networking sites such as Facebook and MySpace.

Part II

Part II offers a critical survey of predominant approaches to privacy, sampling explicit principles guiding law and policy as well as several leading theoretical contributions. It is impossible, in the scope of this book, to provide detailed and systematic accounts of individual theories. Rather, my intention is to explore predominant themes and principles as well as a few of the well-known theories that embody them.

Chapter 4 identifies two general approaches to explaining the sources of privacy's importance as a right, or a value, deserving moral consideration as well as legal protection. One attributes the value of privacy to the crucial role it plays in supporting other moral and political rights and values. The other locates privacy's value in the critical role it plays protecting the sphere of the private. Most of Chapter 4 is devoted to the first of these.

One of the charges frequently leveled against privacy advocacy and scholarship is that its sprawling domain is difficult, if not impossible, to capture with a coherent and distinctive concept. Chapter 5 discusses the approach to containing this conceptual sprawl, based on the private-public dichotomy, which holds that a right to privacy extends only across zones of life considered private. A commitment to this thesis, which has been compelling to both practitioners and scholars, is evident in the literature on privacy as well as in policy formation and key court rulings where privacy protection has attached to private information, private space, and private activities but not to their public counterparts.

Chapter 6, constructing a bridge to Part III, highlights challenges posed by technology-based systems to these theories and paradigms. One recurring skeptical challenge, for instance, cites the lack of concern many people seem to demonstrate in day-to-day behaviors, contradicting claims that privacy is a deeply important moral and political value that deserves stringent protection. Another is the clearly evident cultural and historical variation in commitments to privacy, hard to explain if privacy is supposed to be a fundamental human right. A third points to the difficulty of resolving conflicts between privacy and other moral and political values, such as property, accountability, and security. Most puzzling of all, however, is the problem of privacy in public, which challenges accounts of privacy that rely on the private-public dichotomy. The framework of contextual integrity is able to respond to them all.

Part III
Part III explicates the framework of contextual integrity. The central claim is that contextual integrity captures the meaning of privacy in relation to personal information; predicts people's reactions to new technologies because it captures what we care about when we question, protest, and resist them; and finally, offers a way to carefully evaluate these disruptive technologies. In addition, the framework yields practical, step-by-step guidelines for evaluating systems in question, which it calls the CI Decision Heuristic and the Augmented CI Decision Heuristic.

Chapter 7 introduces key features of the framework beginning with the basic building block of social contexts; the underlying thesis is that social activity occurs in contexts and is governed by context-relative norms. Among these, informational norms govern the flow of information about a subject from one party to another, taking account of the capacities (or roles) in which the parties act, the types of information, and the principles under which this information is transmitted among the parties. We can think of contextual integrity as a metric, preserved when informational norms within a context are respected and violated when they are contravened. Whether contextual integrity is preserved or violated by a newly introduced system or practice is claimed to be predictive of people's reactions—whether they protest, accept, or even welcome it.

Chapter 8 addresses a potential limitation of the framework of contextual integrity, which, to this point, requires compliance with entrenched social norms. To avoid the charge of stodginess and conservatism, it needs to incorporate ways not only to detect whether practices run afoul of entrenched norms but to allow that divergent practices may at times be "better" than those prescribed by existing norms. This requirement is accommodated by an augmented analysis that begins with a presumption in favor of entrenched or normative practices, based on the belief that they are likely to reflect settled accommodation among diverse claims and interests. A presumption in favor does not, however, preclude legitimate challenges, and the approach developed in Chapter 8 looks to a context's internal purposes, ends, and values for benchmarks against which entrenched and novel practices may be evaluated and compared. Accordingly, the augmented framework of contextual integrity tells us that new technologies deserve to be embraced when they help achieve important social and context-based ends more effectively than was possible prior to their use.

In Chapter 9 the book circles back to problems and scenarios that were introduced in earlier chapters, showing how the framework of contextual integrity resolves or avoids them. For instance, because contextual integrity demands appropriate flow and not merely control and secrecy, it predicts the behaviors skeptics cite as paradoxical and it also avoids the problem of privacy in public. It readily explains historical and cultural variability, for although the requirement of contextual integrity is universal, variation naturally enters the picture. First, because informational norms are context relative, targeted to specific ends, values, and purposes of these contexts, they must take local requirements of place and time into consideration, at least in the ideal case. Second, relativity is an inherent feature of contexts themselves because different societies evolve different configurations of contexts, resulting in different configurations of actors, attributes, and so on that create the parameters that characterize informational norms. How and why these configurations differ—across distance, time, ethnicity, religion, and nation—is a fascinating question for historians, sociologists, anthropologists, and others, but outside the scope of this book (and this author's expertise). This all means that historical and cultural variation is not an awkward fact needing explanation but is directly predicted by the framework.

Although chapters 7 and 8 both discuss contextual integrity in terms of real and hypothetical cases, it is Chapter 9 that demonstrates, in detail, the application of contextual integrity to several of the controversial technology-based systems and practices introduced in Part I.

Scope

I have tried, where possible, to incorporate parallel experiences and significant legal and policy milestones in countries beyond the United States, for example, the European Union Directive, Canadian case law, and the UK experience with CCTV. Readers will see, however, that my reference points on policy and regulation, legal doctrine, and case law are drawn from the U.S. experience. The framework was conceived in the United States and informed by local dramas and rhetoric, public experience, technological milieu, media and landscape, and exemplary or inadequate policy choices, decisions, and practices. Does this mean that contextual integrity is applicable only to the United States? I believe not. It is set forth as a justificatory framework for all people and all societies in which information about people has context-specific function and meaning, and it is governed by norms that systematically reflect these meanings and functions in relation to context-specific ends, purposes, and values. Although many actual examples are drawn from the U.S. experience, there is no reason that key themes and principles should not apply wherever people act and transact in social contexts roughly as I have described.

It must also be acknowledged that the book reflects experience only with technologies of the moment (and the foreseeable but near future). Even in the period over which this book was written, on any given day, month, or year, I could have drawn on different sets of cases, depending on what happened to be front and center at that moment, affected by scientific breakthroughs and historical contingencies. Despite this, I like to think that the framework of contextual integrity transcends particulars of the specific technologies selected for detailed analysis and would apply as well to others. The book's purpose, after all, is to articulate a robust conceptual framework for understanding, evaluating, and resolving critical privacy challenges of the day, past and future.

Finally, the research and scholarship that has most directly influenced this book extends across legal, political, and moral philosophy as well as policy analysis though, to be sure, there are gaps in coverage and, perhaps, disputed interpretations. For readers interested in a broader range of works, the References section provides a useful launch point. Beyond this, there is a growing body of important work on privacy in the empirical social sciences, which deserves more attention than this book has been able to give it. This work is particularly relevant because the framework of contextual integrity asserts empirical predictions about actual conditions under which disruptions of flow are likely to draw protest, in contrast with those that are likely to please. Accordingly, important directions for future work on the concept and framework of contextual integrity include checking the plausibility of these predictions against historical findings as well as developing testable hypotheses from them and examining these within research rubrics of the social sciences in natural as well as experimental settings.

PART I

INFORMATION TECHNOLOGY'S POWER AND THREAT

OVER A CENTURY AGO, SAMUEL WARREN AND LOUIS Brandeis started a conversation in the United States about the need for a comprehensive legal right to privacy. They warned, "Instantaneous photographs and newspaper enterprise have invaded the sacred precincts of the private and domestic life; and numerous mechanical devices threaten to make good the prediction that 'what is whispered in the closet shall be proclaimed from the house-tops'" (1890, 195). Although the discussion they provoked in the legal community was and continues to be important, their warning resounds here not so much for its legal ramifications as for its acute insight into the ways new technologies can so disrupt social life and practices as to threaten moral and political values. In Warren and Brandeis's day, the disruptive technical advances were in photography, which enabled the capture of people's images at a distance and without their permission. Combined with efficient printing machinery, this allowed for cheap publication and wide dissemination of these images.

In the past few decades, privacy has been the rallying cry against another family of technologies: computer-based, digital electronic technologies that have hugely magnified the power of human beings over information. We are able, individually and in groups (organizations, institutions, societies), to gather, store, communicate, analyze, play with, and use information in historically unprecedented ways.

These novel actions and practices have aroused a range of reactions from wonder to fear, from hope to indignation, and from resignation to outrage, giving rise to predictable and recurring cycles of public controversy. This book offers a way to understand and evaluate this newfound power.

In predictable and recurring cycles, newly introduced systems and practices stimulate public controversy. Amid swirling disagreement and confusion, opposing sides with differing viewpoints jockey for public support and, ultimately, victory in the relevant venues—marketplace, court, media, or legislature. Part I provides readers a snapshot of the technological landscape, a contemporary sample of socio-technical systems that have raised hackles and often served as spurs for public debate.

To help structure what otherwise is a long and bewildering list, I have found it useful to organize relevant technology-based systems and practices into three rough categories organized around key functional characteristics or capacities.[1] The first is the capacity to monitor and track: to watch over people, to capture information about them, and to follow them through time and space. There is great variability in such devices and systems, not only in how they are embedded in society and the purposes they serve but also in how they function—for example, whether monitoring and tracking is conducted visually, through the recording of sound and touch, or accumulations of biographical information; whether it occurs for a mere instant or for an extended period of time; whether it is in full view or surreptitious.

A second category, labeled "aggregation and analysis," covers the general capacity to store and analyze information. When hashed out in detail, this ability extends across a prodigious array of functions, such as the capacity to store massive amounts of information indefinitely; to merge information from diverse sources; and to search, find, retrieve, organize, scrutinize, and analyze information both from diverse sources and those amassed in a single unit. A third general capacity, which I have labeled "dissemination and publication," includes the highly touted, remarkably effective capacities to distribute information in endlessly varied configurations, engulfing prior forms such as mail, telephone, paper-based publication, and all forms of broadcast media. The dominant and best-known embodiment of these capacities is, of course, the Internet, with the World Wide Web as the most familiar contemporary application.

1 Keeping Track and Watching over Us

THE WORLD IS FILLED WITH DEVICES, SYSTEMS, AND DEVICES embedded in systems that have been designed to notice, watch over, and follow people; to track their actions, take in their attributes, and sometimes simply be aware of their presence. The frequency with which we are monitored and tracked by any given system can vary enormously, from one time only to episodically or continuously, as long as we are in the scope of its sensorium. Although increasingly enabled by technology, monitoring and tracking is not a new addition to the range of human social activities. Nor is it necessarily mediated, as there are countless mundane ways in which people are tracked and monitored: teachers take attendance, parents watch toddlers in a park, and coaches keep track of athletes' performance. Further, although privacy concerns accompany many contemporary monitoring and tracking practices, this does not necessarily need to be a factor, as when physicians monitor the heart rates of their patients or Olympic judges scrutinize and evaluate athletes' routines.

Yet with advances in digital media we have witnessed a dramatic rise in technically mediated monitoring, often emerging as a first-round solution to a wide range of social needs and problems. Not only is there an increase in sheer frequency of technology-mediated monitoring and tracking but a resulting shift in its nature—automated, undiscriminating, and accommodating new subjects, monitors, and motives. Following at the heels of these changes, there is growing discomfort, suspicion, and perplexity. In this chapter a variety of devices and systems, currently in play or under consideration, that have surfaced in the general consternation over information technology and its threats to privacy are surveyed.

A word on terminology: the term *surveillance* is frequently used to cover much of what I discuss in this chapter. The reason I opt for *monitoring and tracking* instead is that *surveillance* is usually associated with a set of political assumptions; namely, that monitoring is performed "from above" as subjects of surveillance are monitored by those in authority or more powerful than them for purposes of behavior modification or social control as sought or determined by those conducting the surveillance. Although surveillance studies are an important neighboring field, my initial goal here is to describe a range of technology-based systems and practices ("socio-technical" systems) without simultaneously theorizing about the uses to which they are put.

Direct and Indirect Monitoring and Tracking

In some cases, monitoring is an explicit and intended feature of a system. In one familiar example, video surveillance (commonly called closed-circuit television, or CCTV in the United Kingdom), video-recording cameras are placed in strategic locations such as the workplace, airports, train and subway stations, public streets, squares and parks, shopping malls and stores, parking garages, and schools (Duong 2005).[1] The CCTV cameras capture visual images, which may be viewed in real time on closed-circuit monitors, recorded and stored for later viewing, or communicated off-site via electronic networks. Cheaper equipment and advances in performance, combined with social and political drivers such as fear of crime and terror, have resulted in the proliferation of video surveillance to the extent that people going about their daily business in urban settings can expect to have their images monitored and recorded an average of 300 times a day by thirty separate CCTV systems (Rosen 2004). In the United Kingdom, an enthusiastic proponent of these systems, estimates suggest that close to one-fifth of the world's CCTV cameras are housed there, with more than 4.3 million installed as of 2004 (Frith 2004). Ongoing improvements in this technology offer higher-resolution images (2048×1536, or 3 megapixels) (Bodell 2007), more comprehensive coverage through greater range of camera motion and wider-angled lenses, digital encoding and compression techniques to enhance storage, ease of communication, and data processing.[2]

Other modalities besides the visual serve as the basis for monitoring. Sound recording and wiretapping, with its long and controversial history, continue to make front-page news and to inspire court cases and legislation (Lichtblau and Risen 2005; "Spying on Americans" 2007; Lichtblau 2008). Less salient, although as much a part of the landscape, are computerized tracking systems that integrate motion, touch, light, and heat detection; chemical sensors primarily advanced for monitoring environmental conditions—which add another sensory dimension to the field (Estrin 2007); and systems based on the transmission of radio frequency signals that facilitate point-to-point communication between receivers and embedded transmitters. (The case of radio frequency identification [RFID] is discussed at length below.) In some cases, the trend is toward systems of networked sensors that are so small as to be imperceptible by humans, some even on the nanoscale (Wolfe 2003).

Although many existing and envisaged uses of sensor networks may hold no relevance for privacy, it takes no great leap of imagination to extrapolate from these to ones that do raise questions. One application, already a step beyond the laboratory, involves integrated monitoring systems incorporating a variety of sensing devices installed in homes. The positive potential of these systems in monitoring the elderly living on their own carries with it a worrying potential of intrusive surveillance in all homes. (Technologies advertised for in-home use for the elderly include ADT Security's QuietCare, SeniorSafe@Home, and iCare Health Monitoring [Larson 2007]; Intel, among other companies, is substantially investing in research in this area [Intel 2007].) Although constructed with benevolent, if paternalistic ends, the potential application to fine-grained multi-modal surveillance with more sinister, less legitimate ends is clear.

Information itself constitutes a modality for monitoring. Aptly captured by Roger Clarke's term *dataveillance* (1988), innumerable interactions and transactions can be monitored and tracked through the exchange, extraction, or capture of information. Border crossings; meticulously kept phone records; swipe-card entry points (e.g., subway turnstiles, proximity or "prox" cards ubiquitous at most U.S. college campuses and places of work); airport check-in counters; and purchases made with credit, debit, and frequent shopper cards capture a dynamic record of people's activities. Because doors, turnstiles, and store checkout registers are already points of restriction, seeping dataveillance has not radically altered how people experience these junctures. The difference is that in the move from lock-and-key and case to magnetic strip, these spaces have become points of information capture and passage; commercial transactions and travel are newly enriched with information.

In many instances, however, monitoring and tracking, particularly the mode we call dataveillance, is not the direct aim but an inadvertent consequence of some other goal for which a given system was originally designed.[3] To give a few mundane examples, the convenience of paying with credit cards can provide evidence of a person's whereabouts; telephone bills primarily intended to extract payment provide information about a person's conversations; prox cards intended to provide security for student dorms enable tracking of their comings and goings; and fine-grain monitoring of usage patterns that provide utility companies with valuable information about load can also indicate the presence, absence, and general activities of building occupants.[4] Manufacturers of consumer devices advertise "smart," networked appliances—refrigerators, toasters, and coffee machines—that can communicate with their owners, and presumably with third parties as well.

Mobile telephony is another instance of a system from which a secondary surveillance capacity has emerged. In order to function, cellular phones must connect with nearby communications towers. It followed from this technical imperative that phone companies would be able to comply readily with the 1996 mandate of the U.S. Federal Communications Commission requiring that a caller's location be determinable to within a radius of 50 to 300 meters for purposes of the "enhanced 9-1-1 emergency call system." This capacity, in turn, enables tracking of telephones (as long as they are on) and their owners to a fairly accurate degree, which raises a complicated set of issues regarding who ought to be allowed access to this information.[5] The urgency of these matters is sure to escalate as new generations of cellular phones come equipped with Global Positioning Systems (GPS), allowing for far more accurate pinpointing of location by GPS service providers, not in an obvious way regulated under the policy rubric governing traditional telecommunications providers.

Although this scenario suggests a classic surveillance relationship in which individual phone subscribers are monitored by powerful, centralized, institutional actors—private and government—mobile telephony has provided a platform for "democratizing" tracking capabilities and, in some instances, even turning the tables. For example, worried parents can subscribe to a service Verizon calls "Chaperone" to keep track of their children's whereabouts. Further, as an inadvertent consequence of equipping the devices themselves with video and still cameras ("cameraphones"), individuals are equipped to monitor and track one another as well as authorities, offering a glimmer of hope at a more level playing field while fueling the worry that watchful eyes are now inescapable.[6]

Public Roadways

Public roadways constitute a telling case of the gradual transformation—still under way—of a venue from one in which monitoring and tracking were largely absent to one in which these processes seem increasingly transparent. This state of affairs follows from the incursion of a diverse range of technical devices and systems either designed explicitly for monitoring and tracking or that allow for monitoring and tracking as an indirect consequence of their primary functionalities.

Public roadways have not been entirely free of social control through monitoring, as driving has required operators' licenses and vehicle ownership has demanded registration with state authorities as well as insurance coverage. Over time, however, incremental changes made and under way imply even closer scrutiny of driving and drivers not only at critical junctures, such as when obtaining and renewing a driver's license, but continuously as one drives. Roadway and bridge tolls, for example, previously paid in cash, are increasingly extracted via automated credit or debit payments. Toll plazas, equipped with RFID systems, log the passage of registered vehicles and deduct payment from an account, typically replenished via credit card payment, which in turn constitutes a point of tracking.[7] Surprised drivers share anecdotes about speeding citations arriving in the mail, based on driving times clocked between plazas A and B, uncertain over the rules, if any, governing information accrued at these toll points.

Other systems that monitor drivers include so-called black boxes. Many people know about black boxes in aircraft, often discussed in the context of air crash investigations, but most of us are unaware of their presence in cars. Originally installed in 1974 to help with the deployment of airbags, these boxes, called event-data recorders or electronic data recorders (EDRs), record general telemetry data such as engine speed, safety belt status, status of brakes during a crash, and acceleration. The precise number of EDRs is not known because while the National Highway Traffic Safety Administration (NHTSA) and the United States Department of Transportation (DOT) ruled in 2006 that automakers must inform consumers that EDRs are installed in vehicles, this ruling applies only to cars manufactured after September 2010 (DOT and NHTSA 2007). While the use of EDR data as evidence in court has been controversial because its accuracy has been questioned, there also has been debate about its admissibility on the grounds that it constitutes an unacceptable invasion of privacy, particularly because drivers are currently not usually informed that EDRs are installed in their automobiles (DOT and NHTSA 2004; Zetter 2005).

The use of GPS navigation systems installed in private vehicles, whose primary function is to direct drivers to their desired destinations, may allow cars and drivers to be tracked, depending on their design. Some systems have allowed police departments to trace stolen vehicles and rental companies to track vehicles and ensure that drivers have complied with company rules (Ramasastry 2005).

On the roads, networked cameras supplement video surveillance systems located in more typical sites, such as public parks and shopping malls. In the United States, cameras are commonly installed at traffic lights to detect and identify red light offenders. In the United Kingdom, automatic number plate recognition (ANPR) systems operating along national roadways, on roadside posts, in police cars, or at gas stations capture and identify number plate images on camera. At least 50 million number plate images per day are centrally processed by the National ANPR Data Center within the Police National Computer in London (Ballard 2006). The ANPR system not only instantly recognizes number plates, enabling interception of targeted vehicles (such as those known to have been involved in a crime), but is capable of tracking the progress of single vehicles along an entire journey by means of date/time stamps and linked GPS data (Evans-Pugh 2006).

Looking into the future, a planning initiative launched under the aegis of the DOT's Vehicle Infrastructure Integration program aims to harness wireless communication technology to promote safety and efficiency in traffic flow rather than aiding law enforcement. One project proposed by this initiative is the construction of a vehicle safety communication (VSC) system, which could also result in comprehensive monitoring of cars on the roadways. Still in planning, the VSC system would equip every motor vehicle with devices capable of transmitting and receiving data to and from roadside units and to other vehicles equipped with similar devices.[8] Vehicles and roadside units would form autonomous, self-organizing, point-to-multipoint, ad hoc, peer-to-peer communications networks able to transmit time- and date-stamped data at a rate of ten messages per second to one another about their respective location, sudden stops or swerves, vehicle speed, and other telemetry data. Drivers (and their cars) could be warned about hazardous road conditions, imminent collisions, upcoming traffic lights, sharp curves, oncoming traffic for left turns, imminent lane changes, or merely congestion.

Although the explicit purpose of the system is to increase safety on the roads, countless design decisions could potentially determine not only its functional efficacy in meeting explicit primary purposes but supporting features as well. One such feature is security. Communication and data requirements designed with the primary goal of road and vehicle safety might make systems vulnerable to security threats, such as inauthentic or bogus messages like spurious "clear the way" signals to ambient traffic from vehicles posing as emergency vehicles. One way to build assurances that data originates from authentic sources into the system is to include some form of identification in the communications protocol. But, depending on how identification is implemented, the inadvertent result could be a comprehensive and inescapable system of monitoring and tracking on the roads. Recognizing this danger, some security experts have offered preliminary approaches to building secure systems that meet functional requirements while maintaining anonymity. Although, at the time of writing, no final decisions have been publicly announced, approaches that emphasize both security and anonymity are not prevailing. In other words, the worry that a well-intentioned roadway safety communication system could turn into a powerful tool for monitoring and tracking seems less salient to interests of law enforcement and private enterprise in a system with effective and transparent identification.[9]

Online Monitoring

Privacy looms large online. The paradox of the online experience is that on the one hand it offers individuals the possibility of communicating and interacting with individuals, groups, and organizations in the privacy of their homes, while on the other hand it exposes them to unprecedented monitoring and tracking (see Lessig 1999, chap. 4). More than ten years ago, Jerry Kang captured some of the distinctive qualities of online monitoring by comparing the experience of shopping online with shopping in a regular mall.

Imagine the following two visits to a mall, one in real space, the other in cyberspace. In real space, you drive to a mall, walk up and down its corridors, peer into numerous shops, and stroll through corridors of inviting stores. Along the way, you buy an ice cream cone with cash. You walk into a bookstore and flip through a few magazines. Finally, you stop at a clothing store and buy a friend a silk scarf with a credit card. In this narrative, numerous persons interact with you and collect information along the way. For instance, while walking through the mall, fellow visitors visually collect information about you, if for no other reason than to avoid bumping into you. But such information is general—e.g., it does not pinpoint the geographical location and time of the sighting—is not in a format that can be processed by a computer, is not indexed to your name or another unique identifier, and is impermanent, residing in short-term human memory. You remain a barely noticed stranger. One important exception exists: The scarf purchase generates data that are detailed, computer-processable, indexed by name, and potentially permanent.

By contrast, in cyberspace, the exception becomes the norm: Every interaction is like the credit card purchase. The best way to grasp this point is to take seriously, if only for a moment, the metaphor that cyberspace is an actual place, a computer-constructed world, a virtual reality. In this alternate universe, you are invisibly stamped with a bar code as soon as you venture outside your home. There are entities called "road providers," who supply the streets and ground you walk on, who track precisely where, when, and how fast you traverse the lands, in order to charge you for your wear on the infrastructure. As soon as you enter the cyber-mall's domain, the mall begins to track you through invisible scanners focused on your bar code. It automatically records which stores you visit, which windows you browse, in which order, and for how long. The specific stores collect even more detailed data when you enter their domain. For example, the cyber-bookstore notes which magazines you skimmed, recording which pages you have seen and for how long, and notes the pattern, if any, of your browsing. It notes that you picked up briefly a health magazine featuring an article on St. John's Wort, read for seven minutes a newsweekly detailing a politician's sex scandal, and flipped ever-so-quickly through a tabloid claiming that Elvis lives. Of course, whenever any item is actually purchased, the store, as well as the credit, debit, or virtual cash company that provides payment through cyberspace, takes careful notes of what you bought—in this case, a silk scarf, red, expensive (Kang 1998, 1198–1199).

Whereas monitoring in unstructured three-dimensional physical space requires significant engineering intervention, giving rise to somewhat clumsy apparatus such as CCTV, monitoring online activities requires relatively minor adaptations of existing functional features. Features like IP addresses, authenticated logins, and cookies, either inherent to the design of the Web or included early in its functional development, have been ingeniously exploited over time as mechanisms for monitoring and tracking individual activities and online social behaviors. As these exploits have seeped into public consciousness, they have periodically erupted into active controversy, such as online advertising companies like DoubleClick exploiting the functionality of cookies to track surfing patterns of individuals across numerous Web sites. By using banner ads and Web bugs to place cookies on people's hard drives, these companies are able to harvest information on Web sites who have contracted with them. Although vocal resistance has not resulted in the prohibition of such practices, it has yielded design alterations in Web browsers and browser interfaces to provide users greater control over cookies (Schwartz 2001).

The banner ad model by no means exhausts online tracking capabilities. Also possible is latent tracking of the time that users spend at various sites as well as comprehensive monitoring of so-called clickstream data. In early 2007 it came to light that Internet Service Providers (ISPs) such as Verizon, Comcast, America Online (AOL), and EarthLink regularly monitor users' clickstream data, linking it with identifiable customer records. Exactly what is stored, for how long, and what is done with it are not matters that ISPs readily disclose (Singel 2007). ISP monitoring of users' online activities is generally analogous to similar forms of monitoring performed by owners of individual online enterprises who monitor the activities of users, customers, or visitors to their sites. For some of the most successful online companies, such as Amazon.com, eBay.com, and Netflix.com, such practices create an uncanny sense of a "soul in the machine" surmising customers' tastes and predilections (Amazon uses a proprietary algorithm called "item-to-item collaborative filtering"; see Linden, Smith, and York 2003). Because these practices lie at the heart of many of these companies' business models, they are unlikely to abate despite discomfort and vocal grumbling by privacy advocates and some of their customers.

Another important instance of online monitoring is conducted by Web search companies such as Yahoo!, AOL, the Microsoft Network (MSN), and the largest such entity, Google. Public interest in privacy of Web search activities was initially aroused in 2006 when the mainstream press revealed that the U.S. Department of Justice (DOJ) had issued a subpoena to Google for one week's worth of search query records, absent identifying information, and a random list of 1 million Uniform Resource Locators (URLs) from its Web index. These records were requested to bolster the government's defense of the constitutionality of the Child Online Protection Act (Bray 2006). When Google refused the initial request, the DOJ filed a motion in a federal district court to force compliance. Before the court, Google argued that the request imposed a burden and would compromise trade secrets, undermine customers' trust in Google, and have a chilling effect on search activities. In March 2006 the court granted a reduced version of the government's first motion, ordering Google to provide a random listing of 50,000 URLs, but denied its second motion requesting search query records (Hafner 2006). Other Web search companies, including AOL, Yahoo!, and MSN, were not named in this legal action because they had complied with the DOJ's request, although details on what exactly they handed over are not known.

A year later another front-page story revealed that certain identities could be extracted from massive records of anonymized search-query data that AOL regularly posted on the Internet for use by the scientific research community. The news media reported on the extent to which search records were logged and revealed some of the ways that the major search companies store and analyze individual search query records to create user profiles (Hansell 2006; Zeller 2006). There are a few key issues that drive privacy worries in relation to this sphere of online activity. One is that Web search companies have provided no detailed disclosures on what they regularly monitor or what they typically do with patrons' information. Another is that these sites provide a constellation of services in addition to Web search capability, including e-mail, calendar programs, online chat, Web portals and directories, digital content, and much more. This means that whatever logging they are doing of Web search activities could, in principle, be combined with this particularly sensitive array of personal record keeping, communication, research, and intellectual exploration. These observations lead some critics to argue that activities such as searching the Web ought not to be monitored at all.

Critics offer similar reasons for resisting technology-based schemes for protecting intellectual property rights in media content such as music, video, and, to a lesser extent, print. Industry incumbents, in an effort to stem unauthorized file sharing by individuals that threaten their property stakes in content, have developed various Technical Protection Measures (TPMs), also called Digital Rights Management (DRM). Certain forms of TPMs or DRM work by identifying consumers and monitoring their content use so they may be held liable for violations of terms of lease or sale. By monitoring the ways one engages with protected content, how frequently, at what times of day, and so forth, these systems encroach into zones of life many consider to be sacrosanct.[10]

Radio Frequency Identification (RFID) Technology

I conclude this chapter with a discussion of RFID technology, which uses radio waves as a modality for tracking and monitoring. This brief case study illustrates key elements at the intersection of technology, tracking, and privacy. Although the range of actual and planned applications of RFID technology has burgeoned in the past decade, experts in the field note that its usefulness as a means of identifying and tracking was recognized as early as World War II, when it was deployed as a way to distinguish American aircraft from enemy aircraft. Since then, its development has accelerated and diversified due to advances in digital electronic technologies. Contemporary RFID systems consist of transponder tags, typically very small microchips with embedded electronic circuits and tiny antennae, that exchange signals with transceivers, usually fixed devices that receive and process information. Present-day offerings fall roughly into two classes. In passive RFID systems, transponder tags with no power source of their own are activated by power broadcast to them by transceivers, emitting radio signals back to the transceiver. In a typical passive system, the information emitted is the tag's own identification, usually linked via the transceiver to a database. Active RFID systems include transponder tags with their own internal power source.[11]

Passive and active systems hold distinct sets of advantages and limitations. Active tags can be read across greater distances than passive tags (up to 1,000 meters versus a few feet) and far more quickly, at a rate of twenty tags moving at speeds of up to 100 miles per hour or thousands at a time versus a few seconds for reading twenty passive tags. Active tags offer 1,000 times more read/write data storage capacity and can incorporate sensor capabilities to monitor environmental variables such as temperature, humidity, shock, and container seal status (to detect item tampering). Finally, active systems are more accurate, more flexible, and less prone to problems of signal interference. So why would anyone choose a passive RFID system? Because active tags are battery operated, have a limited shelf life, and, more critically, cost significantly more—passive tags offered in bulk cost approximately 20 cents each, whereas active tags cost $3 to $15 each (Moore 2005).

Technical improvements in the component technologies of RFID systems have led not only to a steady decline in cost but to a diversified field of applications; some already in place, others anticipated. RFID enabled road-toll systems, such as E-ZPass in the northeastern United States and FasTrak in California, are widespread. These systems use semi-passive transponder tags, which have battery-powered microchip circuitry that transmits information only when activated by system transceivers; tolls are charged to customers' accounts via transponders attached to their vehicle windshields that signal transceivers embedded in toll plazas. Another common use of RFID technology is in the previously mentioned prox card systems used to secure university buildings across the United States; transponders are typically embedded in student identification (ID) cards. Other applications include automobile keys with "immobilizer" chips, keyless automobile entry, tracking of air cargo, RFID-enabled wristbands for newborns, tracking patterns of wildlife migration and spawning, ensuring food safety, and tracking hazardous chemicals (Katz 2007; "Radio Silence" 2007; Weier 2007; Murphy 2008; Priest 2008). In 2006 the U.S. Department of State, along with several other countries, initiated a program to replace existing passports with RFID-enabled passports (O'Connor 2007).[12] The European Union (EU), for example, is planning a comprehensive RFID-enabled biometric surveillance system that would automate EU citizen travel across borders of EU member states (Heath 2008).

Two applications in particular have raised public controversy: implantable transponder chips and the use of RFID in supply-side inventory management. Encased in glass or plastic capsules, implantable chips (both active and passive) roughly the size of a grain of rice can be injected under the skin. Commonly implanted in pets and livestock (see Ti-Rfid Systems, marketed for agricultural use [Texas Instruments 2007], and Pet-ID [2006], targeted at pet owners), they are also marketed for use in humans. VeriChip, which claims to be the first company to offer a patented, human-implantable, RFID microchip approved by the Federal Drug Administration, markets passive tags for purposes of controlling access to resources and spaces, for identifying people with serious chronic diseases needing specific emergency treatments, for infant protection against in-hospital switching, and for preventing residents of long-term care facilities (e.g., those suffering from Alzheimer's) from roaming off the premises (VeriChip Corporation 2006). Highly publicized at the time, the Baja Beach Club in Barcelona, Spain, held an "implant night" where VIP customers were offered the option of a scannable RFID chip to be implanted in their arms. This chip guaranteed access to the club and allowed customers to charge drinks to a debit account (Leyden 2004; Losowsky 2004).

RFID systems, widely touted as an effective tool for managing supply chain assets, are currently used to track cartons and pallets of goods, but the eventual goal is to be able to track consumer items individually. Paving the way to this goal is the Electronic Product Code (EPC) network, a collaboration between industry partners and the Auto-ID Center (currently based at the Massachusetts Institute of Technology). Analogous to the familiar Universal Product Code (UPC) "barcode," which is optically scanned, the EPC would be able to identify products down to the unique individual rather than the product type. Like the UPC network, the EPC network would offer globally standardized EPC tag serial numbers linked to centralized databases that would connect these serial numbers with information about tagged items.

RFID-based asset management systems are expected to provide gains in both efficiency and reliability. With the capacity to track goods along distribution channels from factories to warehouses and ultimately to retail storefronts, supporters assert that these systems will minimize errors and losses. Moreover, for perishable food items, RFID technology could alert store owners to items that may have passed "sell by" dates. In another product-specific application, the U.S. Food and Drug Administration (FDA) is considering RFID as a tool for monitoring the integrity of the U.S. drug supply by ensuring pedigree and authenticity of drugs as they move along the supply chain (U.S. FDA 2004).

Optimism over the benefits of RFID technology is tempered with awareness of potential hazards, even among enthusiastic advocates. Focusing here on hazards bearing directly on privacy, and to security as it relates to privacy, we consider some of the most prominent concerns.[13] One is a trade-off of privacy for efficiency; universal standards like the EPC, for example, increase the efficiency of product tracking but at the same time allow for the possibility that an item can be detected by transceivers outside of a specific system. A similar critique has dogged systems proposed for RFID-enabled passports, as critics demonstrated in early versions of the technology that passport information could be detected and read by unauthorized, rogue readers stationed several feet away (Schneier 2006). Without proper security, such as data encryption, information emitted by primitive tags is vulnerable to interception by unauthorized readers (Garfinkel 2002).

With some applications, such as RFID passports, the major concerns are malfunction and exploitation of loopholes. With others, concerns are provoked by their functional excellence. One such instance is the highly extolled capacity of RFID systems to identify tagged items uniquely, compared with the UPC system, which identifies them only by type. Detractors of EPC for use with consumer items worry that identifiable consumers can be tightly matched with specific items they have purchased via credit cards and consumer loyalty programs. The prospect of retail consumption following the trajectory of RFID-enabled road-toll systems, from a not-traceable, cash-based system to one that tracks people on a per-transaction basis, spurred vocal protests against a pilot project announced by Wal-Mart in which individual Gillette products would be tagged.[14]

Critics have also voiced concerns with RFID's potential for surreptitious tracking. Since readers as well as tags may be hidden from view (in consumer items and even documents), RFID signals are not detectable by human sensory apparatus, and radio frequency waves are able to penetrate many solid materials, systems may operate without detection. Even if we are aware that items we carry and use include RFID tags, we may have no way of knowing when these tags are transmitting information to transceivers embedded inside plastics, cloth, carpets, and floor tiles. Critics warn of discomfiting scenarios in which unsuspecting consumers are tracked beyond checkout, where their purchases "communicate" their whereabouts to strategically placed transceivers, even reporting an inventory of other tagged items in their homes to a central repository.

We do not yet live in a world replete with RFID-enabled consumer items, but these scenarios are not purely the stuff of science fiction. In California and Virginia, for example, where lawmakers are considering the use of RFID-enabled, state-issued ID cards such as driver's licenses, citizens may reasonably wonder whether constitutional constraints are effective against covert, automatic identification at a distance. If not, such cards would enable tracking and monitoring without knowledge or consent. Prospects of identification at a distance are not unrealistic in light of claims that some active tags have sufficient range to communicate with satellites. Although, in this regard, passive tags might seem more benign than active tags that broadcast willy-nilly, in fact, real-time information evoked by land-based readers may be relayed to satellites (Consumers Against Supermarket Privacy Invasion and Numbering, et al. 2003). And since passive tags require no power source, their capacity to communicate is not limited by this. Finally, information captured through RFID tracking may yield a further dimension to growing stockpiles of personal information held by third-party aggregators and information service providers.[15]

In this chapter and the two that follow, my aim is to provide an overview of technology-based systems and practices that are seen as threats to privacy. My focus in this chapter has been on threats generated by new and intensified capacities to monitor and track; however, because it is impossible to survey all such systems and practices, I have described a sample that represents the range of underlying technologies, the range of venues in which we can now expect to be monitored and tracked, and a few instances of controversies that have erupted in the wake of such systems and practices.

2 Knowing Us Better than We Know Ourselves: Massive and Deep Databases

CONTRIBUTING TO THE EXTRAORDINARY POTENCY OF TECHNOLOGY-based systems for monitoring and tracking is the back-end capacity to store information captured by these systems, give meaning to it, and make it readily available for subsequent use. In the United States, these capabilities fueled early public privacy debates in the 1960s and 1970s on the increasing and potentially unlimited uses of computerized databases of personal information compiled by government and large private institutions (Westin 1967; Miller 1972; Burnham 1983; Regan 1995). As the technological possibilities have multiplied in power and complexity and the landscape of threat has become more diverse and sprawling, the debates have continued.

Crowning achievements in three areas of information science and technology have contributed to the landscape of threat. First, in the area of computerized databases, major scientific development, surges in processing power, and a plentiful supply of cheap computer memory have contributed to vastly improved capacities for storing, organizing, and retrieving great quantities of information. Simply put, this has meant that anything about an individual that can be rendered in digital form can be stored over indefinitely long periods of time and be readily retrieved. Second, rapid strides in the science and engineering of digital electronic communications networks, notably the Internet, the World Wide Web, and related wired and wireless networking technologies, have meant that large quantities of information can be moved around reliably and efficiently at lightning speed. As a result, not only can information in databases be communicated across great distances, but information stored at networked nodes can be accessed from multiple places irrespective of geographic distances.

The third significant achievement is the scientific and technological growth in data analysis due to rapid, ongoing developments in information science, information management, theoretical computer science, mathematical and statistical analysis, cryptography, and artificial intelligence. Information can be compressed, sorted, manipulated, discovered, and interpreted as never before, and thus can be more easily transformed into useful knowledge. In sum, these areas of scientific and technological development (which continue to thrive) make it possible for large troves of information to be reliably, efficiently, and meaningfully organized and accessed; to be effectively moved into massive aggregations and disaggregated into usable chunks; and to be transmitted to sites when needed. Furthermore, information begets information: as data is structured and analyzed it yields implications, consequences, and predictions.

In this landscape of possibilities, which excites both enthusiasm and dread, what can we say about implications for privacy? Plainly, these new tools afford new mastery over information: it need no longer be ephemeral, vulnerable neither to the whims and weaknesses of human memory nor to the limitations of paper files; no longer hard to find or prohibitively expensive to disseminate. Beyond one obvious and universal casualty, so-called privacy through obscurity, the particular ways that people are likely to experience the effects on privacy are liable to be neither uniform nor constant. Continuous and rapid technological advances result in an ever-shifting topography of experience, variable across social spheres and subject to adoption rates and the specific information technologies and institutions to which people are exposed. Thus, people living in an urban metropolis, working for multinational corporations, and conducting business online with an array of real and other property (e.g., creative or intellectual content) are likely to experience the impacts of information systems in different ways from people living in rural outposts, owning small service businesses, and traveling very little outside the borders of their hometown.

Instead of developing a detailed matrix of how information systems affect the privacy of these different lives, which would require a detour beyond the scope of this book, I have found that four pivotal transformations form a useful explanatory framework for guiding our thinking generally. These transformations, which are as much social, political, and economic[1] as technological, shape the many different ways computerized record-keeping[2] systems and practices impinge on privacy and affect experiences in diversely shaped lives. Before proceeding it is important to note that the features and transformations discussed in this chapter could be readily adapted to information generally with an eye to understanding the widespread significance of these changes. Our focus, however, will remain on personal information (information about identifiable persons), motivated as we are by an interest in privacy.

Pivotal Transformations

Democratization of Database Technologies

One major transformation is the democratization of access to sophisticated database technologies, facilitated in large part by a dramatic decline in the cost of hardware and software as well as by the efforts of systems developers and vendors to adapt their products to a wide range of users. By "democratization," I mean nothing more than an expansion of access to a broad and diverse community of individual and institutional users. In order to appreciate how this transformation has complicated the privacy conundrum, compare the contemporary scenario with the ways threats to privacy were experienced in the 1960s through the 1980s, as reflected in the framing of the groundbreaking and influential 1973 Report to the Committee of the Secretary of Health, Education, and Welfare, *Records, Computers, and the Rights of Citizens* (U.S. Department of Health, Education, and Welfare 1973). The committee, which included Willis Ware and Alan Westin (leaders in the field in decades following), was charged with recommending public policies that balanced the benefits of computerized databases ("record-keeping systems") with the rights of individual data subjects ("citizens"). The heart of the report is the Code of Fair Information Practices, which articulates five fundamental principles of record-keeping that have shaped privacy policy making throughout the world. These principles expressly prohibit secret databases and the reuse of data for purposes other than those stated at the time of collection, demand adequate data security, and allow data subjects to both inspect and correct their records. Particularly relevant to our discussion, however, is the backdrop of the report—how the committee construed the significant actors and the likely targets of regulation they supported. In particular, they were concerned about protecting private individuals (data subjects) against large government and private sector institutional actors maintaining information about them. The Code, almost like a bill of rights, was an effort to "level the playing field" for individuals in relation to these large and powerful actors. This landscape might have seemed more sinister to the privacy advocates of the day, with its overtones of conspiracy and "big brother," but it was, at least, clearer. Why so?

Leading up to the report, large organizations with the funds to finance equipment and systems were turning, increasingly, to computers and databases to administer, control, and interact with large numbers of people. These businesses included government agencies (e.g., the Internal Revenue Service, the U.S. Census Bureau, and the Federal Bureau of Investigation; see Laudon 1986), banks, insurance companies, utilities, and telecommunications companies. Citing efficiency and waste reduction in government, a number of studies urged further consolidation of record-keeping. For example, in 1965 and 1967, two controversial studies recommended a computerized federal data center and national data center. In the 1970s the General Service Administration issued a report recommending a network linking federal government data systems. Although these proposals were scuttled following energetic protests in the press, trade publications, and in and around the U.S. Congress, the battle lines were drawn during public debates. These deliberations assumed the convergence of two forces: powerful technologies at the service of dominant social and political actors who, realistically, were the only ones who had access to these technologies.[3] This confluence of factors lent a definite shape to calls for privacy protection, because the threat to privacy was the familiar threat of those in positions of power, including agents of government, who had to be prevented from abusing the novel powers of computerized databases. This confluence of technology with a particular power configuration has broken down with the democratization of access to automated record-keeping and related technologies.

In the contemporary picture, the adoption of digital technologies by virtually all organizations—large, small, public, private—places at their disposal affordable, powerful computerized databases for handling a host of functionalities. The major actors continue to be major users. Government agencies, for example, utilize database technologies for administering transactions with citizens and have thus increased their range of applications to include vital records (birth, death, marriage, and so forth), welfare records, real property holdings, drivers' records, census records, and court records, among others (Laudon 1986).

Banks and other financial institutions maintain detailed documentation on holdings and transactions; mortgage and insurance companies keep dossiers on individual clients; phone companies log item-by-item records of conversations; and hospitals and clinics retain detailed records of examinations, procedures, and treatments.

The range of applications has expanded for those who use these technologies—including both small and large retailers and small and large service providers—for managing customer and client relations, marketing, accounting, personnel management, directories, research, and more. Less salient to individual data subjects are specialized records culled from search engine logs, retail purchase records (e.g., supermarkets, drugstores, and hardware stores), magazine and newspaper subscription records, airline records of travelers, rental agency reports of car rentals, and bookstore lists of book orders and purchases. It is no longer surprising that health clubs, pizza parlors, plumbers, and yard service companies can track our interactions with them, such as when a beauty parlor can rattle off recent treatments in addition to the stylists who administered them. Not least, individuals have also become the keepers of electronic records in their computerized calendars and address books, personal digital assistants, and cellular phones. The upshot is an information-rich environment at just about every turn.

Information Mobility

Another transformation is in the mobility of information. Facilitated by easy and inexpensive storage, standardized database formats, and maturation of the networked information infrastructure, the efficiency with which information can be moved around is unprecedented. There is little sense of information being located at any fixed point. Certainly not tied to or limited by geographic location, information collected at one venue may be fluidly transmitted elsewhere either one record at a time or en masse. Mobility of information is not, however, merely a function of network hardware and software, but the enthusiastic upsurge in network adoption and usage by individual and institutional social actors. Unless we choose not to make connections—to engage socially in some way or another—obscurity cannot be achieved through relocation. Information in digital electronic form not only spreads to multiple points, it is also accessible from multiple points. The grapevine is thorough, scientific, and precise; records of whom we are and what we have done follow us around and even sometimes precede us.

Information Aggregation

Another important transformation is information aggregation, facilitated by the first two transformations. Mobility of information means that it can be transmitted from a point of collection to another or other points where it may be needed or simply more highly valued. It can be banked at a third location, pooled with other information, used immediately, or simply remain in storage until a call is made for it. In some cases, the aggregation of information is functionally specific; for example, if a government security agency seeks to draw and pool together information from diverse sources about a group of individuals suspected of terrorist activities or a population health agency seeks to pool medical information on patients with specific conditions from many hospitals in a region. In other cases, information is aggregated strategically, then secured in data banks or so-called data warehouses in anticipation of future need. The transformation is not merely technological; not only do we have the technical competence to format, dispatch, and assemble data for purposes of aggregation, but robust social systems and practices have developed that count on its competence and motivate its continuing development.

To lend precision to the discourse surrounding data aggregation, it will be useful to introduce and specify the meaning of a few terms. Our main interest in this section is with *aggregated databases*, by which we mean assemblages of a number of distinct databases. Even though we generally think of data aggregation as an activity that produces large databases, large databases need not be aggregations. Let us consider two different ways a database can be large: it can be large because it includes many data subjects or it can be large because it includes a great deal of information about data subjects. I will invoke the dimensions of *breadth* and *depth* to indicate the number of data subjects or the numbers of attribute fields, respectively. One can imagine databases—aggregated or not—of many shapes and sizes varying independently along both these dimensions. Quite separately from this, one may want to know how many primary databases contributed to the construction of an aggregated database. Accordingly, there may be very large databases (e.g., the database of results from the U.S. Census Bureau's decennial long-form survey) that are massively broad and reasonably deep but are not aggregations; conversely, there may be relatively small aggregations (e.g., the merger of mailing lists from the Princeton Historical Society with the Princeton Rotary Club) that are shallow and narrow databases. Aggregations that seem to be the most controversial and troubling are those that are broad and deep, and those that are exceedingly narrow (one data subject) but very deep. The latter are frequently called "digital dossiers" (Solove 2002b).

Some of the utility of actual aggregation can be obtained by what we might characterize as virtual aggregation. Although the notion of a data warehouse suggests a large contiguous repository in which information is stored (and often it is), advances in information science, particularly techniques for search and retrieval, enable the extraction of information held in disparate locales. Facilitated by standardized networks and communications protocols, these search techniques allow information to be drawn from multiple sources as it is needed. A familiar case in point is the World Wide Web, which can be conceived of as a huge distributed data repository with public search engines making it possible for people to retrieve targeted information from it. These searches can locate information in a great variety of formats; including music, video, news, blogs, academic papers, images, and so forth. This ability to treat the Web as a virtual warehouse and to extract from it deep profiles on individuals has emerged as one of the perennial privacy issues associated with Web search (Swidey 2003; Hinman 2005; Tavani 2005; Lobron 2006; Weiss 2006). And then there's the (in)famous case of the CNet reporter who dug up personal information on Eric Schmidt using Google, and was subsequently boycotted from Google's press events (Mills 2005; Stross 2005).

Information from Data, Knowledge from Information

The warehouse metaphor is misleading in another way, in that it suggests a large space with information stored passively inside. The value of aggregations, however, lies not merely in their bringing together and making information available, but in a far more dynamic potential. Abetted by brute processing power, increasingly sophisticated mathematical and statistical techniques have made it possible to extract descriptive and predictive meanings from information that goes well beyond its literal boundaries. With sweeping consequences for privacy, this fourth transformation is an unbounded confidence placed in the potential of information processes and analysis to solve deep and urgent social problems. These are problems we may be able to solve by learning whatever we can about people, their attributes, and past actions in an effort to understand their predispositions and predict future actions. This confidence fuels an energetic quest both for information and for increasingly sophisticated tools of analysis.

The potential gains, as well as worries, of cross-analyzing one database with another drew public attention in the 1980s when federal agencies enthusiastically adopted the technique known as computer matching. In one well-known application, computerized files of federal employees were matched with welfare rolls, detecting an embarrassing list of fraudulent welfare applications submitted by people who were, at the time, employees of the federal government (Dallaire et al. 1984; Clarke 1988). Detractors argued that matching not only violated the Privacy Act of 1974, but if unchecked yielded an outcome functionally equivalent to a federal data center, a proposal that had been resoundingly defeated in the 1960s. Although by 1988 the Computer Matching and Privacy Protection Act was passed, skeptics argue that it has merely routinized the protocol for approval and does little to stem government matching and nothing to reduce matching practices in the private sector (see Regan 1995, chap. 4).

Appreciating the power of information to analyze people as well as to predict and even control their actions is not new; it is the very essence of human social relations and interaction. Attentive businesses and curious, observant individuals have always benefited from relying on what they know about people to shape successful—often mutually successful—interactions. If there is a distinctive ambition in this regard prompted by digital technologies of information, it is to develop the means of acquiring this power en masse, efficiently, automatically, and impersonally. Many important works have noted that analysis, or "processing," of data has come a long way since two-way matching of computerized file systems. For example, legal scholar Daniel Solove observed, "But aggregation's power and scope are different in the Information Age; the data gathered about people is significantly more extensive, the process of combining it is much easier, and the computer technologies to analyze it are more sophisticated and powerful" (2006, 506). We may wonder, then, whether commanding information in orders of magnitude greater than before and processing it automatically, efficiently, and impersonally is somehow morally significant. Should numbers, as the philosopher John Taurek (1977) once asked, count? This question, in various guises, will be addressed throughout the book.

One general worry is that the analysis of aggregated data sets generates information about people beyond what is given in the individual data sets. Therefore, circumstances, understandings, or even policies that surround them individually may not apply to them when the information is in an aggregated form. An important example of this is the practice of profiling, in which individuals are assigned to particular categories based on their similarity to members of a comparison class bearing similar clusters of attributes. For reasons ranging from prejudice to unfairness, critics question the legitimacy of decisions based on profiling; regardless, a large number of businesses have adopted the practice. Mortgage companies determine credit worthiness, marketing units distribute particular sales treatments, life insurance companies assess heart attack risk, and national security agencies identify prospective terrorists through this process (Lyon 2003, 2007).

Another well-known cluster of analytic techniques falls under the heading of data mining or knowledge discovery in data (KDD), which also utilizes large data aggregations to draw inferences about individuals. Instead of applying statistical techniques to verify hypothesized correlations, such as ascertaining the likelihood that registered Democrats will vote for a Democratic presidential candidate or the likelihood of dying from kidney cancer if one smokes, KDD techniques search for emergent relationships among attributes in data sets. Individuals are clustered into groups based on common patterns that are discovered in the data, thereby augmenting the range of predictive variables.[4] Exponents tout KDD as transcending both human ingenuity and human prejudice. Although certain applications of KDD and data mining techniques are directly experienced in "recommender" systems such as those of popular Web sites like Amazon.com and Netflix.com, the extent of its success in fields of marketing, national security, and law enforcement is not readily grasped, much like the extent of its full potential.

Setting aside speculations on the ultimate value of profiling and mining in predicting and shaping human action, the hopes placed in their promise has catapulted information—raw and processed—into a dynamic, starring role in social decision making. This faith in information, envisioned as an asset of enormous value, creates a virtually unquenchable thirst that can only be slaked by more information, fueling information-seeking behaviors of great ingenuity backed by determined and tenacious hoarding of its lodes. Inevitably, as our awareness of this landscape grows, so grows a sense of privacy under assault.

Before concluding this chapter with a brief account of several key companies in the information industry, it may be helpful to review a few key points. The transformations facilitated by technology over the past two decades have affected the state and practice of electronic engagement with personal information, which, in turn, are experienced as threats to privacy. The democratization of computerized information storage systems has lead not only to a proliferation of record-keeping systems of personal information but to a diversification in the social actors who maintain and use them. The mobility of information has been enhanced by great strides in the communications powers of digital electronic networks and their enthusiastic adoption worldwide. Abetted by powerful networking capabilities and interoperability in database systems, an active trend has emerged in information aggregation by merging record systems from a variety of diverse sources. Finally, the vast enterprise of meaning-making is motivating a great deal of collection, storage, and dissemination of information, facilitated by the application of computational and statistical techniques of information analysis.

Omnibus Information Providers

The practice of information aggregation drives a thriving industry of information service providers who sell products and services within all sectors of society. Their business success is fueled as much by advances in information science and technology as by social, political, and economic factors. It is interesting to note that despite successful campaigns of the 1960s and 1970s opposing such initiatives as a federal data center, the information industry, which offers much more to both the private and governmental sectors, thrives in relatively unrestrained freedom (Solove 2002b; Birnhack and Elkin-Koren 2003). A focus of concern for much scholarly and popular commentary is what here I will call *omnibus information providers,* also sometimes called online data vendors, information brokers, or information services. Although computerized records of personal information lie at the heart of many enterprises, the distinguishing mark of this sector is that information *is* their enterprise, their currency, and their business model. Financial institutions, credit card companies, insurance companies, and hospitals, for example, maintain massive record systems, but they do so in the service of something else that is their core mission. This is not so for information service providers; their raison d'être is information. The closest governmental comparison might be the Census Bureau, whose core mission is population information.

Because the personal information service sector continues to evolve rapidly, it is important to recognize that what may be true about it at the time of writing may not be true at the time of reading. The landscape has altered significantly over the past couple of decades from a terrain dominated by list-brokers specializing in supplying large directories to direct marketers and credit bureaus specializing in information intended mainly for financial institutions. Omnibus providers have, to some extent, usurped both functions as they have acquired or merged with specialized information providers and one another. For example, eFindOutTheTruth.com also owns OnlineBackground Checks.com, CellularPhoneRecords.com, and emailbreaks.com; 1800Who Where.com is affiliated with PeopleFind.com and PeopleOfAmerica.com; and Addresses.com is part of a conglomerate including Intelius.com, IAF.net, BackgroundRecordFinder.com, PublicRecordFinder.com, and 99Lists.com (Privacy Rights Clearinghouse/UCAN 2006).

Omnibus providers sometimes respond to existing needs but at other times function as consumer product developers, creating information products that they market mostly to institutions but sometimes to individuals as well. Although the vast repository of public and court records is a major source of the information they harvest, they also aggregate credit histories, insurance histories, directories, consumer records, and Social Security numbers en masse. They have carved out a distinctive marketplace in personal information and information products. While this industry is likely here to stay, it draws the attention and fire of privacy advocates, academics, and legislators who would like to see it scrutinized and reigned in (Solove 2002b; Hoofnagle 2004). The following is a snapshot of some of the major omnibus providers taken from self-portrayals on their respective Web sites as well as drawn from accounts in the popular media and academic literature.

Acxiom Corporation

Headquartered in Little Rock, Arkansas, Acxiom is a multinational company operating in Europe, Australasia, China, and Latin America.[5] It advertises many diverse products and services, characterized on its Web site as "customer information management solutions." In the United States, Acxiom's Infobase, for example, contains "multi-source data coverage" on 111 million households and 176 million individuals, including demographics, home ownership, purchase behavior, and "lifestyle," in what it claims is the "largest collection of U.S. consumer and telephone data available in one source," ideal for direct marketing (Acxiom Corporation 2007a). Specifically, it provides "socioeconomic and life-style data," e-mail lists, phone numbers appended to names and addresses, and "predictive and descriptive" models that promise to target household "decision makers" and "eliminate unresponsive households." Another product, Personicx, places *each* (my emphasis) U.S. household into one of twenty-one "Life Stage Groups" and seventy segments "based on the household's specific consumer and demographic characteristics" for the purpose of predicting and guiding action (Acxiom Corporation 2007b).

In addition to information on consumers geared to marketers, Acxiom offers what it calls "Risk Mitigation" services in a mission "to Protect America."[6] This offer is extended to "skip tracers" (whose occupation is locating missing persons, typically, who have skipped bail) and collection agencies, at whose disposal it places "vast amounts of data" and "sophisticated technology" for insight into debtor accounts. To law enforcement agencies, law firms, investigators, and corporate fraud departments, the company offers help tracking down suspects, witnesses, and assets. Its services include assistance in screening people for "personal, workplace, community, and national security" purposes. Acxiom claims access to information on almost all Americans, including sensitive information, "as allowed by law," "FCRA-compliant reports including but not limited to criminal record checks, credit reports and driving records, in combination with others such as past employment, education and professional license verification" (Acxiom Corporation 2006). It identifies potential customers, locates criminals, pinpoints criminal records, and accesses other "vital" information needed for fraud prevention processes. Close inspection reveals that much of what is offered in areas of risk mitigation is derived from public records.[7]

ChoicePoint, Inc.

ChoicePoint has done more than any other company to draw popular attention to the existence of the omnibus information sector. In February 2005 it admitted to inadvertently having sold personal records to identity thieves. In January 2006 the Federal Trade Commission announced a settlement with ChoicePoint in which the company paid a total of $15 million in penalties and consumer redress and publicly acknowledged that records on more than 163,000 individuals had been sold to criminals posing as legitimate customers. According to law enforcement officials, at least 800 cases of identity theft had resulted (Federal Trade Commission 2006).[8]

Headquartered in Alpharetta, Georgia, ChoicePoint claims to be a global leader in the information service industry. Established in 1997 when it broke away from Equifax, one of the largest credit reporting agencies in the United

States, ChoicePoint initially positioned itself as an information broker for the insurance industry.[9] In 2005 they claimed that at least 99 percent of U.S. insurance companies participated in their program; members pool information about customers in ChoicePoint's databases and in exchange they are given access to this pooled data.[10] Since its inception, ChoicePoint has extended its range beyond insurance to other businesses in the private and public sectors by steadily acquiring more than sixty other information collection and technology companies and thus absorbing their data, their technology, and their customer bases.[11] ChoicePoint advertises its ability to integrate information from a wide variety of sources (with "unmatched coverage") and to analyze it in service of wide-ranging interests. It is the "one stop shop" of the information service industry. One advertised product, "The MarketViewSM," aimed at direct marketers, claims to provide "coverage, depth, and accuracy on more than 210 million consumers" (ChoicePoint 2006c). Like Acxiom, it offers screening services, pre-employment and tenant screenings that search public and criminal records, employment and education verification, credit histories, histories of automobile and home insurance "losses," Social Security number verification, drug testing, personality testing, attitude assessments, and biometrics. ChoicePoint advertises a third family of services, identity verification, which uses a variety of approaches and mechanisms including information, passwords, digital certificates, answers to unique questions, and biometrics. In addition to general screening services, it offers individual customers credentialing information about healthcare providers, including their degrees, areas of practice, and lawsuits filed against them.

ChoicePoint offers its services to government agencies, targeting a client pool of local, state, and federal law enforcement groups including the Federal Bureau of Investigation, the Drug Enforcement Agency, and the Department of Homeland Security.[12] ChoicePoint lists its national criminal file, Social Security screen, sex offender search, county criminal search, fugitive tracking, money laundering, and identity verification as solutions for the specialized needs of law enforcement and security. AutoTrackXP is one of several products offered specifically to government security and law enforcement agencies that promises access to huge volumes of information extracted from a diverse array of public and proprietary records, integrated for security related needs. According to the Web site, AutoTrackXP offers "more than 17 billion current and historical records on individuals and businesses. . . . With as little as a name or Social Security number, users can cross-reference public and proprietary records including identity verification information, relatives and associates, corporate information, real property records, deed transfers and much more" (Hoofnagle 2004, 2005; ChoicePoint 2006a, 2006b).

First Advantage Corporation

Headquartered in St. Petersburg, Florida, First Advantage is part of the Lexis-Nexis Group, a global information service company based in New York City and known in academic and legal circles for its vast online repository of legal publications, public and court records, laws, news publications, and periodicals. First Advantage specializes in employment screening; their flagship product, HireCheck, promises "risk mitigation" by matching a candidate against at least nineteen records systems, including criminal records, credit reports, prior employment reports, records of substance abuse, vehicle license reports, and others. According to its Web site, it provides these services in over sixty countries (First Advantage Corporation 2004). It also offers an array of personal information services to firms in the financial sector, insurance companies, marketers, medical providers, collection agencies, government and law enforcement, and more. Its parent company, LexisNexis, advertises the capacity to authenticate identity, assess financial risk, screen applicants, assess customer risk, verify education, and counter fraud, including insurance and healthcare claims and mortgage and credit application fraud. Explicit about the "advanced analytics" it offers on "in depth data," LexisNexis, like many other companies in this sector, is coy about sources from which this data is drawn. We learn only that it trawls "vast databases of public records and non-traditional data," "targeting and contact information," "comprehensive public and private databases," and "consumer records" (LexisNexis 2007).

The burgeoning omnibus information industry is evidence of a spiraling feedback loop: the availability of vast repositories of digitized records of personal information spurs demand in all walks of life, demand spurs further supply, and so on. This industry services, promotes demand, and supplies pools of information with highly focused products and markets. By scouring the electronic environment for records of personal information, these companies add value to them in various ways, sometimes simply aggregating and packaging them for easy access and retrieval, and other times analyzing or mining them for offerings they believe to be valuable for potential customers. The four companies showcased here, though large and highly visible, are by no means unique and the above sketches are intended merely as a momentary impression of an extensive landscape that is evolving continuously and rapidly.

Conclusion

In this chapter, my aim has been to survey a family of systems and practices that are based on the capacity to aggregate personal information in computerized databases and to subject this information to a host of analytic probes. Capturing and analyzing personal information has provoked anxiety over threats to privacy and remains a source of ongoing complaint, protest, and resistance. Omnibus information providers, prominent actors in the burgeoning information sales and service sector, are merely one manifestation of these systems and practices. Others make up in variety and volume what they lack in salience; that is, innumerable information systems holding anything from a single data point to a deep profile on each one of us. It would be incorrect to suggest that all these information repositories, or even most of them, worry us; we even welcome and seek a presence in many of them.

To establish which systems and practices should and do cause alarm, it seems that principles identified in the Code of Fair Information Practices remain a useful guide. Generally, people are unnerved to discover they are "known" when they enter what they believe to be a new setting; we dislike having information about ourselves divulged out of context; we feel indignant when others know more about us than we want them to or when they draw unjustified conclusions about us; we enjoy sometimes escaping the demands of everyday life; and we do not like being surprised at knowledge others have about us. To be sure, none of these anecdotally recorded likes and dislikes can rise to the level of justified claims without detailed argument. To the extent they reflect popular sentiment, however, they reveal the questions we want answered by those who store and use information about us: What information do you have? From where did you get it? To whom do you give it, for what purposes, and under what conditions? Clear answers to these and other questions seem important to judgments whether privacy is threatened or violated; yet they are often not offered, and more often not offered clearly.

3 Capacity to Spread and Find Everything, Everywhere

A S DISCUSSED IN CHAPTERS 1 AND 2, ENHANCED POWERS TO gather and stockpile information have yielded socio-technical practices often experienced as threats to privacy. The subject of this chapter is a third cluster of systems and practices that are also contributing to a sense of privacy's precarious place among societal values. As with the previous two, this cluster is based on digital information technologies; however, in this case, it draws mostly on the extraordinary surge in powers to communicate, disseminate, distribute, disclose, and publish—generally, spread—information. Powerful new capabilities have yielded a continuous flow of systems and practices that challenge expectations and vex our understanding of the sources and extent of their threat to privacy. Consider, for example, a couple of such cases that have garnered public attention.

Street View is a utility of Google Maps, which was publicly announced in May 2007. As described by Google, Street View offers 360-degree photographic "streetscapes" that allow users to "explore neighborhoods at street level—virtually" (Google 2007). Users can control its photographic images by panning 360 degree vistas and progressing along them as if strolling or driving down a road. What is causing the greatest glee and consternation and attracting the public spotlight is a feature that allows users to zoom in and out of particular views. Because the images were photographed in real time, these magnifications sometimes yield personally identifying close-ups of people and their possessions. Already infamous are images of women students sunbathing on the Stanford campus, a man leaving a Manhattan strip club, and a man smoking on his balcony, as well as many clearly visible vehicle license plates (Schroeder 2007). Ironically, these and other images were further publicized by their placement on Web sites expressing vociferous objections to Street View. Critics say that Street View violates privacy; Google denies this on grounds that only public places have been photographed and placed online.

A very different illustration is a project undertaken by a man named George Bell, who decided to digitally archive and record everything in his life, beginning as far back as he could amass material and continuing into the present day and continuing into the future. Bell, an engineering fellow at Microsoft, is one of the visionary developers of foundational computer and networking technology, including the Internet. As recounted in a *New Yorker* story (Wilkinson 2007), Bell's excruciatingly detailed digital scrapbook includes regular sound recordings of conversations with others as well as snapshots taken by a small camera worn around his neck that automatically photographs people when they venture close enough to trigger an infrared sensor. What Bell will do with these photographs and conversations, currently stored in a digital archive along with all his other records, raises questions about privacy, particularly in light of the possibilities he has considered such as making them into a movie, posting them on blogs, and making them available to arbitrary viewers, including the author of the *New Yorker* article. One might wonder whether any of these uses are problematic; for example, it seems that posting photographs and conversations on a blog violates privacy more than, say, allowing friends and family to see and hear them.

These two cases have several things in common. Both involve mundane activities and practices—snapshots and scrapbooks—that appear to undergo moral transformation as they enter the realm of the digital, and their availability on global networks provokes moral indignation and queasiness. What it is about these cases and others like them that provokes moral indignation is a question we take up in chapters 4 through 9. For the remainder of this chapter, I focus on the medium of the Internet and World Wide Web. These media afford unprecedented capacities to communicate, distribute, and publish, enhanced by matching capabilities to organize, search, and find. Such capabilities demand a reexamination and refinement of what it means to disclose or not to disclose something. The Internet and Web are not the only radical enhancements to our capacities to disseminate information, but the degree to which they saturate the lived experiences of so many people in so many parts of the globe make them a suitable target of analysis. Cellular networks not only constitute another widespread, powerful medium for disseminating and communicating information, particularly information that includes a subject's concurrent location (or "geo-positioning"), but amplify these powers on the Web through applications, such as Twitter, which create seamless interfaces between the two.

Following on the themes raised by the brief examples above, I turn now to two controversial cases in which generally positive capacities of information technologies have raised genuinely hard questions about privacy, and well-meaning protagonists struggle to articulate principles to achieve balance among important values. One is the case of whether public records ought to be placed on the Web; the other is social media, specifically social networks, that provide access to personal images and information that participants place online as a matter of course. Although both cases have grown sufficiently broad in scope and complexity to warrant dedicated books and articles, the discussion here is necessarily brief, specifically highlighting how the effects of enhanced capacities to publish and disseminate disturb settled social practices and raise concerns over privacy.

Public Records Online

Public records are government records about individuals that are open to public inspection without restriction. These records, created at federal, state, and local levels of government beginning in the late nineteenth century, have evolved rapidly since the mid-twentieth century (Solove 2002a, 1142–1143). Public records cover a wide range of information, reflecting an equally wide range of transactions with government at all three levels. While some records, such as birth records, include all individuals in a constituency (most often citizens), others include only those who have engaged in particular transactions with governmental agencies, such as individuals seeking welfare. Of greatest salience are "vital records," which include birth, death, marriage, and divorce records. Other types include licensing records, which most commonly relate to the operation and ownership of vehicles, but also relate to professional practice. The government records and makes public information about home and other property ownership, voter registration, tax rolls, immigration, and arrests. In addition, public records can reveal details about people's personal lives, including name, current address, date and place of birth, parents' names, certain medical conditions, aspects of their appearance, employment status and qualifications, and property ownership information, including location, features, and price.

With a few exceptions, court records of both civil and criminal cases are also part of the larger class of public records and contain a great deal of personal information. Beyond the details of the cases themselves, these records incorporate basic identifying information such as name, address, phone number, birth date, and so forth. In addition, these records may divulge medical conditions, lifestyle choices, intimate activities, financial status, work performance, religious and political commitments, and psychological conditions of plaintiffs, defendants, and others involved in a case. But personal information contained in court records is not limited to information about protagonists; it may also cover information gleaned from jurors and members of jury pools during the checking-in process or by their answers to voir dire questions (Barber 2006).

Of course, government holdings extend well beyond public records to include, for example, records of individual tax returns held by the Internal Revenue Service, records amassed by the Census Bureau, and classified files generated by law enforcement and national security agencies. Governed by a complex system of laws and regulations,[1] the degree of their accessibility is generally determined by two regulatory regimes exerting force in opposite directions. One, stemming from the 1966 Freedom of Information Act, defines parameters for creating open access by individuals and nongovernmental organizations to records of all governmental activity, not only records of personal information. The other, stemming from the 1974 Privacy Act, constrains disclosure of personal records held by agencies of the federal government to other agencies, organizations, and individuals.[2] Public records emerge out of a balancing of principles underlying these two statutes: on one hand, a prohibition on disclosure of information following principles of fair information practices embodied in the Privacy Act, and on the other hand, with the determination of what personal information is needed to maintain an open government and to provide citizens with the capacity to understand the workings of government and assure a well-functioning democracy. Court records, a subcategory of public records, are nevertheless governed by specialized statutes and regulations and are overseen by their respective courts.[3]

Until the rise of digital technologies, public records were maintained in material form (typically paper) and dispersed in courthouses and various other federal, state, county, and municipal government buildings. Although access to these records in principle is supposed to be unconditional, in practice, various constraints may be imposed by a combination of physical limitations (as basic as hours of operation) and conditions on access, such as identification requirements, which vary across jurisdictions (Solove 2002a). The variations in the governance of public and court records is a sprawling topic that lies beyond the scope of this discussion. For our purposes, however, it is important merely to acknowledge that public records are ubiquitous, comprehensive, widely dispersed, and dispensed according to a complex and variable set of laws and regulations determined as much by historical and material contingency as by systematic, principled deliberation.[4]

One can mark the impact of digital media on public records in two phases. First, the transfer of paper records to computerized databases made it enormously more efficient to access records in bulk, although it was still necessary to find a means of distribuing this material from its original holding place, such as a court building, to its desired destination. Even in this initial phase, it was clear that the form of distribution was significant. In Higg-a-Rella, Inc. v. County of Essex, for example, a company whose business was selling municipal tax assessment data requested tax assessment data on all municipalities in the county on computer tape, the format in which it had been stored. Essex County refused. Ultimately, the New Jersey Supreme Court ruled in favor of Higg-a-Rella, but noted in their decision that the medium does matter:

> We remain committed to providing citizens with convenient and efficient public access to government information. Nonetheless, we recognize that the traditional rules and practices geared towards paper records might not be appropriate for computer records. Release of information on computer tape in many instances is far more revealing than release of hard copies, and offers the potential for far more intrusive inspections. Unlike paper records, computerized records can be rapidly retrieved, searched, and reassembled in novel and unique ways, not previously imagined. For example, doctors can search for medical-malpractice claims to avoid treating litigious patients; employers can search for workers'-compensation claims to avoid hiring those who have previously filed such claims; and credit companies can search for outstanding judgments and other financial data. Thus, the form in which information is disseminated can be a factor in the use of and access to records. (Higg-a-Rella, Inc. v. County of Essex, 1995, Sec. IV)

In other words, more than ten years ago, well before the push to make public records accessible online, courts recognized the ways in which a medium of storage and presentation makes a difference to what is revealed, even if, in some sense, the content remains unchanged. It is unfortunate that we have not seen greater attention given to the implications of this insight at large-scale policy forums.

The second phase began with government agencies seeking an online presence through such initiatives as e-Government, which are intended to facilitate and streamline interactions between citizens (and residents) and all levels of government.[5] These initiatives not only enable people to conduct transactions such as filing tax returns and paying traffic fines via government sponsored Web sites, they also provide online access to government services and information about those services. As part of this initiative, government offices began systematically placing public records online and the courts sought to follow suit with their records. Prior to the transition to electronic storage and online access, the effort required to visit distinct locales and acquire records one batch at a time made it a cumbersome business. As more and more public agencies place records online, however, seekers are able to retrieve information from myriad locales without leaving their desks. As a consequence, interested parties, from journalists and information brokers to identity thieves and stalkers, are availing themselves of these services.

Similar to the issues discussed in previous chapters, the ones arising here also force us to address moral and political concerns raised by systems and practices transformed by the adoption of new technical media. Why should online dissemination of public records raise new and distinctive privacy problems? One might argue that they do not—that there is no significant change save gains in efficiency and that those agencies are merely providing better, more efficient access to records that were already freely available. Others disagree, offering views that reflect concerns similar to those expressed by the court in *Higg-a-Rella*: different media mean different modes of availability and significance of information, in turn posing different threats to privacy. Holders of this view argue that because placing records online makes them more public than before and, at times, more public than they ought to be, access conditions need to be revisited and strengthened (e.g., Gellman 1995; Solove 2002a; Barber 2006). Despite the fact that a clearly articulated rationale for this difference has not been uniformly adopted, the intuitive sense that online placement makes a morally relevant difference is strong.

In another case decided by the New Jersey Supreme Court, this intuition is given explicit voice. The case in question, Doe v. Poritz (1995), challenged "Megan's Law," which requires certain convicted sex offenders to register with local authorities and, for those offenders considered a high risk, community notification. The court upheld the law while at the same time admitting that community notification does encroach on privacy interests. Although it accepted the argument that individuals have no reasonable expectation of privacy with regard to attributes such as name, address, appearance, and even fingerprints (section VI), the court decision seems to allow that disclosure of such information in the context of a list of convicted sex offenders does implicate privacy interests. "An individual's interest in controlling the dissemination of information regarding personal matters does not dissolve simply because that information may be available to the public in some form" (U.S. Department of Defense v. Fair Labor Relations Authority 1994, 500). Although Doe v. Poritz does not itself raise questions about online access to sex offender records, in anticipation of the conundrum raised by changing modes of access, the court cited findings from another case:

> The Court therefore found a vast difference between the public records that might be found after a diligent search of courthouse files, county archives, and local police stations throughout the country and a computerized summary located in a single clearinghouse of information. Government dissemination of information to which the public merely has access through various sources eliminates the costs, in time, effort, and expense, that members of the public would incur in assembling the information themselves. Those costs, however, may severely limit the extent to which the information becomes a matter of public knowledge. (1995, Sec. 6)

After acknowledging that the mode of access makes a material difference, the court nevertheless concluded that an incursion on privacy is justified, in these circumstances, by the need to protect significant public safety interests.

Worries about the placement of public records online and the threats it poses to privacy have generally gone unheeded. There are some exceptions, such as in the case of drivers' records in which full and unconstrained access to public records was partially revoked (Drivers Privacy Protection Act 1994), but these actions were triggered by other incidents and not directly by a movement of these records to the Web. Another insight that seems to have had little impact on the general course of policy and practice is the one offered by the court in Doe v. Poritz noting the importance of context of appearance in the judgment of whether a privacy interest has been curtailed.

Issues raised by the placement of court records online, including but not limited to privacy, have been evaluated more systematically by presiding authorities (courts and judges), legal scholars, and public interest advocates who continue to grapple with them within individual jurisdictions and in conversation with one another across jurisdictions. Although there is pressure to provide online access to records, there is no automatic presumption that a guaranteed right of access to records in their entirety is equivalent to a guaranteed right of access online. Grayson Barber, an expert on the subject of privacy interests in public records and appointed in 2006 to serve on the New Jersey Supreme Court Special Committee on Public Access to Court Records, supports such caution against making court records "radically public," observing that they contain information many regard as "exquisitely personal" such as social security numbers; income and business tax returns; child support arrangements; home addresses of litigants, witnesses, and jurors; photographs depicting violence and death; the names, addresses, and phone numbers of witnesses in criminal cases; medical and health records; psychological evaluations; and more (Barber 2006). The general sense is that wholesale online "dumping" of court records is inadvisable, but beyond this there is considerable variability across the nation not only in what degree of access is granted and restricted but in what curtailment procedures work best. Some procedures provide for routine blackouts on certain types of information, others provide procedures for lawyers on either side to file for the closing of records, others maintain open records but provide selective access to them; for example, allowing journalist access but relying on their professional discretion to embargo publication of particularly sensitive items (Winn 2004, 2008).

Social Networks and Privacy

The unprecedented degree of accessibility provided by the inclusion of public records in the digital information infrastructure promises great utility while raising disturbing questions about threats to privacy and consequent harms. While it is true that there are good reasons for providing public access, the degree of accessibility offered by the Web seems to alter the terrain in significant ways. Mixed reactions to the burgeoning universe of social networking sites have been strikingly similar in orientation—excitement tempered by worry—despite the significant differences in domain, functionality, and purpose.

Social networking sites constitute a subdomain of the larger social software ecosystem, frequently called Web 2.0, a loose class of Web sites dedicated to creating and maintaining social ties, groups, and networks. Interpreted broadly, this includes individual blogs, blog hosting services like Blogger and LiveJournal, dating services, and collaborative wikis—that is, Web sites whose underlying (wiki) software facilitates creation and collaborative editing of content. For the most part, however, Web 2.0 is associated with communal gathering spots or social networks such as Friendster, MySpace, Facebook, Orkut, LinkedIn, Flickr, YouTube, Piczo, Xanga, and many more.[6] Characteristically, social software enables individuals, even those with moderate technological facility, to express themselves online by posting opinions, information, images, photos, music, and links to other users. Another feature frequently included in these sites is a reputation assessment utility allowing participants to evaluate the quality or performance of the service provided by the site or each others' contributions. The form and governance of these sites varies tremendously in terms of what content can be posted, by whom, and how; whether sites and networks are open or accessible by invitation only; whether large (MySpace has over 120 million accounts) or intimate; and whether oriented around politics, hobbies, interests, content sharing and creation, or generalized socializing.[7]

At least three different types of privacy issues have arisen in the context of social network sites.[8] In one, the typical sequence begins with individuals posting information about themselves; later, when this information is discovered, it gets them into trouble. A spate of these cases has been reported in the popular news media: a family is angered and upset when their daughter, a Brandeis student, mentions smoking marijuana on her Facebook profile (Schweitzer 2005); a middle school student is investigated because of a threat to kill a classmate he posted on MySpace (Mehta 2006); job and internship applicants are ruled out of consideration due to risqué postings on Facebook (Finder 2006). Along similar lines, bloggers have been fired for posting critical or troubling comments about their places of work. For example, Rachel Mosteller was fired from the Durham *Herald-Sun* for critical comments written pseudonymously; Heather B. Armstrong, a Web designer, was let go for writing about her workplace and colleagues; and Ellen

Simonetti, a Delta flight attendant, was fired for posting a photograph of herself in uniform aboard an empty plane (Joyce 2005). A particularly lurid case involved Jeremiah Love, a police officer in Wichita, Texas, who was suspended from his job for posting graphic pictures of dismembered women on his MySpace page and listing his profession as super hero/serial killer (Love defended himself, saying his intentions were humorous) (Associated Press 2006). Cases like these, whether mentioned in dinner party patter or in the hallways of academic conferences, are frequently offered as evidence that "young people" no longer care about privacy—in my view, a grossly mistaken conclusion.

A second type of privacy issue emerging from social networks is raised by the near-universal practice of posting content about others on one's Web page. One colorful instance that predated the upsurge of social networks but raised similar questions involved Web postings of identifiable images of Princeton undergraduate students streaking in the so-called Nude Olympics. (In the Nude Olympics, a tradition started in the 1970s and banned by the university in 1999, undergraduate students streak on campus after the first snowfall of each season; see Stone 1999; Kubik 2001). In the contemporary landscape of social networks, perhaps the clearest illustration of this issue is the countless tagged images posted on such sites such as Flickr and Facebook, captured and posted with or without knowledge or consent. Less direct than the details that are revealed in tagged images is information that is directly and inadvertently shared when subjects list their friends, send them birthday greetings, or write about incidents involving others. Such revelations are not merely careless oversights; they are intrinsic features of social networking sites and very likely part of the attraction (Grimmelmann 2008). Photographs, stories, and anecdotes also can be posted on blogs and open discussion boards, which have come to serve as mutated proxies for personal diaries and private conversations among closed circles of friends and acquaintances. Here, too, we are reminded of Samuel Warren and Louis Brandeis's refrain—technology enabling the exposure of previously closeted aspects of life.

Some of the points considered above come together in a closer look at one online social environment, Facebook. Created in 2004 by undergraduates at Harvard, it spread quickly to virtually all universities and four-year colleges in the United States and many worldwide. Facebook enabled students to post profiles of themselves with photographs and personal information such as academic major, club membership, hobbies, and likes and dislikes that one might share with new acquaintances and friends. The various mechanisms for active socializing are compelling for many participants. They allow one to browse other pages, link to other profiles, and "poke" others (or virtual flirting), which is not simply visiting but letting others know you have visited their profiles. In 2005 Facebook expanded into high schools and in 2006 it opened up to anyone with a work e-mail address. In 2007 it became available to everyone.

Facebook quickly attracted widespread interest, some of it quizzical, including questions about what it might augur for privacy. According to Mark Zuckerberg, the founder of Facebook, privacy had been duly considered in its design, allowing members to control exactly who sees what. Early on, membership restrictions imposed natural limits on whom one might expect to be "roaming about" (since much information was available to only people in a student's network, or university/college), but beyond this, members could adjust settings on their profiles to selectively allow or prevent access. Zuckerberg expressed Facebook's strategy in these terms: "I think that where we come out is that you always want to give people control of everything" (Cassidy 2006, 59).

This disavowal suggests that Facebook's creators anticipated some of the privacy worries raised earlier, assuming one accepts control, in this sense, as providing the tools necessary for assuaging these worries. Even so, two Facebook features bear mentioning. One is tagging, which, as noted earlier, allows users who post photographs to tag them with the names of people in the photograph (and creates a link to their profiles if they have one). Those who happen to learn they have been tagged can choose to delink their profiles but cannot remove the photograph entirely. The other, added in 2006, is the "News Feed" feature, which automatically and conspicuously displays any changes that members make to their profiles on the home pages of everyone in their social network. The storm of protest following the launch of this feature took Facebook's management by surprise. They could not see the sense in this outrage. Why, they wondered, are users incensed by a novel presentation of the very same information they have already made available to their network of friends? (Schmidt 2006).

Facebook's News Feed and tagging features raise similar puzzles in relation to privacy as those we encountered with Google's Street View, the placement of public records online, and blogging one's life experiences on the Web. In support of these activities, some argue that since none of them offers new information beyond what is already "out there," there can be no privacy problem. But consistent and widespread patterns of indignation and worry should be evidence enough that something about these new modes of publication and dissemination is worth further investigation. Why, if information is already "out there" in some sense, is it problematic when it is "out there" in another place? No one is likely to disagree that public records online and Facebook's News Feed alter the degree of "public-ness" or exposure. The disagreement seems to be about what conclusions should be drawn from the consternation they engender in so doing.

I share the enthusiasm of many proponents of the Internet and World Wide Web who have praised its capacity to give voice to individuals and segments of society typically unheard under the regimes governing previous communications and broadcast media. It would not make sense to suppress these capacities. Solutions we seek should be sufficiently fine-tuned to the demands of privacy while doing as little as possible to curtail the communications capacities of the Internet and Web, not to stifle but carefully to direct and divert the flows.

Interactions

The third privacy issue raised by social networks is different from the first two in that it is driven not only by radical shifts in the capacity to share and disseminate information but also relies on capacities to monitor and track (as discussed in Chapter 1). This chapter and the previous two have provided a brief survey of technology-based activities and practices contributing to a growing sense that privacy is "under assault" (Miller 1972). These chapters do not reflect three distinct groupings of technologies and practices, but serve as an analytic framework for organizing an otherwise baffling array. The framework is based on distinct, salient characteristics that may inhere in a single system with the potential for a variety of interactions. Systems that monitor and track (such as keystroke monitoring systems, swipe entry systems, radio frequency identification systems, and clickstream tracking systems) frequently incorporate computerized databases at the backend, where captured information (like keystroke frequencies, entry and egress, movement, and Web browsing habits) is stored. These systems may also include analytic tools, allowing users to chart patterns and draw inferences. The ubiquitous cameraphone, another case in point, is a source of anxiety not only because it snaps away but because the images it captures often wind up online. And amidst the buzz of excitement over social networking Web sites, there is growing suspicion that participant profiles are being harvested directly into databases offered up for commercial profiling. MySpace, for example, is developing a method to harvest user profiles for demographic information that can be provided to advertisers, enabling these advertisers to target their audiences precisely (Kafka 2007), while Hi5 uses software called Zedo to combine user-provided personal information with address, zip code, and personal income to create intensely detailed consumer profiles ("Software Personalizes Advertising" 2007). Compounding and complementing powerful capacities to spread information are the equally powerful tools of search and retrieval that enable harvesting, targeted investigation, and aggregation of findings into "digital dossiers." And so the cycle continues.

In practice, the capacities to capture, hold, and disseminate interact and mutually reinforce one another, but teasing them apart analytically is useful for normative analysis as well as for organizing the baffling array of systems and devices into meaningful categories. When we investigate how well some of these complex systems fare under normative scrutiny, we can expect to evaluate the different components differently. A system whose monitoring function raises no worries may include a questionable storage or dissemination component. A system might not be problematic in the ways it handles information in its database but may include an overly intrusive monitoring component, and so on. Maintaining distinct categories also allows us to tailor normative standards for the respective capacities, not necessarily needing to articulate a single standard for all. There is already a form of branching in ways subfields or discourses have evolved, such as "surveillance studies," a community focusing on—in my terms—monitoring and tracking, or communities interested in "fair information practices" that discuss what I have called aggregation and analysis and the privacy dimensions of media driven by questions about the ethics of disclosure, particularly by journalists.

Analyzing the array of technologies and practices in this way helps to organize it but that is merely a beginning. In all those cases of systems and practices that are met with worry, resentment, and protest over threats to privacy, there remains the question of how systematically to adjudicate them. How do we tease apart the benefits from the threats, how do we evaluate them and craft sensible policies? We seek not only answers, but answers grounded in systematic reasons. Before we describe the framework of contextual integrity in Part III, I will survey some of the most important contributions of philosophical and legal scholarship on privacy for their crucial contributions as well as their limitations in addressing the challenges posed by technology-based systems and practices.

PART II

CRITICAL SURVEY OF PREDOMINANT APPROACHES TO PRIVACY

THE INCREASINGLY PREVALENT SYSTEMS FOR WATCHING over people, the massive storage and analytic capabilities of information systems, and the astonishing powers of dissemination of digital media discussed in Part I are not all controversial. But inevitably, with persisting regularity, certain systems invoke storms of protest and perplexed disquiet as reflected in popular opinion surveys and vocal, sometimes coordinated advocacy by nongovernmental organizations. As often as not, proponents of these systems are the industry representatives and governmental agencies who have implemented them. Popular media have created a record of these antagonistic exchanges, which reveal mutual suspicion, indignation, worried resignation, and something between grudging and trusting acceptance by those who are the subjects of monitoring, profiling, and disclosure.

A number of questions are worth asking. Why do we care? Why do we resist some systems and embrace others? What makes them troubling and controversial? What ought we, as individuals and societies, do about them—leave them be, regulate, or prohibit? And, how do we go about formulating legitimate answers to these questions?

Some believe that people's preferences and interests ought to serve as touchstones for a solution. When controversy arises over a system, it should be possible to map out distinct stakeholder groups and demonstrate how their respective interests are promoted or suppressed. To be sure, such an approach to resolving controversial matters—maximizing preference satisfaction or utility—in a democratic society is not unfamiliar. It is not, however, the approach adopted here.

In contrast, one of my starting assumptions is that preferences and interests, while certainly important factors in considering the impact of escalating practices of monitoring, recording, and disclosure, are not paramount. This approach identifies with a rich, multiple disciplinary literature that views privacy as more than an interest or preference. Privacy's moral weight, its importance as a value, does not shrink or swell in direct proportion to the numbers of people who want or like it, or how much they want or like it.[1] Rather, privacy is worth taking seriously because it is among the rights, duties, or values of any morally legitimate social and political system.

Agreeing that privacy is important for this reason is merely a beginning. To be able to move from the claim that privacy is a value or right to support a particular position on any of the controversial socio-technical systems discussed in Part I, one needs a sufficiently rich substantive account of the value or right. We need an account of privacy that justifies its place among shared, collective values of a community so that privacy is accepted as a legitimate reason for accepting or rejecting a given socio-technical system, even by those members whose interests are not best served by the conclusion.

In Part II I provide an overview of some of the most perceptive and influential theoretical accounts of what privacy is and why it is important. Although covered in less detail than they deserve, the theories are organized according to certain basic similarities and differences among them. In Chapter 4, theories that share the assumption that the importance of privacy stems from its capacity or power to support the attainment of other fundamental political, moral, or human rights and values are grouped together despite differences in detail.

Chapter 5 is organized around a dichotomy that has dominated—and to my mind subverted—a great deal of thinking on the subject of privacy; namely, the private–public dichotomy. The prevalence of this dichotomy in privacy theory, law, and policy, as well as its thoroughgoing ambiguity, is reviewed in detail. Chapter 6 offers a critical discussion of the theoretical landscape, assessing it, specifically, in terms of the practical goals set out in this book; namely, how well they guide understanding and evaluation of the challenges posed by rampant socio-technical systems. In so doing, the discussion brings to light a number of unresolved puzzles and paradoxes, including a challenge to any theory of privacy based on the private–public dichotomy that I identified in previous work as the problem of "privacy in public" (Nissenbaum 1997, 1998).

4 Locating the Value in Privacy

THE LANDSCAPE OF THEORETICAL WORK ON PRIVACY IS VAST, spanning disciplines from philosophy to political science, political and legal theory, media and information studies, and, increasingly, computer science and engineering. This chapter contains a selective look at some of these contributions. Neither an intellectual history nor a thorough scan, I strive to avoid disciplinary prejudice, although as the discussion crosses disciplinary boundaries in an effort to showcase a range of offerings, its perspective (this author's) is necessarily rooted in the analytic tradition.

One point on which there seems to be near-unanimous agreement is that privacy is a messy and complex subject. To bring order to the wide-ranging accounts and theories that may serve to explain why certain of the practices described in Part I are not only disliked but are objectionable, I provide a filter, or organizational scheme, to highlight ideas that are key to the general purposes of the book. This loose scheme incorporates three dimensions of difference within the set of theories: the first distinguishes normative accounts from descriptive ones, the second distinguishes definitions given in terms of access from those given in terms of control, and the third distinguishes accounts that locate the source of privacy's prescriptive power in its capacity to promote other important values from accounts that locate its prescriptive power in the capacity to protect a specific, private realm from access by others. After situating various theories along these dimensions in chapters 4 and

5, I evaluate how successfully they illuminate the challenges of new socio-technical practices in Chapter 6.

Descriptive and Normative Conceptions

Some authors have argued that confusion over the concept of privacy arises from a failure to recognize the difference between descriptive or neutral conceptions and normative ones. To provide a neutral conception is to state what privacy is without incorporating into its meaning that privacy is a good thing, worth having, and deserving moral and legal protection. A normative conception of privacy, by contrast, incorporates a presumption that privacy is something worthwhile, valuable, and deserving of protection. Ruth Gavison's (1980) argument supporting the need for a neutral conception as a sturdy foundation for building moral and legal conceptions is probably the most complete and best known (for others who have supported this distinction, see Powers 1996 and Tavani and Moor 2001). Gavison defines privacy as a measure of the access others have to you through information, attention, and physical proximity. I imagine something like a scale according to which people are described as having more or less privacy based on the degree to which information about them is either secret or known to others, the degree to which they are anonymous and unnoticed or under the watchful gaze of others, and the degree to which they operate in solitude or in the close physical proximity of others.

One of the benefits of starting with a neutral conception of privacy is that it allows one to talk about states of increased and decreased privacy without begging the normative question of whether these states are good or bad. It leaves open the possibility that in certain circumstances less privacy might be better than more and that reductions in privacy need not constitute violations or intrusions or incursions, all terms that signal that something has occurred that ought not to have. Those, like Gavison, who propose a neutral conception do not deny the possibility of normative accounts of privacy, and they may even agree that those are of greater interest to scholars and the general public alike. They maintain, however, that normative accounts are built on the layer of the neutral conception by means of criteria establishing how much privacy is good or required in general, under what conditions the various dimensions of privacy ought to be secured, and at what level. Applied to the cases described in Part I, this conception would indicate that all the examples involved reductions or decreases in privacy; however, whether these reductions in privacy are problematic and must be stopped has not yet been established.

Most experts are drawn solely to issues surrounding privacy's normative significance and simply finesse the question of whether a neutral conception is either plausible or needed. Others, notably Robert Post (1989) in his article on the privacy tort, have explicitly denied both the need for and existence of such a conception, arguing that since there are virtually no uses of privacy with purely descriptive meaning, one should assume that normative intent is integrated into its core meaning. In assessing an action, practice, or system, therefore, whether one says that privacy is reduced or violated comes to the same thing: a prima facie judgment that it is problematic.

It is unclear whether choosing a side in this debate makes a substantive difference for the specific concerns of the project at hand, that of devising a justificatory framework for evaluating the troubling activities, practices, and systems springing up around us. Those who posit a neutral meaning may continue to draw a contrast between descriptive and normative uses, signaling this contrast with terms like "decrease," "diminishment," and "reduction," versus "violation," "intrusion," and so forth. Others, who insist on reserving privacy for normative uses, may refer to changes in circumstances in which access to a person is increased, via information, attention, or physical proximity, by simply stating this directly. The proponent of a neutral definition, like Gavison, must still account systematically—ideally by developing theory—for the circumstances and conditions in which diminishment amounts to intrusion, while proponents of a normative conception, like Post, must still define and theorize what counts as respect for or a violation of privacy. The debate over the meanings of the term *privacy*, though not settled, can for these reasons be set aside as we turn to normative definitions and theories themselves.

Privacy, Access, and Control

Although there is a discernable difference between normative and descriptive conceptions of privacy, these differences are not significant for the purpose of evaluating the systems described in Part I. What is significant is the specific character that various theories claim for privacy, and the conditions they circumscribe for when it is preserved or violated. Two approaches commonly found in the literature include one that characterizes privacy as a constraint on access, and another that characterizes it as a form of control. Although the access and control in question could extend to personal information, as well as to people and their actions, our discussion from here on, given the focus of this project, is limited to personal information. Although a scan of literature, court records, and media reports reveals that most of what is written about privacy assumes it to be a form of control, accounts in terms of access have tended to be more precise and conceptually better developed.[1] Ruth Gavison's (1980) work, referred to above, is an example of this: privacy is a condition that is measured in terms of the degree of access others have to you through information, attention, and proximity.

The philosopher Jeffrey Reiman provides another thoughtful account in this vein, defining privacy as "the condition under which other people are deprived of access to either some information about you or some experience of you" (1976, 30). As with Gavison, Reiman's conception extends beyond information to include other experiential modes. In the case of someone being watched while showering, Reiman insists that even when not absorbing new information as the observer continues to watch, the observer's ongoing perceptual experience of the person showering may constitute a privacy invasion. Although the degree of deprivation of access is a key defining condition of privacy, the issue of who has discretion or control over determining this degree of access is an important area of negotiation between and among individuals and the societies in which they live. Reiman resists a state in which the degree of deprivation of access is fully under the control of others, but he also does not support a definition of privacy according to which individuals are accorded full control. The negotiated state over "who gets to observe one's performance of the excretory functions" (p. 30) illustrates how the degree and nature of access to individuals may be neither fully controlled by individuals themselves, nor by others, but by a combination of these in the context of general societal prohibition. In the end, the requirement of respect for privacy is that others may not have access to us fully *at their discretion.*

For the most part, however, conceptions of privacy adopted in scholarship, law, and policy incorporate control as a component of privacy, or, one might say, constitute privacy as a particular form of control. This view is particularly in evidence in literature on information privacy and the law, where adherents frequently cite Alan Westin's historic book *Privacy and Freedom*

(1967) as their source and inspiration. In it, he defines privacy as "the claim of individuals, groups, or institutions to determine for themselves when, how, and to what extent information about them is communicated to others" (Westin 1967, 7). In another highly influential paper, the legal philosopher Charles Fried writes, "Privacy is not simply an absence of information about us in the minds of others, rather it is the *control* we have over information about ourselves" (1968, 482). Along similar lines, legal scholar Michael Froomkin characterizes privacy as "the ability to control the acquisition or release of information about oneself" (2000, 1464), and legal scholar Jerry Kang's definition is "an individual's control over the processing—i.e., the acquisition, disclosure, and use—of personal information" (1998, 1203).

Another legal scholar, Anita Allen, whose groundbreaking work on privacy brings to light its political complexity, works with a definition that hybridizes control and access. According to Allen, privacy involves three dimensions: physical privacy, characterized as "special seclusions and solitude"; informational privacy, characterized as "confidentiality, secrecy, data protection and control over personal information"; and proprietary privacy, characterized as "control over names, likenesses and repositories of personal information" (Allen-Castellitto 1999, 723; see also Allen 1998). According to Allen's definition, privacy is compromised when, for example, control over information is diminished, or when a person's solitude is broken.

Common usage suggests that intuitions behind both the constraint and control conceptions are sound; namely, that control over information about oneself is an important dimension of privacy, but so is the degree of access that others have to this information, irrespective of who is in control. Intriguing challenges have been posed by those supporting one of these conceptions to those supporting the other. Does a person stranded on a desert island really have privacy? Has a person who intentionally posts photographs of himself to a Web site such as Flickr lost privacy? Does a person who is forced to wear clothing at a public gathering have more or less privacy?[2] In my view, the effect of these challenges, coupled with persuasive arguments, is not to prove that one or the other of these approaches is correct, but that both capture essential aspects of privacy that we seem to care about. A non-arbitrary resolution of this disagreement is not possible, nor, as we shall see in Part III, is it needed. Instead, I conclude this section with a promise to reveal how the conception of privacy as contextual integrity holds onto key insights from both versions, without inconsistency.

Privacy as a Normative Concept

The reason for surveying the body of theoretical works on privacy was to see what help it might offer in crafting well-reasoned responses to the dazzling and disturbing array of socio-technical systems that radically affect how much information about us is gathered, how much is known about us as a result of this, and by how many people and institutions. Those surveyed would, it seems, imply that these systems and practices diminish privacy: more information is being gathered about us—frequently without our knowledge let alone our consent—and therefore more is known about us. Learning that privacy is "diminished" is not as interesting to most people, however, as learning that it has been "threatened," "violated," or "invaded." In short, people want to identify the moral and political significance of any given instance of diminished privacy; they want to know in general terms when privacy claims are justified. Since a right to privacy imposes obligations and restrictions on others, it is important that that right be circumscribed in a non-arbitrary manner. To be sure, this is an important requirement if a right to privacy is to be embodied in policy, law, and regulation of technology, or used as a guide for distinguishing actions and practices that are morally and politically problematic from those that are acceptable or deserving to be embraced.

The need to articulate and give legitimacy to a right to privacy has steered an extensive literature over the course of the past five decades. For many, the provocation has been—as it is here—a need to systematically evaluate and prescribe limits on technology-based systems and practices. In selecting the sample of works to showcase here I was influenced by their stances on two organizing principles; although related, they need to be pried apart. A theory of a right to privacy should include a definition of the right, an account of its nature (e.g., moral, political, legal, etc.), and principles for delineating its scope. It may also provide an account of the source or sources of this right; a meta-principle, if you will. For example, a normative account of privacy based on preferences or interests might claim that people have a right to control information about themselves, or have a right to place restrictions on access to information about themselves, because this best serves their interests or because this accords with most people's preferences.

A contrasting approach searches for the sources of a right to privacy in the framework of moral and political values. Within this rubric, theories may still differ from one another in their definitions, principles, and scope, as well as in the particular values they associate with privacy. What they share, however, is a notion that privacy is bound up in the constellation of values to which most, if not all, societies are committed. Individualized preferences and interests are not irrelevant to privacy, but instead of being defining sources of its importance they would be secondary considerations, the primary considerations being those moral and political values that privacy is presumed to support.

Readers familiar with perennial debates among supporters and detractors of economic accounts of human behavior as well as social, political, and legal systems will rightly place this brief allusion within the larger general debate. They will also understand, therefore, why I choose not to persevere with a general defense of one or the other of the contrasting approaches. While it is important to acknowledge that there are accounts of a right to privacy that point to preferences and interests as its direct sources, these predominantly economic works are not included among those I have showcased below.

Within the rubric of theories of a right to privacy rooted in values, a second organizing principle is how these theories circumscribe its extent and limit. As a starting place, we may all readily agree that no one (except possibly a hermit or someone living in total isolation) can have absolute control over all information about him- or herself. In this regard, we are all at the mercy of those simply passing us by on streets or engaging with us in mundane daily interactions, and more so with others who have virtually unbounded access to us. So, even if we agree that a claim to privacy is morally legitimate, and that privacy is about control or restricted access to information about us, it would be singularly unhelpful to circumscribe a right in such a way that it is violated every time a motorist peers at a pedestrian crossing the street. A plausible theory of privacy that includes an account of its moral legitimacy, therefore, will also include a principled account of its limits.

In the following discussion of some of the theories I have found most useful and important, I have organized them into two rough categories based on the approaches they take in accounting for the extent and limits of morally legitimate privacy claims. In one category, I have included theories that allow morally legitimate privacy claims to range over all information, delineating the extent and boundaries for such claims in terms of their capacity to promote other significant moral and political values. In the other category, I have included theories that attribute the moral legitimacy of privacy to privacy's capacity to protect a private zone for humans. Accordingly, the right to privacy they circumscribe ranges only over a restricted class of (private) information.

The remainder of this chapter will be devoted to a discussion of theories fitting the first category; in Chapter 5 I will discuss those fitting the second.

Before plunging forward with my overview, I pause a moment for clarifications and caveats. A point about terminology: although I am aware of long-standing debates over the meanings of terms such as *rights, claims,* and *values,* I will try to avoid taking substantive positions in any of these. My overriding aim is to achieve consistency while adhering to common usage, to the extent possible. I will refer interchangeably to a *morally legitimate claim to privacy* and a *right to privacy*; where it is necessary to specify the legal status of a claim or right, I will talk of a *legal* right to privacy, or a claim to privacy recognized in the law. The caveat concerns the works I have chosen to discuss, recognizing that the field of privacy, including aspects related to its research, scholarship, and policy making, has blossomed and matured. Therefore, I make no claim to have offered a complete or even representative sampling of the theoretical literature. (My hunch, however, is that unsampled theories will align with my categories.) Interested readers are encouraged to fill in the picture both by delving more deeply into the primary sources listed in the Bibliography and by reaching out to works not included there.

The Value of Privacy

What gives privacy moral legitimacy as a claim to limit access to information or to control information? What is the extent of this right, and what factors might limit it? These questions drive much of the substantial body of theoretical work on privacy. In the remainder of this chapter I will discuss samples that link privacy to important human values by arguing that privacy is either functionally or necessarily related to other more traditionally recognized, entrenched moral and political values. Some of the links drawn between privacy and values pertain to the lives of individuals; others connect privacy with values in human relationships; and yet others reveal an important association between privacy and social values.

Privacy and the Individual

Ruth Gavison's account of privacy locates its value in its functional relationship to valued ends, including human well-being and development, creativity, autonomy, mental health, and liberty (Gavison 1980). Drawing on widely accepted connections, Gavison also points to spheres of life in which people need freedom from close and constant scrutiny to flourish, such as artistic expression and intellectual development. Furthermore, to cultivate sufficient maturity to formulate and pursue life plans and to form independent moral and political judgments, people need leeway to experiment without the distraction of being watched; to be unafraid of disapprobation, censure, and ridicule; and to be free from pressure to conform to popular, conventional standards.

The connections drawn by Gavison are echoed by many others. Jeffrey Reiman, whose definition of a right to privacy we encountered earlier, sets out to demonstrate that privacy is "an especially important and good thing for human beings" (1995, 33) by proposing a thought experiment in which we imagine life in an informational fishbowl, in an "informational panopticon." A key characteristic of this informational panopticon is that like the convicts in Jeremy Bentham's panoptic prison (Bentham 1995), the people inside this fishbowl are visible from a single point. This is not as far-fetched as it initially sounds considering present day analogs of companies like ChoicePoint and other information brokers (discussed in Chapter 2) that make all information about people accessible from a single point. For the people trapped inside an informational panopticon, Reiman speculates that there are four types of risk: risks of extrinsic and intrinsic losses of freedom, symbolic risks, and risks of "psycho-political metamorphosis" (1995, 175).

Extrinsic losses of freedom occur when people curtail outward behaviors that might be unpopular, unusual, or unconventional because they fear tangible and intangible reprisals, such as ridicule, loss of a job, or denial of benefits. Intrinsic losses of freedom are the result of internal censorship caused by awareness that one's every action is being noted and recorded. This occurs as those being watched begin to view themselves and their actions from the perspective of those watching. They are thus deprived of spontaneity and full agency as they self-consciously formulate plans and actions from this third party perspective. Privacy mitigates against both those losses because it functions "as a means of protecting freedom, moral personality, and a rich and critical inner life" (Reiman 1995, 42). Reiman has argued that privacy, when it is asserted as a capacity to withdraw from scrutiny, amounts to an expression of individual sovereignty or self-ownership. The symbolic risk of institutional structures that deny individuals the capacity to withdraw is that they deny them this expression of self-ownership.[3] The fourth risk to individuals, of psycho-political metamorphosis, follows Reiman's speculation that if people are subjected to constant surveillance, they will be stunted not only in how they act, but in how they think. They will aspire to a middle-of-the-road conventionality—to seek in their thoughts a "happy medium."

Similar issues drive legal scholar Julie Cohen's account of the value of privacy. One of her prime concerns is the move to frame privacy as a form of property and, consequently, a marketable commodity (Cohen 2000). Cohen resists this move, insisting that privacy deserves a place alongside values such as equality and freedom, because, she argues, privacy is crucial for the development of moral autonomy, "independence of critical faculty and imperviousness to influence" (p. 1424). With regard to privacy, therefore, "a degree of freedom from scrutiny and categorization by others promotes important non-instrumental values, and serves vital individual and collective ends" (p. 1423). Cohen hypothesizes that absent the space privacy provides for engaging in the "conscious construction of self" (p. 1424), a person's beliefs and desires are more likely to fall within the limited spectrum of the mainstream.

Before exploring the links that have been drawn between privacy and other values, it is worth evaluating two recurrent challenges to privacy's role in promoting freedom. One challenge comes down to this: only those with something to hide have something to fear, or, in other words, to the extent privacy facilitates freedom, it is more likely to serve as a cover for the freedom to do wrong. The second challenge is that privacy does not train strong self-direction but instead gives cover to moral timidity. Rather than hide unpopular choices, we should learn to be strong enough to resist social pressure and stand up for the right to be different. Being open about unpopular and unconventional choices (e.g., when a gay man chooses to reveal his homosexuality) has the secondary benefit of giving others the courage to do the same and might even promote tolerance and understanding of those choices in surrounding societies.

In rebutting these two challenges, Gavison and Reiman remind us that in liberal, nontotalitarian societies significant areas of life are protected from public regulation (the classical source of these ideas is, of course, John Stuart Mill's *On Liberty* [1859, 9]). In these areas, people are (in theory) let alone to decide and act as they please, as long as they do not directly harm others. In the United States and many other western democracies, these areas encompass religion, diet, sexual orientation, selection of friends, what one reads, what music one listens to, the use of birth control, consumption of alcohol, and so forth. Although it lies outside the scope of this book to assess, in general, how liberal societies ought to delineate these areas, they are committed to freedom from interference in areas we might call "zones of liberty" (whatever they might be in a given society). Pursuit of lifestyles and life choices that run afoul of particular community mores are not only tolerated in liberal societies but, according to classic traditions, are potential sources of advancement and development.[4] Privacy is important because it protects the diversity of personal choices and actions, not because it protects the freedom to harm others and commit crimes.

What of the second challenge, that openness requires moral courage because it forces societies to confront difference, and that, by contrast, privacy promotes moral timidity? To this Gavison and Reiman respond that morality does not require supererogatory acts of its adherents. Prejudice, hatred, and irrational suspicion of others are known to persist even in societies explicitly committed to political principles of toleration for racial groups, religious affiliations, ethnicities, lifestyle choices, and sexual orientation. Demanding openness as a show of character and as a means of "educating" the rest of society is calling for a sacrifice where positive results are not assured. "The absence of privacy," Gavison notes, "may mean total destruction of the lives of individuals condemned by norms with only questionable benefit to society. If the chance to achieve change in a particular case is small, it seems heartless and naïve to argue against the use of privacy" (1980, 454). Similarly, Reiman reminds us that "laws and social practices generally have to be designed for the real people that they will govern, not for some ideal people that we would like to see or be" (1995, 36). He continues, "Even if people should ideally be able to withstand social pressure in the form of stigmatization or ostracism, it remains unjust that they should suffer these painful fates simply for acting in unpopular or unconventional ways. In any actual society we will need privacy to prevent this injustice" (p. 36).

Privacy and Other Values

In the following passage, James Nehf (2003) encapsulates the web of anxieties we may confront as a result of diminishing privacy:

> The more cognizable and immediate problem with a loss of information privacy, and the problem that is most likely to produce a political resolution, is our inability to avoid circumstances in which others control information that can affect us in material ways—whether we get a job, become licensed to practice in a profession, obtain a critical loan, or fall victim to identity theft. We cannot avoid the collection and circulation of information that can profoundly

affect our lives. We feel that we have little or no voice or choice in the data collection and sharing process. We do not know who has what information, how they got it, what purposes or motives those entities have, or what will be done with that information in the future. Even if the information in databases is accurate and complete in all relevant respects, it can still harm us if it falls into the wrong hands or if it is used for a purpose we did not envision when we disclosed it. (p. 26)

One finds these and other anxieties systematized in the work of philosopher Jeroen van den Hoven, who offers one of the clearest accounts of the value of privacy for individuals.[5] He sorts moral reasons for why privacy deserves protection into four types: (1) information-based harm, (2) informational inequality, (3) informational injustice, and (4) encroachment on moral autonomy (2001, 433). Van den Hoven arrives at these distinctions by asking what gives moral legitimacy to public policy that would restrict the collection, retrieval, and dissemination of data not simply because it satisfies idiosyncratic desires and preferences, but because it furthers moral ends, prevents harms, and promotes equality, justice, and autonomy. These distinctions deserve closer examination.

Informational Harm.   As an increasing array of critical transactions are mediated via Internet or phone (e.g., banking, travel, interactions with government agencies, and shopping), the unrestricted availability of information such as Social Security numbers, mothers' maiden names, passwords, and home addresses enables fraudulent construction of identities in a crime now commonly called "identity theft." (The three-year Javelin Strategy and Research Identity Fraud Survey Report, conducted with the Better Business Bureau, found that identity fraud affects from 8 to 10 million Americans a year, with a financial average of $5,720 in harms per victim in 2007. See Privacy Rights Clearinghouse 2007b.) Harms to victims range from financial to reputational, and include wasted time, frustration, fear, anxiety, and ultimately reluctance to engage in socially beneficial activities. Information that is too freely available from school and government records or media reports sometimes falls in the hands of stalkers, pedophiles, and others with harmful intent. A poignant case, which ultimately led to restrictions on access to drivers' records, was the murder of actress Rebecca Schaeffer, whose address was gleaned from then freely available drivers' records. Data protection is needed to protect against harms like these, and many others (Solove 2004).[6]

Informational Inequality.   When the flows of personal information are not systematically constrained, the benefits may accrue disproportionately to some parties over others. This is what van den Hoven calls informational inequality. Take, for example, the existing market in personal information in which corporate and governmental actors agglomerate transactional and biographical information on customers and consumers. Individuals engaging with these providers of goods and services may be unaware that information is being systematically collected, have no idea what happens to it beyond the point of the initial transaction, and not realize that information they share freely has a value in the information marketplace. Institutional structures in society generally do not provide individuals with mechanisms for engaging as agents in this marketplace[7] and they generally have few realistic opportunities for gaining equivalent access to information about the corporate actors with whom they interact. As a result, the information marketplace is far from level, with insufficient protections in place to ensure that exchanges are governed by "openness, transparency, participation, and notification on the part of business firms and direct marketers to secure fair contracts" (van den Hoven 2001, 435).

The problem of informational inequality was explicitly placed on the policy agenda at least as early as 1973 by the Secretary's Advisory Committee on Automated Personal Data Systems of the U.S. Department of Health, Education, and Welfare. When charged with a study of problems arising from the use of computers for personal record-keeping, the committee conceived of their task as assuring some leverage to individuals interacting with far more powerful government agencies and large corporations:

> The report explores some of the consequences of these changes and assesses their potential for adverse effect on individuals, organizations, and the society as a whole. It concludes that the net effect of computerization is that it is becoming much easier for record-keeping systems to affect people than for people to affect record-keeping systems. Even in nongovernmental settings, an individual's control over the use that is made of personal data he gives to an organization, or that an organization obtains about him, is lessening. (U.S. Department of Health, Education, and Welfare 1973, "Summary and Recommendations")

In his influential book *The Panoptic Sort* (1993), Oscar Gandy also draws connections between inadequate privacy protections and inequalities. From initial positions of vast inequalities in power and status that are exacerbated by unequal access to information, systems and practices of aggregation, profiling, and segmentation yield a "panoptic sort." Inequalities of starting position, filtered through the panoptic sort, result in an insidious form of discrimination among individuals and groups, with some deemed worthy of various privileges, such as special offers on consumer products, mortgages, discount coupons, credit cards, and so forth, and others deemed unworthy.[8]

Informational Injustice.   By informational justice, van den Hoven means the extent to which information remains in its proper sphere. Building on Michael Walzer's (1984) concept of "spheres of justice," van den Hoven argues that information belonging in one sphere should not be allowed to migrate into another or others because if it does, informational injustice will have been perpetrated. An example of such injustice would be if a job candidate's medical history or religious affiliation found its way into the files of a company considering him for employment.[9] Data protection laws should scrutinize practices that involve spreading information from one sphere into others in which it does not belong.

Theorists besides van den Hoven have understood how important context is in judging whether the spread of information constitutes an injustice. Consider another recurrent counter to calls for stronger privacy protection.[10] This one reflects on an idealized past (or distant present) in which people in small towns live happily together knowing a great deal about one another. This scenario is supposed to show that calls for privacy should not be understood as a means to resist the intrusion of newfangled, technology-based systems and practices that would make our lives dangerously transparent, but as a material change from this idealized past and possibly the source of social alienation and loneliness. Jeffrey Rosen and Priscilla Regan have challenged the significance of this sentimental idyll, pointing out that to the extent that people did indeed live happily together, key interacting elements cannot be overlooked. First, what people knew about one another was set in a rich social context; second, power differentials were relatively small; and third, knowledge was reciprocal (Regan 1995, 223). Take context, for example; it lends meaning and significance to information. An impression formed about someone when you hear he has been arrested is affected by knowing the charges were dropped, or that it was for political protest, or administering marijuana to a cancer patient, or sexual assault. Imagine what you might infer about someone, upon learning that she defaulted on a loan, whether or not it occurred during a time of major economic recession (Rosen, 2000, 8; see also Laudon 1986). To minimize informational injustice, well-crafted data protection rules stanch the movement of information from one sphere into others where it does not belong.

Encroachment on Moral Autonomy. A fourth reason for data protection is moral autonomy, which, according to van den Hoven, is "the capacity to shape our own moral biographies, to reflect on our moral careers, to evaluate and identify with our own moral choices, without the critical gaze and interference of others and pressure to conform to the 'normal' or socially desired identities" (2001, 439). Van den Hoven's depiction of the relationship between privacy and moral autonomy resembles Cohen's, Reiman's, and Gavison's: according to the liberal vision, the actions of ideal moral agents are guided by principles arrived at through critical reflections. According to van den Hoven, because privacy constitutes one of the conditions for developing critical faculties and moral independence, a liberal state ought to make a political commitment to privacy: "Data protection laws thus provide protection against the fixation of one's moral identity by others than one's self and have the symbolic utility of conveying to citizens that they are morally autonomous" (p. 440).

Privacy and Autonomy

The vital role that autonomy is believed to play in arguments for adequate privacy protection deserves closer inspection.[11] There appears to be support in the literature for at least three forms of this relationship. One is conceptual. If privacy is understood as the claim or right to control or determine access to information about oneself, and autonomy is understood as self-determination embodied in the individual "whose actions are governed by principles that are his own" and who "subjects his principles to critical review, rather than taking them over unexamined from his social environment" (Benn 1971, 24), then privacy is, in fact, partially constitutive of autonomy. In other words, in the relationship between privacy and autonomy so conceived, the connection is not a causal one. Instead, privacy is to be understood as a form of autonomy: specifically, it is self-determination with respect to information about oneself. Two related but slightly different forms of this idea draw connections between privacy and self-presentation, and privacy and identity formation. According to those theories, privacy constitutes the capacity to shape how individuals define themselves and present themselves to others in the variety of life's circumstances and as such, the capacity to express an important dimension of autonomy, or self-determination (Goffman 1959; Austin 2007).

Second, insofar as privacy, understood as a constraint on access to people through information, frees us from the stultifying effects of scrutiny and approbation (or disapprobation), it contributes to material conditions for the development and exercise of autonomy and freedom in thought and action. There are many ways that unfettered access to information may, directly, thwart self-determination. Seeking approval and trying to avoid disapproval, people may feel compelled to act in certain ways; as long as we are being observed, monitored, and possibly judged, constantly taking others into consideration in determining courses of action and decisions, our actions are not truly voluntary. But there are also indirect disciplining effects that we know to be embodied in the fundamental notion of a panopticon, for even when we are uncertain whether or not we are being watched, we must act as if we are. When this happens, when we have internalized the gaze of the watchers and see ourselves through their eyes, we are acting according to their principles and not ones that are truly our own (Bentham 1995; Foucault 1995). But panoptic effects might be even more insidious than this, leading to a diminishment in our capacity to formulate principles, plans, and desires with which we truly identify. According to this framing of the relationship between privacy and autonomy, it is not conceptual but causal for privacy is claimed to be an important aspect of an environment in which autonomy is likely to flourish, and its absence likely to undermine it.

A third form of the relationship between privacy and autonomy, while also causal, draws on a different or augmented understanding of autonomy, referring not only to the capacity to review principles of action critically and the freedom to act on them, but also to the capacity or wherewithal to follow through. We have already seen that autonomy is curtailed when we are limited in our capacity to ground our actions and decisions on beliefs, desires, and goals with which we fully identify. But this dimension is further stunted when people are not provided the basic means to follow through. An example might be the person who, upon critical reflection of her life's goals, forms the ambition to become a lawyer, but lives in a society that does not provide basic education to members of her social group. Under conditions like these, writes Gerald Dworkin, we "feel used . . . as an instrument of another's will" (1988,

14). Due to the manipulation by others of a people or their circumstances, their autonomy, in the form of follow-through, is stunted.

To see how this connects to privacy, it is necessary to return to the world of pervasive monitoring, data aggregation, unconstrained publication, profiling, and segmentation—Oscar Gandy's world of the panoptic sort. In this world, the manipulation that deprives us of autonomy is more subtle than the world in which lifestyle choices are punished and explicitly blocked. Widespread surveillance and the aggregation and analysis of information enhance the range of influence that powerful actors, such as government agencies, marketers, and potential employees, can have in shaping people's choices and actions. Bearing a disturbing resemblance to the techniques of con men or blackmailers, these techniques of influence may exploit people's weaknesses, bargain from positions of unfair advantage, target us for certain treatments, and, perhaps even more problematically, withhold information about opportunities if the people in question have been deemed unworthy (Gandy 1993). If, as a result of these manipulations, people choose jobs, banks, or products not primarily because they comply with our own values, but because they have been kept in the dark about more relevant options, they are victims of a form of deception or coercion, even subtler than that of the con man or blackmailer. According to Dworkin, being deceived or simply kept in the dark has implications for autonomy: "Both coercion and deception infringe upon the voluntary character of the agent's actions. In both cases a person will feel used, will see herself as an instrument of another's will" (1988, 14).

It would be absurd to insist that only the person who is utterly impervious to all outside influences is truly autonomous; that person would simply be a fool. Although the line between morally acceptable and unacceptable ways of shaping, manipulating, and influencing people's actions is a fine, even fuzzy one, the distinction is nevertheless real and worth insistent probing. According to Dworkin, it is important to distinguish

> those ways of influencing people's reflective and critical faculties which subvert them from those which promote and improve them. It involves distinguishing those influences such as hypnotic suggestion, manipulation, coercive persuasion, subliminal influence, and so forth, and doing so in a non ad hoc fashion. Philosophers interested in the relationships between education and indoctrination, advertising and consumer behavior, and behavior control have explored these matters in some detail, but with no finality. (1988, 18)

Gandy's worry is that the opportunities offered and withheld as a result of the careful process of sorting (the "panoptic sort") more often than not constitute forms of subversive manipulation because they have little to do with assessing what is needed based on goals people have set for themselves, or the achievement of values and ends to which we are committed.[12] Instead, they are predicated on the exploitation of people and their circumstances for the benefit of others.

My purpose here has not been to settle the question but to reveal a potential connection between unbridled data collection, aggregation, and profiling and a subtle erosion of autonomy. As far as I can see, there is insufficient evidence to claim that these systems and practices, in general, lead to coercion, deception, and manipulation, only that they may. I do not believe we can avoid the demands of difficult line-drawing to which Dworkin refers, and, to this end, a readiness to embrace the details of case-by-case analysis. I return to these issues later in the book.

Privacy and Relationships

Permeating many prominent philosophical works on privacy is a preoccupation with the role it plays in human relations. In one of the earliest and most oft-cited articles incorporating this theme, the legal philosopher Charles Fried asserts a dependence on privacy of valuable human relationships that is not merely instrumental and contingent, but necessary. He writes, "It is my thesis that privacy is not just one possible means among others to insure some other value, but that it is necessarily related to ends and relations of the most fundamental sort: respect, love, friendship and trust. Privacy is not merely a good technique for furthering these fundamental relations; rather without privacy they are simply inconceivable" (1968, 477). There are two sides to this coin: our closest relationships of love and friendship are defined by our willingness to share information, yet we signal our trust in and respect for others by not insisting that they relinquish control over information to us. Although Fried conceives of privacy as control over information about oneself, his claim that information serves as "moral capital" for "relationships which we would hardly be human if we had to do without—the relationships of love, friendship and trust" (p. 484) does not extend to all information, but to private information only. What falls in this category, according to Fried, is determined by a rough ordering conventionally designated and very likely culturally and historically contingent, whereby information ranges from the most general facts about people to those considered private and personal. If we grant that friendship, intimacy, and trust are fundamental goods without which human life would be intolerably degraded and accept that "in developed social contexts love, friendship and trust are only possible if persons enjoy and accord to each other a certain measure of privacy" (p. 482), Fried's thesis follows and privacy protection is endowed with moral legitimacy.[13]

The idea of privacy as a necessary context for important relationships has been developed in various directions. One such theory suggests that its value lies not only in regulating closeness, but also in regulating the distinctiveness or variety of relationships. Ferdinand Schoeman, who has developed one of the deepest and most subtle philosophical accounts of privacy and its value to humans, writes, "People have, and it is important that they maintain, different relationships with different people. Information appropriate in the context of one relationship may not be appropriate in another" (1984, 408). This assessment is echoed in the work of philosopher James Rachels, who attributes to privacy a key role in differentiating the variety and distinctiveness of relationships people need to maintain: "the value of privacy [is] based on the idea that there is a close connection between our ability to control who has access to us and to information about us, and our ability to create and maintain different sorts of social relationships with different people" (1975, 326). Privacy makes it possible for people to share information discriminately, which in turn enables them to determine not only how close they are to others, but the nature of their relationships:

> businessman to employee, minister to congregant, doctor to patient, husband to wife, parent to child, and so on. In each case, the sort of relationship that people have to one another involves a conception of how it is appropriate for them to behave with each other, and what is more, a conception of the kind and degree of knowledge concerning one another which it is appropriate for them to have. (Rachels 1975, 328)

Privacy and Society

When arguing in support of a moral right to privacy and articulating its scope, most discussions emphasize privacy's importance for individuals— their personal well-being and relationships with others—and for its capacity to support other moral and political rights firmly rooted in liberal, democratic traditions. Amid these discussions, however, have been a few persistent voices calling attention to the social value of privacy; that is, the value of privacy to society.[14] The argument put forth by political scientist Priscilla Regan in *Legislating Privacy* (1995) is the most thoroughly developed and innovative. In a fastidiously drawn history of approximately five decades of privacy regulation in the United States, Regan lists case after case of well-justified initiatives to protect privacy through legislation and rule making that have fallen by the wayside. These failures, according to Regan, are the result of associating privacy with the interests of individuals, which, in the end, are usually outweighed by countervailing social needs—dire or otherwise (e.g., business efficiency, national security, law enforcement, or economic prosperity). Furthermore, focusing on the value of privacy for individuals fails to recognize its importance as (1) a common value, (2) a public value, and (3) a collective value.

> Most privacy scholars emphasize that the individual is better off if privacy exists; I argue that society is better off as well when privacy exists. I maintain that privacy serves not just individual interests but common, public, and collective purposes. If privacy became less important to one individual in one particular context, or even to several individuals in several contexts, it would still be important as a value because it serves other crucial functions beyond those that it performs for a particular individual. (Regan 1995, 221)

In claiming privacy to be a common value, Regan is not merely suggesting that it is valued by many individuals. She is claiming that in promoting the interests of many individuals, the particular types of interests and benefits that privacy brings to individuals translate into a societal good. Too often, societal goods are seen to be consonant with the interests of corporate and governmental organizations that mediate many critical aspects of life, such as medical care, education, financial transactions, employment, and security; these organizations are hungry for information. Conversely, when we credit privacy with the role it plays in promoting values such as autonomy, human development, and freedom of thought and action, we stop at the good of the individuals. It is time, Regan argues, to emphasize how crucial these values—values such as freedom of speech, association, and religion—are to the flourishing of liberal societies. As such, privacy is to be grasped as a common value.

In claiming privacy as a public value, Regan has in mind the various ways it supports democratic political systems, particularly liberal democracies. First, it is constitutive of the rights of anonymous speech and freedom of association, and is implicated in the institution of the secret ballot. Second, privacy shields individuals against over-intrusive agents of government, particularly in spheres of life widely considered out of bounds. Third, inspired by the works of Hannah Arendt, John Rawls, Oscar Gandy, and Carl Friedrichs, Regan (1995, 226–227) argues that privacy allows people to separate and place in the background aspects of their private lives that generally distinguish them from others, such as distinctive preferences, personal interests and relationships, religious commitments, habits, hobbies, and tastes. As a result, when people come together in a public realm, they are able to place in the foreground what they have in common with their fellow citizens. This state of affairs affirms their equality as citizens; equal consideration is given to others and is expected in return.

Although the various freedoms form a common starting place, there is a difference between the collective value and public value of privacy. The former refers to the shared benefits of living in a society in which people develop distinctive personalities, can develop and express creativity, and are educated and independent minded. In defending the public value of privacy, Regan stresses its importance for key institutions of democracy such as the assumption of autonomy in promoting healthy democratic elections, the assurance of a secret ballot, and the existence of a vibrant public realm.

In touting privacy as a collective good, Regan invokes yet a third social dimension, that of privacy as a nonexcludable, indivisible collective good like clean air and national defense. In my view, Regan has a tougher time establishing this connection than the other two, arguing that like other collective goods, privacy is best protected through public regulation rather than through mechanisms of private ordering, notably, a competitive free market.[15] Even though many of the benefits of privacy accrue to individuals, just as those of clean air, there are three reasons why the marketplace solution for privacy protection is not viable. First, there is little incentive to allow or facilitate participation or desertion on an individual basis, as is required for a competitive free marketplace, because much of the value in personal information for corporations and government actors lies in its completeness and because value of the end product is depleted by administrative overhead. Second, only a fraction of useful information is, in fact, provided with explicit consent of subjects; most of it is either yielded under terms that are effectively nonvoluntary, such as in the context of taxation, banking, and health care where full participation is required, or gleaned from secondary sources as by-products of transactions or systems of monitoring. The ideal of a free market exchange, which requires openness and choice, is inimical to both these circumstances. Finally, in mediated communications systems, a key source of personal information gathering, the level of privacy is a function of technical design and administration, such as the ability to track the geographic location of wireless callers or the ability to block Web cookies. Once these features are settled for the system as a whole, it becomes difficult, if not impossible, for individuals to determine a particular level for themselves.[16]

Conclusion

This chapter offered a brief overview of several key theoretical works on privacy that conceive of the value of privacy instrumentally in terms of its value to individuals, relationships, and society at large. One way to connect insights from these works to the mission of evaluating socio-technical threats is to study how the systems in question, in reducing levels of privacy, might be blocking or reducing the attainment of these other values.

5 Privacy in Private

ONE OF THE CHIEF REASONS FOR UNCOVERING THE SOURCES OF moral legitimacy for privacy claims is to guide our responses to encounters with socio-technical systems. According to the theories surveyed in Chapter 4, the right to control information and to limit access—the right to privacy—is grounded in the cluster of values that privacy underwrites. When we formulate resistance (or capitulate) to specific socio-technical systems, it is frequently with reference to these values. However, there is another influential approach that derives privacy's value from the role it plays in delineating a protected, private sphere for individuals. We can tease apart two strands in this approach, one a positive strand, the other, if you will, a negative one. The positive strand stresses the importance to individuals of a private sphere or zone in which one is able to avoid scrutiny, approbation, accountability, and so forth, drawing on a similar set of assumptions and arguments to those reviewed in Chapter 4. A right to (informational) privacy, by imposing limits on access to information, is one means of creating or asserting such a sphere. In other words, as before, we recognize privacy's instrumental value but specifically focus here on its role in circumscribing a private sphere.

The negative aspect of this thesis looks critically at a great deal of work on privacy, judging it to be overly inclusive. Legal scholar Tom Gerety concedes that privacy is important and worth protecting, but only once its conceptual sprawl has been radically trimmed. Focused predominantly on the legal concept of privacy, Gerety asserts, "A legal concept will do us little good if it expands like a gas to fill up the available space" (1997, 234). He holds that the effectiveness of privacy in legal discourse and practice has waned as a result of its becoming overbroad, vague, and burdened with incoherent requirements: "The doubt in this regard comes not from the concept's meagerness but from its amplitude, for it has a protean capacity to be all things to all lawyers, and, as often defined and defended, it lacks readily apparent limitations of its own" (p. 234). Gerety's remedy is to reign in the concept, to snip away at meanings and applications that have cluttered it and allowed it to leach into areas and cases where it does not belong. To frame his proposal, Gerety taps into the familiar private/public dichotomy that pervades political and legal discourse: thus, privacy holds sway, or has prescriptive power, in the realm of the private, but not in the realm of the public. In taking this step, Gerety shares a path taken by a number of privacy scholars.

It is a path, moreover, even more pervasive outside the academy, where it is deeply engrained in public policy, serves as a guide in the courts, and is a reference point for government and commercial practices. Given the prominence of the public/private dichotomy as the basis for distinguishing legitimate privacy claims, its role in privacy discourse deserves closer scrutiny. The dichotomy itself, although both useful and well entrenched in legal and political thought, is the subject of ongoing study. There seems to be general agreement, however, that although the terms *private* and *public* vary in meaning from one arena to another (and I take this assertion to be relatively uncontroversial among scholars in law and politics), they invariably demarcate a strict dichotomy. In some arenas, the term *private* signals the realms of the familial, the personal, or intimate relations, while the term *public* signals civic actions (e.g., the Habermasian "public sphere") beyond the home and the personal. In other arenas, public invokes the realms of government and other public institutions in contrast to the realms of private citizen and private institutions (such as corporations). In the arena of law, private law generally marks the realm of practice engaged in settling scores between and among people in their private capacities, while public law generally covers disputes involving government actors and institutions.[1]

Clearly, a family of concepts that have preoccupied great thinkers from Plato to Hannah Arendt cannot be adequately captured in a paragraph, but the need to stay on course demands that we focus on those aspects of the public/private dichotomy most relevant to privacy. For this purpose, Judith DeCew's characterization strikes a useful balance: "The public/private distinction has sometimes been taken to reflect differences between the appropriate scope of government, as opposed to self-regulation by individuals. It has also been interpreted to differentiate political and domestic spheres of life. These diverse linguistic descriptions capture overlapping, yet nonequivalent concepts. Nevertheless they share the assumption that there is a boundary marking off that which is private from that which is public" (1997, 10).

A symbiotic relationship has evolved between the private/public distinction on the one hand, and privacy on the other. In one direction, privacy is invoked when fleshing out distinctive characteristics of the private and public spheres, as one of those characteristics is that the private sphere warrants protection against intrusion. In the other direction, according to scholars like Gerety, privacy protection applies in the private sphere alone. Gerety is neither alone nor the first scholar to assert this position. Dating well before contemporary anxieties over technically mediated intrusions, the nineteeth-century British legal theorist James Fitzjames Stephen wrote in his treatise on law, "there is a sphere, nonetheless real because it is impossible to define its limits, within which the law and public opinion are intruders likely to do more harm than good" (1873, 160). Samuel D. Warren and Louis D. Brandeis also recognized the need to protect the sanctity of the private sphere against unjustified intrusions, asserting, "The general object in view is to protect the privacy of private life" (1890, 215).

A closer examination of this relationship reveals not just one, but at least three ways in which the private/public dichotomy has shaped the way *privacy* is defined, as well as the way it has been applied in prescribing behavior and policy. First, privacy functions as a protective barrier between behavior and policy, and calls into play the private/public distinction defined as a line between private individuals and government actors. Second, regarding the line between the political and domestic or personal spaces or realms, privacy protects what Warren and Brandeis might call the sanctity of the latter. Third, the private/public distinction is applied to information; privacy is called into play as a protection against access to private information. Each of these contributions to the meaning of privacy is elaborated below.

Actors: Privacy and Government

Attention to privacy often centers on its role as a protective barrier for private citizens in relation to government: a robust right to privacy, in various manifestations, is thought to tip the balance of power slightly more in favor of individuals by maintaining a distance between citizens and agents of government. Among the checks and balances that a liberal society sets in place to curtail governmental domination and tyranny are strict limits on incursions into the private lives of citizens. Accordingly, interest in privacy as a right of private individuals against the government gains traction from a considerable body of political scholarship in the liberal, democratic tradition. The checks and balances that constitute the right to privacy against government, such as limiting surveillance and placing restrictions on access to personal records, function to curtail such evils as government intimidation and totalitarian-style incursions into private life.[2] The upshot is well-deserved attention to privacy of private individuals in relation to government that manifests in a variety of ways, including a set of principles that informs the design of government institutions as well as a complex and highly developed body of law and regulation.

One source of legal protection against government intrusion is the U.S. Constitution. The Constitution, whose drafters were influenced by English common law and the historical canon of political philosophy that has inspired democracies worldwide, sets out fundamental principles defining and limiting the powers of government.[3] Some of the most important rights and liberties for individual citizens in relation to government are developed in the set of constitutional amendments that form the Bill of Rights. Despite the fact that the term *privacy* is nowhere explicitly used, privacy protection is embodied in several of these amendments.[4] In legal scholarship and case law the amendments most frequently cited as evidence of Constitution-based protection for privacy are the First (concerning freedoms of speech, religion, and association), Third (protection against compulsory quartering of soldiers in private homes), Fourth (a measure against unreasonable search and seizure), Fifth (protection against self-incrimination), Ninth (general liberties), and Fourteenth (protecting personal liberties against state action) (Regan 1995; Cohen 1996; Froomkin 2003; Solove 2004).

Not all protection of citizens in relation to government, however, is rooted in the Constitution. Other safeguards have been embodied in federal, state, and local statutes, which were initially prompted by the spike in interest in privacy in the mid-1960s when escalating use by government agencies (and others) of computerized databases for administrative and statistical purposes became a topic of intense scrutiny in Congress; the media; and the popular, trade, and scholarly presses. According to Priscilla Regan's detailed account of privacy policy in the decades leading up to the 1990s, one of the key provocations was a proposal in 1965 by the Social Science Research Council to create a federal data center, a central repository that would coordinate the uses of government-held personal information.[5] Intense deliberations across a variety of public forums ultimately reached a resting place with passage of the Privacy Act of 1974.[6] The act placed significant limits on the collection, use, and transmission of personal information by federal agencies, although, in an omission that disappointed privacy advocates and ignored the recommendations of the secretary's committee, it did not incorporate the private sector in its scope.[7]

To pursue the central concern with the private/public dichotomy, it is necessary to step away from this historical narrative to focus on the efforts that drove some of the more successful attempts during that period to protect privacy through legislation.[8] (Readers interested in following up on the detailed narrative of privacy regulation during this period will find Regan's [1995] astute account well worth consulting.) In particular, one unifying theme seems to have been a principled commitment to maintain a check on government in the name of individual autonomy and liberty. From the 1950s until the end of the Cold War, regimes in the East loomed vividly in public consciousness, and fictional constructions like George Orwell's Big Brother in 1984[9] were lively in the public imagination.[10] Moves to protect privacy against government intrusion could be convincingly portrayed as insurance against totalitarian tendencies such as these.

Although the rhetoric of "keeping government in check" was successfully parlayed into privacy protection, the more generalized rhetoric of leveling the playing field was not quite as successful, at least during the active period of the 1960s and 1970s. As mentioned previously, in response to growing public anxiety, the secretary of the U.S. Department of Health, Education, and Welfare formed an Advisory Committee on Automated Personal Data Systems in 1972 to evaluate the use of computerized record-keeping systems and develop policy guidelines for them (Center for Democracy and Technology 2000). The resulting landmark report, *Records, Computers, and the Rights of Citizens*, on the impacts of computerized record-keeping on individuals, organizations, and society as a whole (U.S. Department of Health, Education, and Welfare 1973),[11] stressed the need to protect privacy as a powerful mechanism for leveling the playing field in the grossly unequal pairings of the state (and state actors) with individual citizens, and individual citizens with large institutions of the private sector (e.g., insurance companies, banks, and other financial and commercial institutions). Warning that "the net effect of computerization is that it is becoming much easier for record-keeping systems to affect people than for people to affect record-keeping systems," the committee recommended that "[a]lthough there is nothing inherently unfair in trading some measure of privacy for a benefit, both parties to the exchange should participate in setting the terms" (U.S. Department of Health, Education, and Welfare 1973). The proposed framework for mutual participation in "setting the terms" was the Code of Fair Information Practices, whose five principles included forbidding secret databases, requiring that people know what records are kept about them, requiring a statement of clear purpose and consent if purposes shift, requiring the ability to correct and amend, and enjoining adequate security and reliability. Intended as a set of guidelines for powerful organizations across the board, the code as embodied in the Privacy Act of 1974 applied only to agencies of the federal government.[12]

This section explores just one of the ways the private/public distinction functions in legitimating a right to privacy. In particular, as a distinction between actors—private versus public or government actors—it draws on normative principles embodied in liberal democracies that prescribe limits on incursions into the lives of individuals by agents of government. Although the influence of the dichotomy is evident in other forms, it continues, to the present day, as one of the key influences defining privacy protections in relation to government actors. Contemporaneously with the writing of this book, for example, has been the unfolding of intensive scrutiny of the Bush administration over monitoring U.S. citizens' phone and financial records and tracking their travel and other activities (Lichtblau and Shane 2006; Sanger 2006; "Spying On" 2007).

Realms: Private Versus Public

Another way that the private/public dichotomy has both guided and limited the normative scope of privacy is as a dichotomy of spaces—not only geographically defined spaces, but abstractly conceived realms, spheres, or domains (Curry 2002, 502). Generalizing from the age-old maxim, "a man's home is his castle," the dichotomy recognizes the sanctity of certain private or personal realms where people are sovereign, where they may demand to be shielded from the gaze of others, from surveillance, and from unwanted

intrusions. Serving as a framework for privacy, this inte
chotomy is adopted by scholars, such as the political sci
when claiming the purpose of legal privacy protection
protecting the private sphere against intruders, whether g
(Friedrichs 1971, 105). Philosopher Robert Gerstein, echoing lega.
Charles Fried and philosopher James Rachels, contends that zones of "intimacy simply could not exist unless people had the opportunity for privacy. Excluding outsiders and resenting their uninvited intrusions are essential parts of having intimate relationships" (1984, 271). Ferdinand Schoeman also asserts a distinct zone of life that warrants privacy protection: "one's private sphere in some sense can be equated with those areas of a person's life which are considered intimate or innermost" (1984, 412); privacy's purpose is to insulate "individual objectives from social scrutiny. Social scrutiny can generally be expected to move individuals in the direction of the socially useful. Privacy insulates people from this kind of accountability and thereby protects the realm of the personal" (p. 415).

Law and policy have unequivocally acknowledged the need for specific protections for distinct zones. Within the Bill of Rights, the Third and Fourth amendments, for example, define limits on access to the home by the government—whether quartering soldiers in the Third, or securing it against unreasonable search and seizure in the Fourth. The Fourth Amendment, particularly, has featured in countless cases accusing government actors (frequently law enforcement agents) of having illegitimately breached private domains.[13] It should be noted, however, that Constitutionally defined private domains include not only home and personal effects, but also certain areas of life such as family, "conscience," communications, sexual and marital relations, and reproduction.[14]

Although the U.S. Constitution provides protection for individuals against agents of government, other laws and policies maintain the integrity of these private zones against private actors as well. In the rhetorical flourish with which Warren and Brandeis conclude their article, they call for the expansion of a privacy tort that would clearly recognize broad-based protections of a private zone against intrusion: "The common law has always recognized a man's house as his castle, impregnable, often, even to its own officers engaged in the execution of its commands. Shall the courts thus close the front entrance to constituted authority, and open wide the back door to idle or prurient curiosity?" (1890, 90).

Seventy years later, in an article that remains influential to this day, William Prosser, a leading expert in the law of torts, surveyed court decisions in the sprawling array of cases generated by the tort of privacy and found that four torts could be distinguished among them. Of the four, one in particular, intrusion upon seclusion, assumes a dichotomy of spheres, including a personal sphere to which access is permitted only by consent. As with Constitutional protections, Prosser allows that this personal sphere need not be geographically specified but normatively defined: "It is clear . . . that the thing into which there is prying or intrusion must be, and be entitled to be, private" (1960, 391). Textbook cases have included a hospital room in which a woman is giving birth, a home, a hotel room, a stateroom in a steamboat, a conversation, and boundaries defined by the physical body (pp. 389–392). The remaining privacy torts that Prosser identified include false light and appropriation of name or likeness, which will not be discussed here, and public disclosure of private facts, the subject of the following section.

Information: Private Versus Public

A third way the public/private dichotomy is called into play to define the scope and extent of privacy protection is in the realm of information. Accordingly, information (or following Prosser, "facts") is either private or public; privacy protection extends to private information only. Delimiting the scope of privacy protection in this way is an approach taken in arenas of policy and legal practice, extensively supported in scholarship, and regularly assumed as an organizing principle in public deliberations.

Consider some of the many instances in which law and policy in the United States reflect a commitment to this dichotomy of information: the Family Education Rights and Privacy Act of 1974 (FERPA, known as the Buckley Amendment), protecting the privacy of educational records; the Right to Financial Privacy Act of 1978, protecting information about financial holdings; the Video Privacy Protection Act of 1988, restricting access to and the dissemination of video rental records; and the Health Insurance Portability and Accountability Act of 1996 (HIPAA), with privacy rules developed by the U.S. Department of Health and Human Services regulating the flow of medical records. In the common law, Warren and Brandeis sought restrictions on access to and publication of information about "the private life, habits, acts, and relations of an individual" (1890, 216), which later emerged as one of

Prosser's four privacy torts protecting against access to and revelation of "embarrassing private facts about [a] plaintiff" (1960, 389). To qualify for relief under this tort, one of the key conditions is that "the facts disclosed to the public must be private facts, and not public ones. Certainly no one can complain when publicity is given to information about him which he himself leaves open to the public eye, such as the appearance of the house in which he lives, or to the business in which he is engaged" (p. 394).

A number of influential philosophical accounts of privacy have sought to delineate reasonable boundaries for the extent of its protection by means of the public/private dichotomy. Charles Fried (1968), who suggested that privacy is a necessary condition for love, friendship, and trust, endorses that a limit be placed on the moral and legal right to privacy. This right, which he defines as a right to control information about oneself, applies not to all information but only to a special class of personal information. According to Fried, prevailing social order "designates certain areas, intrinsically no more private than other areas, as symbolic of the whole institution of privacy, and thus deserving of protection beyond their particular importance" (1968, 487). Narrowing the scope in this way still leaves sufficient "currency" to differentiate among relationships of differing degrees of intimacy: "The most important thing is that there be some information which is protected" (p. 487). Fried's rationale for restricting the scope of a right to privacy is to minimize interference with other social and legal values that might be threatened if it were not curbed; the "inevitable fact that privacy is gravely compromised by any concrete social system" is due to "the inevitably and utterly just exercise of rights by others" (p. 493).

Other noteworthy philosophical accounts of a right to privacy that limit the scope of its application to a privileged class of personal information include those of William Parent, Raymond Wacks, and Tom Gerety. Parent defines privacy as "the condition of not having undocumented personal knowledge about one possessed by others. A person's privacy is diminished exactly to the degree that others possess this kind of knowledge about him" (1983, 269). Parent delimits the scope of privacy in two ways. First, to personal information only, by which Parent means "facts which most persons in a given society choose not to reveal about themselves (except to close friends, family) or facts about which a particular individual is acutely sensitive" (p. 270). In contemporary America, Parent speculates, this usually covers "facts about a person's sexual preferences, drinking or drug habits, income, the state of his or her marriage and health" (p. 270). Second, a right to privacy in information requires that the information in question be undocumented, by which Parent means that it has not appeared or been published in a "newspaper, court proceedings, and other official documents open to public inspection" (p. 270). This second requirement taps into the private/public distinction as it applies not only to information but, as discussed in the previous section, to domains, requiring not only that the information be private (or personal) but also that it should not have been reported in a publicly accessible document.

Raymond Wacks, a British legal philosopher whose work is discussed in chapter 6 in greater detail, contends "that at the core of the preoccupation with the right to privacy is protection against the misuse of personal, sensitive information" (1989, 10). For Wacks, the key to determining whether privacy has been violated is determining whether " 'private facts' about the individual are respectively published, intruded upon, or misused" (p. 22). Gerety, claiming that an all-encompassing definition such as Alan Westin's (that "on its face includes *all* control over *all* information about oneself, one's group, one's institution") is too hopelessly vague, concludes that a viable legal right to privacy be limited to "an autonomy or control over the intimacies of personal identity. Autonomy, identity, and intimacy are all necessary (and together normally sufficient) for the proper invocation of the concept of privacy" (1997, 226).

Interactions, Gray Areas, and Applications

Whether one believes privacy to be control over information or a limitation on the degree of access to information, the task remains to delineate the extent and boundaries of a morally legitimate claim to it. In Chapter 4, an approach that traces necessary and contingent links between privacy and other fundamental human values was discussed. These links define privacy's own value and give moral weight to its claims. The approaches surveyed in this chapter, however, take a different tack, resorting to the private/public dichotomy as a framework for discerning legitimacy: privacy in private warrants protection, otherwise its status is unclear. As far as I know, a point not elsewhere explicitly noted or fully appreciated is that accounts in this class may further be distinguished according to their interpretations of the private/public distinction, whether primarily in terms of actors, realms, or information. Therefore, to conclude this chapter, I examine some interesting interactions among these interpretations, as well as consequential ambiguities.

The three ways that the private/public dichotomy shapes the definition and scope of a right to privacy are to be understood as conceptually independent; however, they may factor into concrete cases in various combinations. In cases of a person peering into someone's bedroom window, or a police wiretap connected to a suspect's telephone line, there are at least two potential sources of privacy violation. One is due to breaches of the two private domains. A second is due to the content of what may have been seen or heard; that is, information that might have been personal and sensitive—the subject undressing or discussing medical problems—or it might have been perfectly mundane and impersonal. It may be unclear which of these dimensions prevails: Does the status of the information in question trump the status of realm, or vice versa? Parent (1983) requires that both dimensions be given equal consideration—that private information must have been taken from a private domain (i.e., never before revealed or documented in public). Other theories are incomplete in this regard and do not define their stances on interactions among the three dimensions. This lacuna can regularly become a serious one when parties, unguided, arrive at conflicting viewpoints, sometimes enacted in courtroom struggles.

Teasing apart these three dimensions of the private/public dichotomy can shed light on several of the famous Fourth Amendment cases cited in discussions of privacy. The independence of realms (or space) from content was clearly endorsed in cases about—of all things—garbage. The courts have consistently found that garbage itself does not warrant a place in the category of "personal effects," but is protected if located within spaces recognized as private (within the "curtilage"). In California v. Greenwood (1998), for example, a case that has served as precedent for many that followed, the U.S. Supreme Court concluded: "[a]ccordingly, having deposited their garbage in an area particularly suited for public inspection and, in a manner of speaking, public consumption, for the express purpose of having strangers take it, respondents could have had no reasonable expectation of privacy in the inculpatory items that they discarded" (37; see also LaFave 1996, 603). In other words, the Court agreed that people have no privacy interests in the content or constitution of their garbage but that such interests are a function only of location—whether inside or outside of what is considered a person's private domain. Thus, courts are, in effect, recognizing the independence of these two dimensions of the private/public dichotomy, as well as, in this case, privileging the spatial dimension over content.

Skirmishes among stakeholders with competing interests have arisen in the wake of policy shifts that have made evident the independence of the dimensions. In one case, the Individual Reference Services Group, Inc. (IRSG), an industry association of information brokers and credit bureaus, brought suit against the Federal Trade Commission (FTC), challenging new administrative rules drafted by the FTC. This followed passage of the Federal Financial Modernization Act (also known as the Gramm-Leach-Bliley Act of 1999), which, among other matters, redrew conditions under which financial institutions disclosed nonpublic personal information about consumers. In carrying out Congressional mandates and formulating detailed administrative rules, the FTC shifted the designation of "credit headers" from public to nonpublic (FTC 2000). Previously, under the Fair Credit Reporting Act (FCRA 1992), credit header information, including name, address, social security number, and phone number, which happened to be listed at the "head" or top of a person's credit record, was not subject to the restrictions FCRA imposed on the collection, use, and dissemination of financial information. This shift meant that the header section of a credit record, which had implicitly been understood as a public zone with all of its contents up for grabs, could no longer be designated as such. Members of the IRSG were indignant that header information, now falling under the ambit of the rules, could no longer be freely traded with one another and other interested parties, such as direct marketers.[15]

It may not be surprising, but still worth noting, that the line dividing public and private, for any of the three dimensions, is neither static nor universal. For instance, consider FERPA's switch in status of student records from public to private. In so doing it prohibited disclosure of student information, such as performance and staff recommendations, without the explicit permission of students and their parents. It also distinguished practices in the United States from those in other countries that regularly allow for public dissemination of student grades.[16] Sometimes a switchover can occur as a result of a public incident and an examination of public sentiment, whether or not followed by legislation. This was the pattern of events after a newspaper published the videotape rental records of Robert Bork, then-nominee for the Supreme Court. Congress acted swiftly, passing the Video Privacy Protection Act of 1988 to switch the status of video rental records from public to private (Electronic Privacy Information Center 2002; see Regan 1995 for a more complete discussion). A switchover in the opposite direction occurred with "Megan's

Law," a 1999 amendment to the 1994 Jacob Wetterling Crimes Against Children and Sexually Violent Offender Registration Act requiring local law enforcement to make information about perpetrators of sexual offences against minors more vigorously publicized (e.g., requiring that neighbors be explicitly notified) and more comprehensive (e.g., publishing offenders' residential addresses) than before. Historically, one of the most significant switches was accomplished in 1967, when the U.S. Supreme Court overturned the 1928 ruling in Olmstead v. United States. Whereas in *Olmstead* the Court found that wiretapping the telephone conversations of a suspected bootlegger did not constitute an illegal breach of a private sphere (1928, 466), in Katz v. United States (1967) the Court found that the Federal Bureau of Investigation (FBI) had acted illegally in attaching a bugging device to a telephone booth to gather evidence on a suspected gambling operation. Framing this landmark ruling in terms of the dichotomy of realms, it can be understood as effectively transforming telephone conversation into a constitutionally protected private zone (1967, 359).

One can now see more clearly why new information technologies, such as many of those described in Part I, are so disorienting as they reveal the inconstancy of boundaries and fuzziness of definitions. In the workplace, for example, there has been a complete reversal in the status of employee online activity from the early 1990s, when the "space" of e-mail, Internet, and Web usage was conceived as personal and inviolate, to the present day, when it is widely accepted (some anticipate soon to be mandated) as open to monitoring by employers and their representatives. Except in a few philosophical discussions, there has been little public opposition to court decisions that have consistently found that businesses' or systems' owners claims to control and monitor usage of their servers trump the privacy claims of their employees.[17] These findings seem to have resulted in the shift of presumption in favor of monitoring employee e-mail and Web surfing (Cohen 2000).[18]

A few more examples illustrate the continuing debate over line-drawing. One is the ongoing tussle over online space both in relation to government law enforcement and security agencies and in relation to private actors like online advertisers, as each assumes an entitlement to enter into agreements with private Internet Service Providers (ISPs) in order to monitor identifiable clickstream data. It remains unclear whether systems like the FBI's Carnivore software, installed at ISP access points for purposes of analyzing incoming and outgoing traffic, violates Fourth Amendment protections.[19] Another tussle over line-drawing, arising in the wake of the September 11, 2001, attacks, has been sparked by executive rules and laws such as the USA PATRIOT Act that give government agencies greater leeway to infiltrate a broad variety of zones previously considered private, including bank and telephone records and even library lending records (Lichtblau and Risen 2005). Finally, there is the unsettled controversy over whether what people post on social network sites constitutes private or public information (because it is available unprotected over the public Web). The framework of contextual integrity I present in Part III does not take sides in these controversial line-drawing exercises; rather, it reveals them to be symptoms of the deeper problem of invoking the private/public dichotomy to inform our understanding of privacy.

Conclusion

This chapter has discussed approaches to defining and delineating a right to privacy that align it with the public/private dichotomy. Generally, a right to privacy is associated with the private. Privacy is associated with not one but three dimensions of the public/private distinction: (1) the dimension of actors, divided into government and private actors; (2) the dimension of realm, including space, which can be divided into the public and the private; and (3) the dimension of information, which can be divided into the public and the personal. In philosophical and legal writings in which this approach is taken, and in the court rulings, law, and policy that incorporate it, one can usually detect an emphasis on one or the other of these dimensions, but for the most part the dimensions are not explicitly recognized and are sometimes conflated, resulting in disputes and controversies.

6   Puzzles, Paradoxes, and Privacy in Public

IN CHAPTERS 4 AND 5 I DESCRIBED, IN BROAD BRUSHSTROKES, A FEW of the exemplary theoretical works representing two general approaches to defining a morally and politically defensible right to privacy. In this chapter I evaluate their general contributions and shortcomings. It is important, however, to qualify the nature of this evaluation: it is offered not as a detailed assessment of all aspects of these theories and approaches, but is focused on the quality of guidance they offer in addressing the bewildering array of socio-technical systems and practices that individually and in sum portend a radical erosion of privacy. The focus, therefore, is on their practical merits and the structure of reasons they incorporate for distinguishing the morally and politically acceptable from the unacceptable systems and practices that unrelentingly enter our lives and alter, shape, and mediate social experiences. The conclusion I reach is that they fall short on various fronts.

The shortcomings of these approaches are manifested in various ways but most importantly in not being able to provide sufficiently finely tuned responses to many of the challenges to privacy posed by these systems and practices. New practices, in some cases, are met with great anxiety and resistance yet do not register as privacy violations; in other cases they may, according to theory, register as privacy violations but, by other measures or in practice, may seem unproblematic. Certain theories respond in heavy-handed ways, with insufficient sensitivity to significant details, not because their principles and theses are wrong but because they are "blind" to relevant elements and differences. These direct and indirect challenges to predominant approaches to privacy are grouped into three clusters. The first calls attention to the persistent puzzles and paradoxes confronting any account of privacy, to which existing approaches seem unable to provide adequate responses. The second questions how well existing approaches, particularly those that attribute value to privacy based on its functional relation to other important values, are able to meet challenges posed by countervailing values. The third points to difficulties inherent in any definition of a right to privacy whose contours follow the private/public dichotomy.

Puzzles and Paradoxes

Imagine a debate between a privacy skeptic on the one side and, on the other side, a proponent of any of the theories that reserve an important place for privacy among the social, moral, and legal values worthy of vigorous protection. The skeptic draws attention to several points that weigh against the proponent's vision.

One is a paradox, a stark contradiction at whose heart is this: people appear to want and value privacy, yet simultaneously appear not to value or want it. Those who support vigorous protection point to countless polls and surveys in which people express the importance of privacy, how worried and indignant they are over its erosion, and how dissatisfied and suspicious they are about current levels of protection. In 1998, for example, 94 percent of people responded "somewhat" or "very" to the question: "How concerned are you about threats to your personal privacy in America today?" (Louis Harris & Associates and Westin 1998). In 1990, 79 percent of respondents agreed that if the Declaration of Independence were rewritten today they would be willing to add "privacy" alongside "life, liberty, and the pursuit of happiness" (Louis Harris & Associates 1990). Eighty-five percent of respondents in a survey conducted by the Pew Internet and American Life Project said they were "very" or "somewhat" concerned about "businesses and people you don't know getting personal information about you and your family," and 54 percent objected to Internet tracking (Fox et al. 2000). In a 2003 University of Pennsylvania study, 86 percent of respondents supported a law that would give individuals the right to control how Web sites use their information (Turow 2003); in a 2003 Harris Poll the majority of respondents maintained that it is extremely important to be in control of who can get personal information

(Harris Interactive 2003); in November of the same year, 95 percent of respondents indicated that they were "highly concerned with websites' collection of personal information" (Kandra and Brant 2003); and a 2002 poll recorded 83 percent of respondents willing to end business dealings with a company if the company misused customer information (Krane, Light, and Gravitch 2002).

Privacy skeptics are unimpressed with these survey responses. What people do counts more than what they say, and what they do expresses quite the opposite of what is indicated by the polls. In almost all situations in which people must choose between privacy and just about any other good, they choose the other good. The list is long: credit cards over cash, E-ZPass over traditional toll payments, discount shoppers' cards over cash, subscriptions to caller ID over call blocking, traceable search engines over self-directed Web surfing, and so forth. People choose the options that offer convenience, speedy passage, financial savings, connectivity, and safety rather than those that offer privacy. Only 20 percent of people claim to read privacy policies "most of the time" (TRUSTe and TNS 2006) and even fewer complain about these policies: only 7 percent, according to a *PCWorld* survey (Kandra and Brant 2003). On these grounds, computer scientist Calvin Gottlieb concludes, "I now believe that most of the populace really does not care all that much about privacy, although, when prompted, many voice privacy concerns. The real reason that the trade-offs referred to above have been made, have been possible, is that they are in line with the wishes of the large majority of the population" (1996, 161). Citing all the above as evidence, skeptics would have us conclude that people's actions convey the message loudly and clearly that privacy is not of great value after all; or, at least not of comparable value to other goods.

Countering this logic, privacy advocates argue that what skeptics claim to be choices are not truly choices, not truly deliberate or free. One reason for this is that people often are not fully aware that at certain critical junctures information is being gathered or recorded. Nor do they fully grasp the implications of the informational ecology in which they choose and act. Some claim that it is unfair to characterize a choice as deliberate when the alternative is not really viable; for instance, that life without a credit card, without a telephone, or without search engines requires an unreasonable sacrifice.[1] There is evidence that goes partway to confirming this reasoning. A study conducted in early 2003 revealed that 57 percent of those polled believed that if a company has a privacy policy it will not share information with other entities, and that 59 percent were unaware that Web sites collect information even if there is no registration requirement on the site—both false assumptions (Turow 2003). Another survey, published in 2005, indicated persistent ignorance: a significant majority of the respondents believed that the presence of a privacy policy on a Web site means that the company cannot sell customers' information (75 percent); that banks are barred by law from selling personal information without permission (73 percent); and that supermarkets are barred by law from selling customer data (64 percent). Furthermore, 47 percent believed that online merchants give consumers an opportunity to see their own data—again, all false statements (Turow, Feldman, and Meltzer 2005). Moreover, a study conducted by a team of researchers at Carnegie Mellon University brings to light key variables affecting people's information-sharing tendencies. In one of the few empirical studies of privacy behaviors (as opposed to attitude surveys and polls), a controlled investigation demonstrated that when online merchants' privacy policies are made salient, consumers prefer to purchase from those with better privacy policies even if, in some instances, this means paying more for the goods (Tsai et al. 2007, 35).

Proponents of a right to privacy that is limited in scope to the private spheres of life, as discussed in Chapter 5, might follow the debate between skeptics and advocates about toll plazas and shoppers' cards with an air of detached superiority. Thus far, they would agree with the skeptics, though for different reasons: the problem is not that people do not care about privacy; the problem is in assuming that privacy extends over such a wide range.

Skeptics point out another phenomenon that belies people's deep concerns with privacy, what one might call "media exhibitionism." People are ready, even eager, to bear their souls to the world. These trends have been clearly evident for many years in many mainstream television talk shows, whose guests—both celebrities and ordinary folks—share lurid details of their personal lives and intimate relationships. In many reality shows, contestants, often ordinary people, vie for the chance to live or compete in full view of millions; and their audiences exhibit seemingly unlimited appetites for such entertainment.[2] In what could be called "new media exhibitionism," these trends have democratized, expressing themselves in a variety of forms online. In 1996, Jennifer Ringley, a pioneer of this genre, set up a Web cam in her dormitory room at Dickinson College in Pennsylvania. The camera posted unedited images of her to her Web site, Jennicam.org (later Jennicam.com), which were refreshed every few minutes. Ringley's Jennicam, which predated even early reality television shows such as "Big Brother" and "Survivor," inspired many others ("camgirls") to follow suit (Allen 2001; Wikipedia Contributors 2006b). Beyond the Web cam genre, other revelatory forms of self-expression have emerged in blogs, personal Web sites, and, as discussed in Chapter 3, social networking sites (such as MySpace.com and Facebook.com). In all of these, the skeptic argues, no matter what people say about their desire for privacy, they reveal little regard for privacy in what they do. Clear evidence is the abandon with which millions of users of all ages and demographics from around the world disclose, with abandon, personal and sensitive information (Barnes 2006; Edwards and Brown 2009).

Further evidence that privacy does not rise to the height of other core values, such as those embodied in the U.S. Constitution, is its great variability, or relativity, across historical periods, societies, and even individuals. What might Samuel Warren and Louis Brandeis, whose indignation was ignited by uninvited photographers publishing snapshots of private social gatherings, say about contemporary forms of media and new media exhibitionism? How does one who claims for privacy the status of a fundamental, universal human right account for vast differences among societies, communities, cultures, and nations in what each state knows and does not know about its citizens, what people freely ask about each other, what institutions can reveal about individuals, and what people reveal in public settings?[3] How does one account for the enormous variability at the individual level, where some people seem happy to expose to others the details of their public and personal lives, while others prefer discretion? Is it even possible to solve this conundrum within the life of a single individual, who at one moment deplores a particular practice, such as video surveillance in the workplace, yet at another location comfortably accepts a very similar situation, for instance, surveillance cameras in airports (Grudin 2001)?

What can we make of this assortment of findings and observations? Privacy skeptics have proffered them as evidence that people, generally, do not care about privacy very much or, when they do, it is more as they would care about a trend, sensibility, or preference than as a moral value.[4] Even Anita Allen-Castellitto, a strong proponent of privacy protection, worries that the phenomenon of public and new media exhibitionism demonstrates a shift in norms, an eroding of our taste for privacy (1999).[5] Of course, the data do not universally or conclusively favor the skeptic; there is enough evidence to suggest that people lack crucial knowledge about privacy practices, and results like those achieved by the team at Carnegie Mellon reveal a more nuanced connection between what people say and what they do. This may call into question the skeptic's charge that people are downright fickle when it comes to privacy, but the problem of how to systematically integrate these messy findings into existing theoretical frameworks that posit a right to control or restrict access to information is unclear.

Trade-Offs

The skeptical position enunciated above questions whether privacy warrants the status of a distinctive moral value. The skeptical interlocutor is less concerned with ontological status than with privacy's relative standing among other values. Targeting the family of theories discussed in Chapter 4, the skeptic accepts that privacy is a value with functional connections to other values, but denies that it is a very important value by demonstrating in many paradigmatic circumstances that privacy claims are appropriately trumped by other, more important ones. Even the technology-based systems and practices that thus far have been conceived as *problems* for a viable theory of privacy to solve, the skeptic sees as *solutions* to the attainment of other valued ends. In sum, privacy advocates do not adequately recognize the force of countervailing interests and values, and privacy theories offer scant resources with which to systematically resolve conflicts that result from them.

One of the most frequently cited conflicts, particularly in the wake of the September 11, 2001, attacks, is between privacy and security. Following much talk of the vulnerability of Americans to threats of terror on their home soil and the need for changes in the American way of life, there has been a steady rise in institutionalized watchfulness. Due process requirements, diminished with the passage of the USA PATRIOT Act, allow for more video surveillance of public spaces; more eavesdropping on mediated conversation; more identity checkpoints; and closer scrutiny of activities, transactions, purchases, travel, and financial flows. Those who might object to these incremental incursions as privacy violations are easily shamed into capitulation by the illogic: privacy, as described in Priscilla Regan's book *Legislating Privacy* (1995), is a "selfish" value which needs to be sacrificed for the collective benefits of security.[6]

Another challenge pits privacy against freedom of expression. Arguably, the best known version of this challenge is from legal scholar Eugene Volokh. In the name of free speech, Volokh opposes policies that would prevent private entities from freely sharing with other private entities personal information they may have acquired in direct transactions with a subject, or indirectly from third parties (2000a). According to Volokh, the First Amendment allows this restriction no more than it would allow a restriction on what one individual can say to another about a third in private communication, such as common gossip. A move to restrict speech via privacy policies is only permissible in circumstances in which clear countervailing values are at stake; for example, to curtail the overzealous exercise of power by government actors, or to protect against disclosures that may pose dire threats to individuals.[7]

A right to property has also been pitted against privacy in the sometimes antagonistic relationship between the owners and consumers of intellectual content stored in digital form. Radical changes in digital media technologies used for creating, storing, and distributing intellectual content—images, music, written word, and video—have been a source of equally radical changes in customer relationships with creators and owners as well as with the creative works themselves. These changes have not all been hailed by creators and owners, particularly by industry incumbents such as record companies, publishing companies, and art museums whose traditional business models have been challenged. Experiencing unprecedented threats to their customary dominance, organizations that have traditionally controlled distribution of these works have sought remediation through both law and technology. Although it is impossible to cover the terrain of countless books and articles that have recounted the tale of these struggles, my intention is merely to set the backdrop for an approach taken by and on behalf of content copyright holders to control distribution through mechanisms known as digital rights management systems or technological protection measures.[8] Privacy scholars and advocates have vociferously objected to versions of these mechanisms that function by monitoring not only individual purchases of music, movies, text, images, and so forth, but also episodes of listening, watching, reading, and viewing (Cohen 1996, 2003). Sure, this is an incursion on privacy, the skeptic admits, but one trumped by property rights.

Finally, privacy is regularly challenged by a desire or need for greater efficiency, which has been a significant driver in the collection, aggregation, and analysis of personal information. One of the most common applications has been marketing; businesses wishing to identify suitable customers seek as much information as possible about the demographics of a population, as well as the habits, socioeconomic standing, interests, past activities, and purchasing choices of identifiable members. In a clash of interests and opinions, privacy advocates and consumers complain that these practices should be stopped or severely curtailed because they violate privacy; conversely, supporters insist that businesses should not be stopped in their pursuit of information (as long as it remains within legal limits) because individual privacy interests in consumer information is no match for the business interests of companies gathering, selling, and using it. These practices not only promise greater profits through greater efficiency, they also protect businesses against high-risk customers.[9] Furthermore, these benefits to business interests may "trickle down" to customers in the form of lower prices and, replacing the scattershot of so-called junk mail, enable more effectively targeted ads and special offers.

The clash of privacy with other values is not unique; such clashes are endemic to any pluralistic system of values. Developing general approaches to resolving these conflicts, or even finding uncontroversial resolutions to particular instances, can be difficult, if not impossible. Demonstrating how theories cope with intractable values conflicts is a common struggle for ethicists and political and legal theorists; accepting them as an inevitable feature of moral and political life is described with poignancy by the great political theorist Isaiah Berlin:

> These collisions of values are of the essence of what they are and what we are. If we are told that these contradictions will be solved in some perfect world in which all good things can be harmonized in principle, then we must answer, to those who say this, that the meanings they attach to the names which for us denote the conflicting values are not ours. We must say that the world in which what we see as incompatible values are not in conflict is a world altogether beyond our ken; that principles which are harmonized in this other world are not the principles with which, in our daily lives, we are acquainted; if they are transformed, it is into conceptions not known to us on earth. (1969, 13)

Even though values conflicts are normal features of moral and political deliberations, and some of the most compelling are precisely those that elude resolution by straightforward application of general principles, this does not mean that all bets are off. Systematic reasoning informed by practical wisdom and artful judgment that guides us away from missteps, suggests heuristics and rules-of-thumb, and clarifies what is at stake in these dilemmas, may point the way to better if not certain judgments.[10] In my view, many of the dilemmas stemming from values conflicts with privacy may benefit from clarification and guidance of this kind.

One way a conflict may be misconstrued is if interests are presented as values. Unraveling this conflation may clarify what is at stake and affect how one assigns relative weights to conflicting factors. For example, cases of non-consensual collection, aggregation, and sale of personal information by businesses are often presented as a direct conflict of values, efficiency, or liberty with privacy. In many instances, a closer look reveals that costs and benefits are unevenly distributed and that because benefits accruing directly to businesses come at a cost (or potential cost) to individuals, this conflict is more aptly understood as a conflict of interests. This fact is glaringly overlooked by many defenders of these practices, including Richard Posner (1978a, 1978b), who fail to acknowledge that costs and benefits of alternative policy options not only yield different outcomes, but, on balance, accrue to different parties unevenly. For a resolution to be morally defensible it should at least rise above brute competition among interest-based constituencies; it should also limit consideration only of demonstrably legitimate claims, and should be constrained by the requirement that the distribution of costs and benefits be a just one.

The presentation of value conflicts may also be misleading if the values in question are inadequately conceptualized. One case in point is the conflict between privacy, presented as a value whose benefits accrue to individuals, and security, presented as valuable for society at large. Adopting Priscilla Regan's conception of privacy as a social value may result in a recalibration of trade-offs since it presents a fuller picture of what is at stake in alternative resolutions. In particular, as long as privacy's social value is ignored, we are likely to see it consistently, and mistakenly, undervalued. A similar correction may be required in proposals to trade privacy off against free speech. In Volokh's presentation of the clash, protecting privacy is conceived as placing constraints on speech. But drawing from the arguments of Julie Cohen (2003) and Michael Froomkin (2003), privacy also supports freedom of speech. Accordingly, any policy that strives to resolve conflicts between privacy and speech needs to take into consideration not only the potential chilling of speech due to privacy, but the chilling of speech due to reductions in privacy.

It is commonly taken for granted that when values conflict, the only way out of the conflict is a trade-off, one value "traded" for another. This is Berlin's message in the passage quoted above, suggesting that "incompatible values" cannot be harmonized except in some "perfect world" that is not ours. Not all conflicts, however, fit this mold; they are not baked into conceptual incompatibilities but are contingent outcomes of particular social arrangements, or even technical design. In cases such as these, the horns of the dilemma need not be quite as sharp—shift to Berlin's perfect world or make hard choices in trade-offs—rather, there may be gentler alternatives. One would be to seek compromise, a bit of one and a bit of the other in suitable measures. Another is to look for adjustments in arrangements or the design that allow us to have our proverbial cake and eat it too. In my view, applying this mindset to conflicts can result in creative solutions. The conflict between privacy and security, frequently presented as a fundamentally incompatible couplet, is a case in point: there are instances when redesign might give extra leeway to both. In the context of air travel, for example, the full-blown surveillance that might emerge initially as the obvious solution could give way to alternatives that preserve privacy in varying degrees, such as careful screening of luggage and fully securing the cockpit door. Along similar lines, those objecting to permissive grants for wiretapping might propose to try other investigative strategies instead, ones that might be equally effective and less invasive.[11]

In sum, I have considered here how those who champion a right to privacy for its capacity to promote other important moral and political values may respond to radical privacy threats of technology-based systems and practices, such as those discussed in Part I. Their response is likely to begin with an assessment of the degree to which systems or practices diminish control individuals have over personal information.[12] Accordingly, because diminishing control over the flow of information is precisely what many of these systems accomplish, proponents would say that it is no wonder they raise fear, indignation, and protest. Yet this is not the whole story. It is surely the case that reasons exist for developing and deploying the systems in question, and while some of these reasons might not carry moral weight, many of them do, frequently referring to values that happen to conflict with the privacy of affected information subjects. In order to grapple with these cases, it is not enough for proponents to point to the connections between privacy and values like autonomy, freedom, and democracy. They must be able to address, in systematic ways, conflicts between privacy and competing values served by the offending technologies. Although it might turn out that the connections drawn will be compelling enough to win the day for privacy (or require capitulation), the numbers of systems and practices that continue unabated in spite of the hostility they provoke suggest there is a significant chunk missing in this approach. In Part III I revisit this theoretical approach, explaining, for purposes of application, the ways it is partial or incomplete.

Privacy in Public

Theories that restrict the right to privacy to the domain of the private may potentially avoid the challenge of conflicting values. As discussed, one reason why the technical systems of monitoring, aggregation, and publication pose difficulties for what we have called functionalist theories of privacy is that while these theories do an estimable job explaining the value of privacy, they typically lack the conceptual, normative, and sometimes even rhetorical resources to discern cases in which privacy legitimately overrides the values and purposes promoted by these systems from those that do not. By contrast, theories that rest on the private/public dichotomy and reserve privacy protection for the realms of the private arguably provide firmer support for privacy claims, even though these claims extend over a reduced area. Positing a less promiscuous right to privacy, so to speak, selectively asserted against government actors, within private domains, and about private information, these theories effectively stake out territories that are more easily defensible while giving way on those in which privacy claims are likely to be more tenuous. The promise of aligning the scope of legitimate privacy claims with the private/public dichotomy is that it might provide a meaningful cutoff between privacy claims that are sustainable against conflicting claims and those that are not. The dichotomy theories are spared having to explain why video surveillance of public spaces or trawling public records for purposes of aggregation is problematic because, according to them, they are not in the private sphere and therefore are not a privacy problem. In those theories that align the scope of legitimate privacy claims within the private/public dichotomy, the dichotomy marks a cutoff between privacy claims that can be sustained against competing claims and those that cannot. A stark way of expressing this alignment is that the private warrants privacy protection while the public does not; in the public, "anything goes." Yet as promising as this approach might appear for avoiding proliferation of conflicts (and, as Gerety argues [1997], for defining a concise legal concept), it falls prey to a different set of challenges—those posed by a right to "privacy in public" (Nissenbaum 1997, 1998).

In Chapter 5 I observed that there are three ways in which the private/ public dichotomy serves as a framework for articulating a right to privacy. The first focuses on specific claims against incursions by government actors (as distinct from private), the second against incursions into private domains, and the third against collection and dissemination of private information. These three interpretations of the dichotomy circumscribe domains of actors, spaces, and information that warrant privacy protection; for anything that lies outside these protected domains, the implication is that "anything goes." In my view, the trouble with this approach is that it neglects a range of situations—from those involving nongovernmental actors, to spheres not typically deemed to be personal or private, to collecting or disseminating in- formation not typically deemed personal or private—in which many people perceive robust and legitimate privacy claims. And, of greatest relevance to the central themes and purposes of this book, these neglected circumstances incorporate many of the troubling technology-based systems and practices described in Part I.

A quick terminological point before proceeding: I use the term *public sur- veillance* to refer to systems and practices that are outside the scope of a right to privacy defined by the private.

Agents

Hardly controversial, it still bears mentioning that many systems and prac- tices considered unacceptably intrusive involve private actors. Although, for reasons discussed in Chapter 5, laws and statutes addressing intrusions by government actors are more fully developed, few experts now deny that con- straints need to be imposed to limit violations by private actors of one anoth- er's privacy. Nevertheless, the political and legal sources for justifying the en- trenchment of limits on private actors in law are more diverse, and frequently more controversial, than those imposing limits on government actors.

Realms

My contention is that invoking the private/public dichotomy to afford privacy protection for private realms while resisting privacy constraints in realms outside of these is deeply problematic. To support this contention, it is neces- sary to evaluate a common set of arguments offered in defense of this limited application of constraints to zones of the private. One argument, so compel- ling on its face that I have dubbed it the normative "knock-down" argument, proceeds as follows. When people move about, act, and transact in public arenas, they are implicitly consenting to be seen and noticed. Even philosopher Jeffrey Reiman, who favors a strong right to privacy and for whom respect for privacy is expressed as "a complex of behaviors that stretches from refraining from asking questions about what is none of one's business to refraining from looking into open windows one passes on the street" (1976, 43–44), concedes that the social demands of privacy do not include "the right never to be seen even on a crowded street" (p. 44). Practically speaking, it is not only implausible that one would not be noticed, but imposes an unreasonable burden on others, requiring that they actively restrain themselves by averting their gaze or not telling others what they saw. Larry Hunter, another supporter of a strong and comprehensive right to privacy, grants that "although we consider it a violation of privacy to look in somebody's window and notice what they are doing, we have no problem with the reverse: someone sitting in his living room looking *out* his window" (1985, 295). Analogously, restrictions on "public" records, which place on similar public display a broad swath of information including vital records, drivers' records, vehicle ownership license records, real estate records, court records, and so forth, seem both impossible to impose and morally indefensible. In other words, if people make no effort to cover, hide, or remove themselves or information about themselves from public view, if they willingly yield information into the public domain, if they let the proverbial "cat out of the bag," it is unreasonable for them later to "get it back" or suppress it.

There is a strong temptation to draw a direct parallel between conceptions of privacy that rely on the private/public dichotomy and the well-entrenched legal standard of a "reasonable expectation of privacy." Formulated in an opinion by Justice John Harlan for the landmark Supreme Court case Katz v. United States (1967), the standard established that an expectation is reasonable if (1) a person exhibited an actual expectation of privacy, and (2) the expectation is one that society is prepared to recognize as reasonable (Katz v. United States, 1967, 360–361; Regan 1995, 122; Solove and Rotenberg 2003, 21). In *Katz*, this meant that a conversation in a public telephone booth could be declared a private zone, covered by the Fourth Amendment, even though it took place outside a person's home. Relying on a dichotomy of realms to delineate the scope of a right to privacy does not require that one commits to one specified space—the home—as private, only that a dichotomy exists of private and public zones and that only in private zones can one have an expectation of privacy. This reasoning is evident in the defense offered for the use of video cameras connected to a facial recognition system at the 2001 Super Bowl. Tampa police argued that scanning the faces of spectators, one by one, when they entered the stadium did not violate privacy as "the courts have ruled there is no expectation of privacy in a public setting" (Slevin 2001).

A twist on this reasoning, in my view, emerged in Florida v. Riley (1989), when the same standard *denied* a reasonable expectation of privacy in the home, a space considered quintessentially private. In this case, the Supreme Court decided that police had not conducted an illegal search when an officer observed from a helicopter, at a height of 400 feet, what he thought were marijuana plants. In a separate but concurring opinion, Justice O'Connor wrote, "I agree that police observation of the greenhouse in Riley's curtilage from a helicopter passing at an altitude of 400 feet did not violate an expectation of privacy" that society is prepared to recognize as "reasonable" (p. 452). Just as it is unreasonable for citizens to expect police to shield their eyes so as to avoid seeing into private property from public thoroughfares, so is it unreasonable to expect to be free of aerial observation at altitudes where the "public travel with sufficient regularity" (pp. 452–455). One could argue, however, that O'Connor's reasoning merely complicates the parallel between the dichotomy and the reasonable expectations standard because she does not challenge that privacy applies only in the realms of the private but only whether all parts of private property fall within this realm.

I would suggest, however, that expectations of privacy are even further out of alignment with a dichotomy of zones, even one allowing for shifts. While hardly anyone would claim a right to not be observed attending the Super Bowl, "none of your business" is a perfectly reasonable answer to a passerby on a sidewalk asking your name, even though the sidewalk is most surely a public space and by any standard one's name is not considered private information. Whereas hardly anyone would assert a right not to be seen on a crowded street, the prospect of radio frequency identification device tags implanted in our clothing, personal effects, or bodies that connect our whereabouts—even in public places—via transceivers and across networks to remote databases is discomfiting, though the source of this discomfit would seem to elude courts such as those deciding *Riley*, and theorists like Gerety, Parent, and possibly Fried.

The crucial point I am arguing here is not that the private/public dichotomy is problematic, per se, but that it is not useful as the foundation of a normative conception of privacy. Although, in the past, it might have served as a useful approximation for delineating the scope of a right to privacy, its limitations have come to light as digital information technologies radically alter the terms under which others—individuals and private organizations as well as government—have access to us and to information about us in what are traditionally understood as private and public domains.

In the period before such technologies were common, people could count on going unnoticed and unknown in public arenas; they could count on disinterest in the myriad scattered details about them. We see this assumption at work as the fictional detective Alexander Gold interrogates a murder suspect:

> "You certainly sounded as though you hated him enough to kill him."
>
> "Not hated, Mr. Gold, despised. If I had killed him, would I have told you how I felt?"
>
> "Maybe. You could be trying reverse psychology."
>
> "Yes, but Professor Moriarty, you know that I know that you really know that I really know . . ." Kirsch let his voice fade away.
>
> Alexander had to smile. "All right. Let's talk about something else. Where were you when Talbott was killed?"
>
> "Jogging. In Central Park."
>
> "Witnesses?"
>
> "Hundreds." . . .
>
> "So you have an alibi."
>
> "Not exactly . . ." (Resnicow 1983, 116–117)

Seen by hundreds, noticed by none. Or, if we are noticed, it is by disparate observers, each taking in only discrete bits of information. As such, the information would be sparse and disjointed, limited by the capacities of a single human brain. Why would we care that on a particular day, say Monday July 31, 2006, a woman is observed by one person to be wearing a pair of black pants, black pumps, and a red shirt commuting into New York City on New Jersey Transit; by another, to be purchasing coffee from a café; by a third, overheard discussing her son's progress with his school teacher; later that day, spotted in a rally for gay marriage; and that evening buying drinks and leaving a bar in the company of another? Although all these activities occur in the public eye, no single one of them would be considered particularly threatening or intrusive. But with digital information technologies, the observers might be coordinated: networked systems of video cameras, footage stored and analyzed at a central point, able to be recorded and conjoined with past records. The murder suspect, Mr. Kirsch, could have his alibi, and someone would possess a multidimensional profile of a conservatively dressed mother going about her business on July 31.

A defender of the dichotomy might argue that the problem is not with the dichotomy itself, but with the creeping extension of privacy's scope. Replying to this charge, I say that the standard for privacy has not changed; rather, the threats are different. The rough cut implied by the dichotomy incorporated a set of material assumptions about what was and was not possible—in terms of observations, intrusions, and monitoring—in both private and public realms. As these assumptions have been undermined by technical systems, so the inadequacies of the dichotomy have emerged. Under the prior material constraints "anything goes" meant one thing when applied to privacy; today, under altered circumstances, it means something different. This point is similar to one information law scholar Lawrence Lessig makes when he calls for a "translation" of constitutional principles in light of altered material conditions. Lessig presents the altered status of wiretapping and bugging from *Olmstead* to *Katz* as a case where the courts need to reinterpret a rule not in an attempt to alter anything but in order to preserve a principle. He writes, "This form of argument is common in our constitutional history, and central to the best in our constitutional tradition. It is an argument that responds to changed circumstances by proposing a reading that neutralizes those changes and preserves an original meaning. . . . It is reading the amendment differently to accommodate the changes in protection that have resulted from changes in technology. It is translation to preserve meaning" (1999, 116).

Preserving meaning in an altered media landscape may be a relatively uncontroversial aim, but what this amounts to in practice may be more open to dispute. The status of public records, discussed in Chapter 3, emerged as a subject of such disputation when it was discovered that the murderer of a popular screen actress, Rebecca Schaeffer, had located her whereabouts through the address in her drivers' license record. Responding to public worry, the Drivers Privacy Protection Act of 1994, incorporated into the Violent Crime Control and Law Enforcement Act of 1994, imposed new restrictions on access to drivers' records held by state departments of motor vehicles.[13] New restrictions shifting certain types of information from the realm of the public to the realm of the private, supported by privacy advocates and opposed by direct marketers, information brokers, and many journalists, can be understood as a recalibration of values, with privacy slightly edging out public access. Another interpretation, however, reveals a different meaning: the scope of a right to privacy has not been expanded. Rather, in order to counteract material changes wrought by new technologies, new regulations were imposed on public records simply to stay true to the original balance of interests that public records struck. In other words, because of radical changes in our capacities to conduct public surveillance, there is a need to protect privacy even in public. Endorsing this conclusion, once and for all, breaks the binding of privacy with the private.

The private/public dichotomy is further strained by online social networking, also discussed in Chapter 3. Observations of the activities and interactions mediated by social networking sites indicate that, for now, they seem to defy obvious categorization as either public or private. Without ruling out the possibility that these spaces are merely undergoing transition and soon will settle into traditional private and public realms, expectations of privacy remain complex and contested at present, at some times allowing that everything is up for grabs, at other times indignantly demanding respect for privacy. In this case, we may at least conclude that whatever expectations of privacy are in play, they do not appear reducible to whether a network, or a space in a network, is deemed public or private.

Information

Those who have relied on the public/private dichotomy as the foundation for a right to privacy may concede that the right to privacy does not align perfectly with a dichotomy of actors. They may grudgingly also concede that it does not, strictly, line up with a dichotomy of realms. But, they might argue, the dichotomy of information is surely so deeply entrenched in the public's thinking about privacy that it will resist even the seismic shifts in information systems and practices caused by digital information technologies and media. What this means is that the scope of a right to privacy extends across the segment of private (personal, sensitive) information, but when it comes to the rest, to public information, anything goes!

In 1990 executives at Lotus Development Corporation and Equifax, Inc., advanced this understanding when defending the legitimacy of their joint venture, Lotus Marketplace: Households. The Lotus Marketplace: Households database was to contain actual and inferred information about approximately 120 million individuals in the United States and was to be distributed on CD-ROM. It was expected to be a boon to marketers and mail-order companies, except that it provoked a vigorous public outcry, including an estimated 30,000 e-mail protests. In January 1991 the partners announced the cancellation of Lotus Marketplace: Households, citing public relations concerns as the sole reason. They insisted that privacy was not an issue as Households would have been compiled only from information already "out there," using no intrusive means (e.g., no hidden cameras in bedrooms) and no private information. The only information in the database was to have been harvested from public records and other records of transactions conducted in the public domain, including name, address, type of dwelling, marital status, gender, age, estimated household income, lifestyle, and purchasing propensity.[14]

For William Parent, an advocate of limiting the scope of privacy (see Chapter 5), this would be an easy case: as long as the information in question is neither personal nor undocumented it "cannot without glaring paradox be called private" (1983, 271). This conclusion is consistent with positions taken in other scholarly literature, as well as in policy and the courts. So why did Households provoke such vociferous opposition? I maintain that such strident opposition reveals a fundamental flaw in the notion that information can be divided into two categories, public and private, and that we need only worry about imposing constraints on the flow of private information. As with the dichotomy of spheres (or realms), technology-based systems and practices that radically have altered access and flows of information have revealed fault lines that had not before been significant, at least for practical purposes. It might have been possible in the past to live happily with privacy policies roughly following the contours of the dichotomy (i.e., impose constraints on the flow of private information, and for the rest, nothing much is needed); but with the prospect of a CD-ROM that would broadly aggregate and widely disseminate many fields of information, this heuristic was revealed to be inadequate (and how much more so with networked environments and even more fields of information?). Here, too, even if one can agree that there is a class of public information that can be discerned from the private, there remains a belief that there is a right to privacy in public.

Let me examine a bit more deeply why a dichotomy of information serves poorly as the basis for a right to privacy. Some may find it problematic that the dichotomy is socially drawn and therefore socially relative, it is sometimes explicitly defined (as in law) and at other times implicit (as through convention and practice). Defining the class of private information is less an onto-logical task than a task of discovering what elements a particular society considers private. As legal philosopher Raymond Wacks suggests, "Personal information consists of those facts, communications, or opinions which relate to the individual and which it would be reasonable to expect him to regard as intimate or sensitive and therefore to want to withhold or at least to restrict their collection, use, or circulation" (1989, 26). Parent concurs: "Let us, then, say that personal information consists of facts which most persons in a given society choose not to reveal about themselves (except to close friends, family) or of facts about which a particular individual is acutely sensitive and which he therefore does not choose to reveal about himself, even though most people don't care if these same facts are widely known about themselves" (1983, 270). From Charles Fried's standpoint (discussed in chapters 4 and 5), limiting the scope of a legal right to privacy to personal or intimate aspects of life is largely determined by social and cultural convention or prevailing social order, which "designates certain areas, intrinsically no more private than other areas, as symbolic of the whole institution of privacy, and thus deserving of protection beyond their particular importance" (1968, 214).

These accounts may strike critics as hopelessly circular or arbitrary; privacy protection is reserved for private information; private information is that which people believe to be private. They are saved, however, by the further claim that private information is information *legitimately considered* to be private and that one may discover, as a matter of substantive fact, what information is so considered in a given time, for a culture, society, or even for an individual. One could imagine such questions being studied by social scientists using a standard array of investigative methods, such as surveys and ethnographic studies. But there are other systematic ways of answering such questions; for example, through legal precedent, jury determinations, and the application of reasonable person standards. In reality, however, this question has not been formally studied with great frequency and scholars and practitioners alike tend to rely on what might be called "informed speculation," a combination of careful, if anecdotal, observation.[15] Thus, although the dichotomy of private and public information is socially constructed and as a result variable across societies, this need not be the root of its problem as a foundation for a right to privacy.

A more serious problem with building a right to privacy atop a dichotomy of information is that not only are the definitions of *public* and *private* relative across societies, but the dividing line within societies is virtually impossible to draw. I am not here referring to the potentially fuzzy borders one inevitably encounters with any classification scheme—particularly rich and interesting ones—based on natural terms. There is, rather, a deeper ambiguity and confusion over the principles underlying classification of information into one or the other of the two categories.[16] Moreover, it is not the absence of principles that is problematic, but the presence of at least three plausible contenders, dividing the universe of information into irreducibly different schemes. These are: (1) a dichotomy of information rooted in the relation of individuals to the liberal state; (2) a dichotomy rooted in the intimacy of information; and (3) a dichotomy rooted in the sensitivity of information.

The Relation of Individuals to the Liberal State.   In the introduction to his book devoted to the classification of information for purposes of privacy protection, Raymond Wacks writes,

> The modern distinction between public and private realms arose out of a twin movement in modern political and legal thought. On the one hand, the emergence of the nation-state and theories of sovereignty in the sixteenth and seventeenth centuries produced the idea of a distinctly public realm. On the other, a delineation of a private sphere free from the encroachment of the state emerged as a response to the claims of monarchs and, subsequently, parliaments, to an untrammeled power to make law. (1989, 7–8)

From the idea of a distinctly public realm hospitable to government action, and its opposite, a private realm inhospitable to government interference, Wacks infers a principle for determining two parallel spheres of information: public information, the legitimate business of the state, and private information, which is normally off-limits except under strictly laid out conditions. Information withheld from the state supports the quest for self-determination of private citizens as well as the pursuit of a variety of liberties; public information supports the business of state administration, economic viability, security, and so forth. In the United States, for example, the state is not entitled to information about religious affiliation, political association, personal communications, and intellectual activity, but it is entitled to information about income, vehicle ownership, and vital statistics.

The Intimate and Personal.   A principle that leads to the division of information into that which is accessible to government and that which is off-limits captures one important rationale for a private/public dichotomy of information, but it does not capture all possible ways of defining a dichotomy that are relevant to privacy. A second principle, embodied in both law and scholarship, marks off a distinctive realm of information that is private because it is considered intimate or personal—"the intimacies of personal identity" (Gerety 1997, 281)—about which we might reasonably respond to a nosy outsider, "That's none of your business," or that might feature in a tort of "public disclosure of embarrassing private facts" (Prosser 1960, 389). For Gerety, it is this class of information that forms a sound underpinning of a rigorously defined legal right to privacy:

> Invasions of privacy take place whenever we are deprived of control over such intimacies of our bodies and minds as to offend what are ultimately shared standards of autonomy. Intimacy itself is always the consciousness of the mind in its access to its own and other bodies and minds, insofar, at least, as these are generally or specifically secluded from the access of the uninvited. . . . We should be able to share our intimacy with others only as we choose. It is the value of sharing such knowledge that is at stake in the right to privacy. Whenever intimacy is made indirect—that is, impersonal, secondhand, and involuntary—and public, its value is lost or diminished. (1997, 268)

These intimacies of personal identity may include (and do include, in many Western democracies) such matters as close relationships, sexual orientation, alcohol intake, dietary habits, ethnic origin, political beliefs, features of the body and bodily functions, the definition of *self*, and religious and spiritual beliefs and practices. The exact content of this set is less important than an acknowledgment that such a set exists and defines relationships not only between private individuals and government actors, and private actors and private organizations, but between private individuals and other private individuals. Also belonging in the class of personal information conceived of as "intimacies of personal identity," is information considered trivial yet still not anyone else's business. I have in mind information about such matters as how often one flosses one's teeth, how much one weighs, where one buys one's groceries, how many spoons of sugar one takes in coffee, and which side of the bed one prefers.[17]

Sensitivity.   The second principle defines private information that warrants privacy protection as that which is personal and intimate. Yet there is a third principle, one that marks information that is sensitive for special consideration. In this case, sensitive information is defined as information whose collection, disclosure, or use may result in harm to its subjects. Wacks (1989) has offered the most systematic and thorough scheme for classifying information according to its sensitivity, using it as a basis for determining law and regulation pertaining to information in the United Kingdom. He suggests a taxonomy according to which information is classified by its degree of sensitivity: high, moderate, and low. The degree of sensitivity depends not only on the type of information in question, but on numerous circumstantial factors as well, such as the scale of its disclosure, the age of the information, and likely recipients. Degree of sensitivity of particular types of information will also vary across historical periods and social contexts. Writing about the United Kingdom in the late 1980s, Wacks's sizeable taxonomy classifies medical history, sexual life, political opinion, and criminal convictions as highly sensitive; monthly mortgage payments, what credit cards one possesses, and trade union memberships as moderately sensitive; and name, address, and copyrights in literary productions as information of low sensitivity (pp. 238–239). Thus, information that is of high or moderate sensitivity deserves privacy protection, while that which is of low sensitivity does not. In the present-day United States, information such as sexual orientation, Social Security number, the fact that one has undergone an abortion, medical information, and any jail time served is often pegged as highly sensitive. A similar dichotomy recognized in the European Data Directive identifies "special categories of data," including "personal data revealing racial or ethnic origin, political opinions, religious or philosophical beliefs, trade-union membership, and the processing of data concerning health or sex life" (European Parliament and Council of the European Union 1995, Article 2).

Which Information Dichotomy?   To be sure, there would be plenty of overlap in the classes of private and public information that the three principles yield, respectively, yet there would be significant dissimilarities in plumbing distinctive sets of values. Consider the following quick test cases: a Social Security number, password, and the code for a combination lock are all potentially harmful in the wrong hands and therefore sensitive, but they are neither personal and intimate nor off-limits for government; the number of spoons of sugar taken in one's coffee, whether one has undergone liposuction, where one purchases underwear, and the name of one's high school sweetheart are all personal and intimate but unlikely to be sensitive; one's income is decidedly not off-limits to government but considered personal, at least in the United States; and membership in a local church community is off-limits to government but not (usually) deemed private in either of the other two senses.

These observations do not pose problems in themselves unless we are pressed to choose one of the principles as a foundation for morally legitimate claims to privacy. They cannot all be applied because their discrepancies result in conflicts. No single principle seems perfectly suited; yet each embodies themes that are importantly related to privacy.

Conclusion

My aim in Part II was to consider how existing theoretical works on privacy might approach the challenges of an ever-growing array of technology-based systems and practices that have radically altered the flows of personal information. While all these works recognize that privacy is affected by systems and practices that wrest control away from information subjects, or dramatically increase the access others have to information, they differ in how they account for the rights people have in relation to it. For those who rate privacy rights over information to the attainment of other valued ends, there is a presumption against systems or practices that diminish peoples' capacities in relation to potentially all personal information, particularly when this capacity bears on whatever valued ends are of particular concern. A different approach limits a right of privacy to the realms of the private, drawing on the public/private dichotomy to demarcate these realms.

In this chapter I listed a number of objections to these two approaches. Those generally skeptical about the moral significance of privacy cite apparent contradictions between what people say and what they do, as well as clearly evident cultural differences in dealing with information, as their objections. Others target the specific characteristics of the two approaches. Although philosophically insightful, the first approach runs into trouble as an applied framework when confronting the challenges of countervailing values embodied in the technology-based systems and practices in practice. In my view, these challenges reveal an important gap that needs to be filled.

Approaches to privacy that restrict its sphere of legitimacy to the private, though commonly supported in academic work and adopted in law and policy, are founded on a set of assumptions about the relationship between privacy and the public/private dichotomy that ultimately are incoherent. I have argued in this chapter that no matter what principle—actors, spheres, information—is adopted for dividing the world into public and private, it cannot hold ground against a growing host of socio-technical systems in which radically expanded powers over information have been implemented. Because of these powers, there are no actors, no spheres, no information that can be assigned unconditionally to the domain of the public, free of all and any constraints imposed by rights of privacy; none are "up for grabs."

However, my critique does not amount to total rejection. Many of the insights driving the private/public dichotomy approach are sound, even though flaws have been exposed by socio-technical systems and practices. It seems natural for privacy restrictions to be tailored to the actors in question and to vary according to the spheres or realms in which activities or transactions are occurring. One would also expect a range of varying restrictions to apply to information of different types depending on whether or not its release may cause harm, whether or not it is about intimate activities and relationships, and whether or not it is the legitimate business of government. But these are not the only variations that conceivably may affect restrictions we may wish to prescribe on the flows of personal information.

The framework of contextual integrity, presented in Part III, builds on valuable insights of the theoretical and other works discussed above. Many of the complexities that revealed gaps and oversights in these works are readily absorbed in the framework: contextual integrity situates privacy restrictions on information flows in a much richer social milieu, and thus is able to draw on a richer domain of variables for characterizing realms, actors, and information.

PART III
THE FRAMEWORK OF
CONTEXTUAL INTEGRITY

THE CENTRAL THESIS OF THIS BOOK IS THAT A RIGHT TO privacy is neither a right to secrecy nor a right to control but a right to *appropriate* flow of personal information. The framework of contextual integrity, developed in Part III, makes rigorous the notion of appropriateness. Privacy may still be posited as an important human right or value worth protecting through law and other means, but what this amounts to is a right to contextual integrity and what *this* amounts to varies from context to context.

In Chapter 7 I lay out the fundamental building blocks of contextual integrity: social contexts and context-relative informational norms. The norms, which prescribe the flow of personal information in a given context, are a function of the types of information in question; the respective roles of the subject, the sender (who may be the subject), and the recipient of this information, and the principles under which the information is sent or transmitted from the sender to the recipient. When these norms are contravened, we experience this as a violation of privacy, here labeled as a violation of contextual integrity. The problem with many of the controversial socio-technical systems discussed in Part I is that they flout entrenched informational norms and hence threaten contextual integrity.

For the framework of contextual integrity to have moral clout, however, it must offer more than an ability to determine whether novel systems and practices contravene entrenched norms. If not, one could not distinguish between those that ought to be resisted and those, including many beneficial new systems and practices enabled by advances in information science and technology, that ought to be embraced. The framework, as further developed in Chapter 8, incorporates an approach to evaluating novel systems and practices against entrenched norms they violate, allowing for the possibility that the former might legitimately challenge and lead to reform of the latter. Here, too, the framework draws from the wealth of ideas developed in prior work on privacy but adds into the mix the notion of values, ends, and purposes around which social contexts are oriented.

In Chapter 9 I demonstrate how the framework of contextual integrity may be used to analyze and evaluate specific cases, including several introduced in Part I. Privacy advocates may rightly suspect those who claim to support privacy while insisting that it must be "balanced" with needs to collect and share personal information for the sake of law and order, efficiency, or security of thinly veiled expediency. By this light, they may accuse the call of contextual integrity for appropriate flow and not the stoppage of flow of similar expediency. This would be a mistake. The framework of contextual integrity does not allow privacy to be compartmentalized at the margins of social and political life, to be called on from time to time to merely contain overzealous government intrusion or discipline corporate indiscretion with personal data. By contrast, privacy as contextual integrity is a complex, delicate web of constraints on the flow of personal information that itself brings balance to multiple spheres of social and political life. Systems and practices that radically disturb this web of constraints are not merely threatening a marginal newcomer to the stage of values and rights, but potentially tearing at the very fabric of social and political life.

7 Contexts, Informational Norms, Actors, Attributes, and Transmission Principles

OBSERVING HOW PRIVACY NORMS VARY ACROSS AND WITHIN social groups, some critics have concluded that privacy is at best a culturally relative predilection rather than a universal human value. The framework of contextual integrity begins with the same observation, but draws a different conclusion; there is, indeed, great complexity and variability in the privacy constraints people expect to hold over the flow of information, but these expectations are systematically related to characteristics of the background social situation. Once these characteristics are factored into an account of privacy expectations (hereafter referred to as norms of information flow), the law-like character of these privacy expectations, or norms, is much more evident. Variability in norms, in other words, is far from idiosyncratic or arbitrary. The heart of the framework of contextual integrity is an elaboration of its key construct: context-relative informational norms. Context-relative informational norms function descriptively when they express entrenched expectations governing the flows of personal information, but they are also a key vehicle for elaborating the prescriptive (or normative) component of the framework of contextual integrity. In this chapter I introduce key notions of a context and an informational norm and elucidate the descriptive component of the framework of contextual integrity.

In the course of people's lives we act and transact not simply as individuals in an undifferentiated social world, but as individuals acting and transacting in certain capacities as we move through, in, and out of a plurality of distinct social contexts. By contexts, I mean structured social settings with characteristics that have evolved over time (sometimes long periods of time) and are subject to a host of causes and contingencies of purpose, place, culture, historical accident, and more. Familiar to those of us living in modern industrial societies are contexts of health care, education, employment, religion, family, and the commercial marketplace. In these contexts we act and interact with others, individually and collectively, as coworkers, professionals, clients, teachers, students, citizens, family members, club members, congregants, and neighbors. We relax with family, commune with neighbors, go to work, seek medical care, attend school and religious services, visit friends, consult with psychiatrists, hire lawyers, cast votes, and go shopping, banking, dancing, and to concerts.

I am not inventing the idea of a social context. Instead, I rely on a robust intuition rigorously developed in social theory and philosophy that people engage with one another not simply as human to human but in capacities structured by social spheres. Inspired by various goals and specialized concerns, this idea has spawned a host of formal accounts populating a range of academic fields, including social theory, social psychology, sociology, social philosophy, and political science. Influential accounts are associated with leading figures in sociology, from founders of the field such as Talcott Parsons, Erving Goffman, and Max Weber (who coined the term "spheres of value" for this purpose), to contemporary scholars of institutional theory, including Paul DiMaggio and Walter Powell, whose account of institutions as "a pattern of regularized conduct" (Martin 2003, 40) captures aspects of the basic intuition. In institutional frameworks, such as marriage and parenthood, actors' expectations of each other are set out in rules and social mores that do not just stem from individuals.

Pierre Bourdieu's field theory is another highly developed account of structured social settings defined by a set of constructs that are consonant with those I have informally associated with contexts. Bourdieu, a French philosopher and social theorist who emerged to prominence in the latter half of the twentieth century, was preoccupied with hierarchy and the uneven distribution of power within what he called social fields, "familiar divisions of action [divided] into self-contained realms of endeavor" (Martin 2003, 23; see also Bourdieu 1984). Social fields are differentiated, structured social systems in which individuals are defined by their position in the field. Although fields are autonomous, they can be affected by outside events in ways that vary according to the internal logic of each field. Individuals in their respective positions have unequal possession of and access to the species of capital valued in their respective fields. Governed by an internal "law" that regulates their actions and practices, social agents are arrayed in deeply entrenched power relationships within fields. Although agents may engage in antagonistic or competitive relationships with one another, they are also, as players, bound by the rules of the fields. As sociologist John Levi Martin writes, "What is at stake in a chess, tennis, or sumo tournament is not simply which individual will be the winner, but what *kind* of chess, tennis, or sumo (and hence what *kinds* of players) will dominate the field in the future" (2003, 23).[1] In the course of developing these general ideas, Bourdieu paid considerable attention to the professional fields of law and journalism, as well as photography, literature, and academia, as he shaped his ideas on the constitutive theoretical constructs.

Social philosophers proffering accounts of social ontology have also defined a family of constructs analogous in function to those associated with fields and institutions. In the analytic tradition, Raimo Tuemelo, John Searle, Margaret Gilbert, and Seumas Miller account for the social world and the activities of human agents within it not only in terms of their individual or shared properties as human beings, but in terms of their properties as social actors, in social roles, and within social structures, be they "fields," "institutions," or "contexts" (Searle 1995; Miller 2001). So robust are these paradigmatic social spheres in the ways even ordinary people conceptualize their lives that leading psychologists Roger Schank and Robert Abelson (1977) postulated the existence of cognitive structures, or knowledge representations of stereotyped actions such as eating at a restaurant, which they called "scripts." The elements of these scripts include paradigmatic actors (e.g.. waiters), activities (e.g., reading a menu, ordering), typical environments (e.g., restaurants), and sequences (e.g., order-eat-pay). Another influential work that assumes social differentiation is the political philosopher Michael Walzer's theory of justice, which posits that there are distinct social spheres—politics, workplace, marketplace, family, state, school, and so forth—defined by distinctive social goods with special meanings distributed in their respective spheres according to distinctive sets of principles (Walzer 1984).

In the Continental tradition, Theodore R. Schatzki posits "practices" as basic building blocks of social order: "Social orders . . . are arrangements of people and of the artifacts, organisms, and things through which they coexist, in which these entities relate and possess identity and meaning. To say that orders are established within practices is to say that arrangements—their relations, identities, and meanings—are determined there" (2001, 53). According to Schatzki, practices are constellations of activities constituted by a pool of understandings, constituent actions, and practitioners (identities, roles); a set of rules that "enjoin or school in particular actions"; and "a mix of teleology and affectivity" (p. 51). Schatzki's teleology is reminiscent of the more familiar values, or ends, and affectivity of beliefs about the constellation of activities that will bring those ends about. He writes, "In sum, a practice is a set of doings and sayings organized by a pool of understandings, a set of rules, and a teleoaffective structure. . . . that can change over time in response to contingent events. But it is by virtue of expressing certain understandings, rules, ends, projects, beliefs, and emotions (etc.) that behaviors form an organized manifold" (p. 53).

Contexts

Contexts are structured social settings characterized by canonical activities, roles, relationships, power structures, norms (or rules), and internal values (goals, ends, purposes). I have not fully adopted any one of the standard theories as a framework for the intuitive notion of a context, though all share a remarkably similar array of key theses and characteristics, starting with the basic idea that social life comprises structured, differentiated spheres, whether labeled and theorized as "fields," "institutions," "structured social systems," "spheres," "social structures," "practices," or "contexts." Further, although *contexts* are tuned specifically to the task of framing a response to socio-technical systems and practices that have radically altered information flows, most of their key characteristics can be roughly matched with corresponding characteristics of their more formally developed counterparts. The idea of canonical activities, for example, corresponds to institution theory's patterns of regularized conduct, Schank and Abelson's stereotyped actions, and Schatziki's practices; the idea of roles corresponds to Bourdieu's positions and several of the philosophers' social actors and social roles; power structures correspond to Bourdieu's hierarchies and entrenched power relationships; contextual norms correspond to DiMaggio and Powell's rules and social mores, Bourdieu's internal law, and Schatzki's sets of rules; and internal values correspond to Bourdieu's capital, Walzer's social goods, and Schatzki's ends or teleology.

Of most immediate relevance to the development of the framework of contextual integrity are the constructs of roles, activities, norms, and values, each briefly explained below.

Roles. Contexts incorporate assemblages of roles. By this I mean typical or paradigmatic capacities in which people act in contexts. Teachers, physicians, lawyers, store managers, students, principals, congregants, rabbis, voters, cashiers, consumers, receptionists, journalists, waiters, patients, and clients are among some of the most familiar roles.

Activities. Contexts are partly constituted by the canonical activities and practices in which people, in roles, engage. Examples include browsing goods in a store, singing hymns in church, completing homework assignments, lecturing in a classroom, conducting and undergoing physical examinations, writing reports, entering a vote at a polling station, and interviewing job applicants.

Norms. Behavior-guiding norms prescribe and proscribe acceptable actions and practices. Some of them define the relationships among roles and, in this way, the power structures that characterize many familiar social contexts.[2] Consider how the various elements interact in the case of a grade school, which functions in an educational context. Attending the grade school are children in the role of students, taught by adults in the role of teachers, managed by an adult in the role of a principal. Schools also usually include administrative staff, clerical workers, and janitors, and are overseen by a district superintendent. Norms prescribe that teachers expound on subjects in the curriculum and prepare report cards; students pay attention, write notes, ask questions, complete homework assignments, and take tests; the principal keeps a close eye on things and sometimes disciplines unruly students or lackadaisical teachers. In other educational contexts, such as universities, the assemblages of roles, activities, and norms are similar, though not identical. Academic departments, for example, include chairs, tenured faculty, assistant professors, students, and administrators who engage in typical activities and interactions. Norms define the duties, obligations, prerogatives, and privileges associated with particular roles, as well as acceptable and unacceptable behaviors. (Much more is said about norms below.)

Values. Many of the canonical activities of a context are oriented around values—sometimes more aptly called goals, purposes, or ends; that is, the objectives around which a context is oriented, something akin to Schatzki's "teleology."[3] Values are crucial, defining features of contexts. Imagine visitors from Mars landing on Earth at a school, university, or, for that matter, a hospital, with instructions to report to their leaders back home all they have learned about life on Earth. Like all good ethnographers, they make extensive sightings and recordings, take copious notes on all of the hustle and bustle, engage in sensitive conversation with earthlings, and observe roles, regularities, and rules, but they will be missing something crucial in their reports on these contexts unless they have grasped the set of ends, values, and objectives around which these contexts are oriented; in sum, the teleology of education or health care. They would be unable to understand or properly explain what they have observed without appreciating that the purposes of educational contexts include transmitting knowledge, knowhow, and, arguably, social values to a society's young; imparting training; and, sometimes, preparing students for occupations beyond school. They would need to have grasped that among the values of health care are alleviating physical suffering, curing illness, and promoting the health of individuals as well as collectives. Although settling on a definitive and complete list of contextual values is neither simple nor noncontentious, the central point is that contextual roles, activities, practices, and norms make sense largely in relation to contextual teleology, including goals, purposes, and ends.

To simplify usage, hereafter I generally use the term *values* or *contextual values* to refer to this cluster of teleological notions.

Contexts are not formally defined constructs, but, as mentioned earlier, are intended as abstract representations of social structures experienced in daily life. In saying what contexts are and itemizing their key characteristics I should not be taken as stipulating that contexts, by definition or necessity, take a particular form. Rather, I am attempting to create a generalized snapshot of a context based on attributes observed across concrete instances, ultimately testable in the real world. In other words, the activity of fleshing out the details of particular types of contexts, such as education or health care, is more an exercise of discovery than of definition. Because contexts are essentially rooted in specific times and places, their concrete character in a given society, reflected in roles, practices, norms, and values, is likely to be shaped uniquely by that society in relation to the arrangement of other contexts in that society as well as to its culture, history, politics, and economics, and even to physical and natural contingencies (e.g., war, famine, and earthquakes). Disparities across societies, cultures, and historical periods may manifest in differences between contexts of the same type (e.g., differences in characteristics of educational contexts across societies), or perhaps even divergent contextual structures. It is therefore worth discerning how similar the constellation of contexts (educational, political, familial, etc.) is across societies. Such questions, however, lie outside the purview of this book, belonging rather in the territory of anthropologists and other empirical social scientists.

Even within a given society, there can be great variability in how key characteristics manifest across contexts. One dimension of variability is how finely articulated these characteristics are. Certain contexts are articulated in great detail, for example, voting stations, courtrooms, and highly ritualized settings such as church services. In these contexts the roles, actions, and practices are thickly specific and guided, in detail, by a rich set of norms. In the context of a polling station during democratic elections, roles are clearly specified, and what one says and does in that context is constrained by law, regulation, and possibly local custom. In contrast, contexts such as business meetings or open-air markets may be relatively sparsely and incompletely (or partially) specified. Accordingly, although certain roles are specified, no one is surprised to encounter great variation in others; likewise, what people say and do and what transactions are performed are somewhat, but far from fully, constrained. At a cocktail party in the United States circa 2009, for instance, the norms of propriety generally demand that guests arrive more or less at the appointed time and be fully clothed (perhaps, more specifically, in "cocktail attire"), that they eat and drink in the appropriately polite manner, and that they thank the hosts upon departure. Within these sparse requirements, the scope of action is quite open-ended. Variation we may encounter in individual instances is not always a result of open-ended, partial, or incomplete specification. It may reflect contention within a society over the structural characteristics of a given context. In the context of sexual relations, for example, historically there has been strong disagreement about the legitimate presence of marketplace norms, leading some members of a given society to eschew the buying and selling of sex, while others deem it acceptable.

Another difference among contexts is in the degree to which they are institutionalized or recognized formally and explicitly. Law is one such mechanism, important for according formal sanction as well as imposing explicit governance over a context. There also are mechanisms for institutionalizing contexts, or fragments of contexts, such as the rules of a professional society, club, or religious community. There can be interactions among these mechanisms; laws setting out a basic framework for certain types of contexts, such as for corporations or professions, are further fleshed out by rules or professional codes applying to particular corporation or professional societies, which may specify officeholders (roles), goals, practices, and norms of acceptable or expected behavior. There may be a further amalgam of elements that are explicitly and officially sanctioned with others that are only tacitly and gradually incorporated into the contexts. In my view, many persistent specific disagreements over the nature and extent of the right to privacy are the result of this particular form of variability across contexts. Defenders of one position are prepared to accept only those elements (roles, activities, norms, and values) that are explicitly recognized in the law of privacy, whereas others accept as legitimate constraints that originate from a broader array of sources, including customary expectations, art, literature, ethics, and even etiquette.

It is useful to highlight possible relationships among and between contexts. One of these is nesting. The example discussed earlier of a grade school context is nested within the more general education context. Referring to a high school is further specification within the nested contexts of grade school; an inner-city high school, more so; and a particular high school, say the Washington Irving High School in Manhattan, even more. The education context also includes universities and their distinctive substructures, which may, again, be further specified down to individual instances, as in "the context of New York University" with its particular rules and traditions overlaid upon the more generalized education elements. The implications for privacy of such nesting might be that the governing norms of the commercial marketplace may be differentiated from richer, more specific norms for food markets, and even more differentiated for an individual store.

Contexts may overlap and possibly conflict with one another. What does this mean? In the course of daily life, people regularly find themselves negotiating multiple contexts, sometimes simultaneously. A mother takes her children shopping, a physician is called to treat a friend's medical condition, a job applicant is interviewed by her uncle, and one has friends who also are workplace colleagues. Observing that practices do not exist in isolation from one another, Schatzki says this about how they may be formally and informally interwoven: "Arrangements established across practices, say, farming and commercial ones, interact and thus form an arrangement at, say, the general store; or when chains of action pass through different practices, for example, those of farming, commerce, cooking, and state surveillance, and thereby set up arrangements that embrace farmers, shop owners, spouses, and Internal Revenue Service officers" (2001, 53–54).

Overlaps need not necessarily involve conflicts. Thus, a community health center may collaborate with school authorities to promote health and nutrition within schools.[4] It is not so much that contexts themselves conflict as that, occasionally, when and where they overlap the norms from one context prescribe actions that are proscribed by the norms of an overlapping context. In such instances, actors face tough choices: the uncle is inclined to offer the job to his niece out of love and a sense of family loyalty but is also disposed to select another candidate with more relevant work experience; the physician might be inclined to warn a patient sternly to refrain from patently unhealthful eating habits but as a friend is reluctant to adopt such intrusive paternalism about lifestyle choices.

Even though careful consideration of the details in specific contexts may favor one action over the other, there may be no general solutions to these general types of conflicts and it may be that some are simply intractable. Collisions among contexts giving rise to conflicts do not, in themselves, refute the context-based structure of social life any more than value conflicts, as discussed by Isaiah Berlin, constitute a refutation of values pluralism. Although some of the conflicts we face can be clarified and even resolved by adopting sound strategies (too many to enumerate here), others are simply entrenched in the world as we know it, not necessarily a fault of theory but one of the challenges of living. Numerous conflicts, as they arise regularly in relation to privacy, will be discussed later at greater length.

Norms

Norms may be construed in a variety of ways, but because they are central to the account of contextual integrity, it is necessary to specify my understanding here before defining the concept of a context-relative informational norm. Like many other interesting and contentious concepts, the idea of a norm is rich with intuitive meanings drawn from popular usage in lived experience. At the same time, it has provoked considerable interest in applied and scholarly investigations in law, philosophy, and the social sciences, where scholars and practitioners have attempted to imbue it with greater rigor. To attempt comprehensive coverage of the range of works would be both a presumptuous and impractical undertaking for this book; instead I strive for an interpretation that is as close as possible to a natural one, disambiguated and made somewhat more precise through the insights of a small selection of relevant scholarship.

One point of disambiguation is choosing between two robust interpretations of the term. According to one, norms are part of the larger category of rules that prescribe, mandate, or require that certain actions be performed; according to the other, norms are used merely descriptively to refer to behavioral regularities, habits, or common practices, with no underlying expectation or prescription. The ambiguity is described in this way by philosopher Cristina Bicchieri:

> Still, the term social norm may refer to two very different things. One is what people commonly do in certain situations or what constitutes 'normal' behavior. The other is what people believe ought to be done, what is socially approved or disapproved. The first may be dubbed descriptive norms, the latter injunctive norms. . . . Conformity to a descriptive norm does not involve an obligation or mutual expectations. . . . It is important to notice that the behavioral regularities we call descriptive norms are supported by unilateral expectations. Though we expect others to follow the norm, we do not feel any pressure to follow it ourselves. (2000, 156)

I adopt here as a default the prescriptive interpretation, what Bicchieri calls injunctive, highlighting the thematic link between norms and the normative instead of the link Bicchieri asserts between norms and the normal. Although this is not the place to launch a full defense of this choice, the normative meaning strikes me as dominant, as one is hard pressed to think of actual situations in which at least some hint of prescription is not lurking behind the term *norm*, even in situations in which it is used ostensibly to refer merely to *normal* practice. I also tend toward the normative sense of the term because it links this work with dominant interpretations adopted in general canonical works on norms by philosophers and legal theorists such as H. L. A. Hart and Joseph Raz (Hart 1961; Raz 1975; Richardson 1990; Miller 2001). Accordingly, when I say that an action or practice is norm-governed, I mean not only that most people generally follow it but they do so because they believe they ought to. Furthermore, I adopt the anatomy of norms that Raz adapted from Georg Henrik von Wright (1963, chap. 5; Raz 1975, 50), attributing four key elements to norms: (1) a prescriptive "ought" element; (2) a norm subject—one upon whom the obligation expressed in the norm falls; (3) a norm act—the action prescribed in the norm; and (4) a condition of application—the circumstances in which the norm act is prescribed for the norm subject.

Even with the focus narrowed to prescriptive norms, great variability in norm types remains. One dimension of variability that is relevant to contextual integrity is the degree to which norms are explicitly expressed in a given society, ranging from those that are only implicitly understood and accepted, to those that are explicitly formulated and sanctioned by authoritative individuals and institutions, to those that are explicit, formal, and enforced, such as norms embedded in formal legal systems. Seumas Miller, a social philosopher, is interested in a particular class of norms he calls social norms, distinguished from the others in that they are neither explicitly expressed nor enforced: "They are not, qua social norms, explicitly formulated; nor do they, qua social norms, emanate from any formal authority or have any formal sanctions attached to them" (2001, 123). Context-relative informational norms, discussed below, can have all of the above.

Another dimension of variability recognized in the philosophical literature, beyond formal expression and official sanction, is in norm type. Familiar instances of norm types are moral norms, proscribing activities such as lying, inflicting physical harm, and stealing; social conventions of etiquette proscribing actions such as interrupting others while they are talking, walking unclothed in public places, and addressing nobility with inappropriate familiarity; and rules or procedures in formal committee meetings, such as Robert's Rules. Norms also vary in their degree of seriousness, from those that, as Raz has remarked, relate to "fundamental features of human societies and human life" to those that "like many rules of etiquette, are of little importance and carry little weight" (1975, 51). Further, norms may vary according to their historical legacy, universality, and source of origination. Religious norms, for example, may have an impressive heritage but limited range of applicability versus newfangled fads, which may be widespread but fleeting. Some norms originate as the imperatives of authority figures (or institutions), while others seem to have evolved along with cultures, histories, and political traditions, and, in fact, are partly constitutive of them.

One final general point, relevant to the framework of contextual integrity, is that the norms that guide our lives are, for the most part, embedded in systems. As Raz notes, "certain groups of norms are more than haphazard assemblages of norms. Normative systems are understood to have some kind of unity" (1975, 9). Rules of a game, laws of a country, bylaws of an association or club, principles in a code of professional ethics, and contextual norms are all cases of normative systems. To fully appreciate and find norms that are elements of normative systems compelling, one needs to consider them against the backdrop of the system itself. Otherwise, in isolation, they might appear arbitrary or even dubious. Certain rules of the road, for example, make sense only holistically: directives such as "stop on red" and "drive on the right" are arbitrary on their own but function integrally in relation to "go on green" and, more generally, the complex socio-technical system of roads, vehicles, and drivers. Norms proscribing marital infidelity that seem immediately robust draw their import from the broader meaning of family and the institution of marriage in a given society. And norms guiding professional conduct might seem positively unethical except in relation to the broader functioning of the profession in society.

Context-Relative Informational Norms and Contextual Integrity

Given the myriad norms that govern activities and practices within and across contexts, consider those that are specifically concerned with the flow of personal information—transmission, communication, transfer, distribution, and dissemination—from one party to another, or others. I will call these *informational norms* when speaking of them within individual contexts and *context-relative informational norms* when referring to them generally.[5] *Contextual integrity* is defined in terms of informational norms: it is preserved when informational norms are respected and violated when informational norms are breached. The framework of contextual integrity maintains that the indignation, protest, discomfit, and resistance to technology-based information systems and practices, as discussed in Part I, invariably can be traced to breaches of context-relative informational norms. Accordingly, contextual integrity is proposed as a benchmark for privacy.

The Structure of Context-Relative Informational Norms
Context-relative informational norms are characterized by four key parameters: contexts, actors, attributes, and transmission principles. Generally, they

prescribe, for a given context, the types of information, the parties who are the subjects of the information as well as those who are sending and receiving it, and the principles under which this information is transmitted. In other words, informational norms regulate the flow of information of certain types about an information subject from one actor (acting in a particular capacity, or role) to another or others (acting in a particular capacity or role) according to particular transmission principles.

Contexts

As discussed above, contexts are the backdrop for informational norms. It is crucial to bear in mind, particularly because it is so easy to forget when one enters the fraught territory of privacy, that informational norms are always elements of a context-based system of informational norms as well as context-based normative systems, generally. Further, according to Raz's adaptation of von Wright's anatomy of norms, contexts are what he would call the condition of application, or the circumstances in which an act is prescribed for a subject. The co-constitutive relationship between informational norms and contexts is conveyed with the term *context-relative information norms* (hereafter frequently abbreviated to *informational norms*).

As a brief aside, connecting back to the discussions in chapters 5 and 6, the public/private dichotomy can be understood as a cruder version of contextual integrity, postulating only two contexts with distinct sets of informational norms for each—privacy constraints in the private, anything goes in the public. The framework of contextual integrity, by contrast, postulates a multiplicity of social contexts, each with a distinctive set of rules governing information flows.

Actors

Informational norms have three placeholders for actors: senders of information, recipients of information, and information subjects. Sender and receiver placeholders might be filled respectively by single individuals, multiple individuals, or even collectives such as organizations, committees, and so forth. (Other terms, including *parties* and *agents*, will be used to refer to those communicating, transmitting, sharing, or sending information as well as those receiving it.) For the subject placeholder, I will only be seriously considering single individuals, though in many instances, the subject and sender of information will be one and the same.[6] In specifying an informational norm, it is crucial to identify the contextual roles of all three actors to the extent possible; that is, the capacities in which each are acting. In a healthcare context, for example, there are numerous informational norms prescribing information sharing practices where the subjects and senders are patients themselves, and where the recipients are physicians. We might express this more formally by saying senders/subjects are acting in their capacity as patients seeking medical attention, and recipients are acting in their capacity as physicians. Other norms apply in cases where the recipients are receptionists, bookkeepers, nurses, and so forth. In healthcare contexts there are informational norms governing the transmission of information about patients from physicians, as senders, to other recipients (such as medical students under their tutelage, fellow practitioners, insurance companies, and their spouses).

In requiring that actors' roles are fully specified as a default condition, the framework of contextual integrity provides a more expressive medium for highlighting variables that are relevant to privacy. Actors' roles are among those critical variables that affect people's rich and complex sensibilities over whether privacy has been violated or properly respected. Other attempts to articulate privacy principles go awry because they neglect or under-specify actors' roles in explicating both policies and the problematic scenario under consideration. As a result, we are called to adjudicate incompletely specified situations because rarely, if ever, is the flow of information prohibited, or required, in a way unconditioned by the capacities in which sender, subjects, and recipients are acting. In structuring informational norms with placeholders for actors, the framework of contextual integrity affirms intuitions that the capacities in which actors function are crucial to the moral legitimacy of certain flows of information. This holds true even when it appears that it does not—as when people remark that certain information is secret when they usually mean it is secret in relation to some actors, or constrained by a particular principle of transmission rather than absolutely. Usually, when we mind that information about us is shared, we mind not simply that it is being shared but that it is shared in the wrong ways and with inappropriate others. Although most of the time these requirements are tacit and the states of all parameters need not be tediously spelled out, in controversial cases, elliptical expressions of people's expectations can be taken too literally and serve as sources of common misunderstandings.

The relevance of actors to whether a particular system or practice violates privacy is often implicit in our reactions even if not systematically theorized. Among the exceptions, James Rachels's account of the value of privacy cited in Chapter 4 makes this connection explicitly: "businessman to employee, minister to congregant, doctor to patient, husband to wife, parent to child, and so on. In each case, the sort of relationship that people have to one another involves a conception of how it is appropriate for them to behave with each other, and what is more, a conception of the kind and degree of knowledge concerning one another which it is appropriate for them to have" (1975, 71). Just as contexts generalize the dichotomy of realms to a rich multiplicity, the notion of people acting in capacities generalizes a dichotomy of actors; it is relevant to know whether the actors are government or private, and in what capacity they act, among an innumerable number of possibilities.

Attributes (Information Types)

In the passage quoted above, Rachels affirms the critical relevance of actors to a sense that privacy has been violated. Another parameter of equal importance is the nature of the information in question: not only who it was about, and to whom and from whom it was shared, but what it was about; or, as Rachels puts it, the "kind and degree of knowledge" (1975, 71) . The framework of contextual integrity incorporates *attributes* or *type* or *nature* of information (terms I will use interchangeably) as another key parameter in informational norms. (A technical term with similar meaning is *data field*.) In a healthcare context, for example, strictures on information flow vary according to roles and to the type of information in question, whether it be patients' medical conditions, their attire, their addresses and phone numbers, the name and code number of their health insurance carrier, or the balances on their accounts. Here, too, analysis in terms of contextual integrity is a radical but clearly essential generalization of approaches that assume a private/public dichotomy of information. These approaches also recognize the importance of information types, but only two types; analysis in terms of contextual integrity, in principle, recognizes an indefinite array of possibilities.

Informational norms render certain attributes appropriate or inappropriate in certain contexts, under certain conditions. For example, norms determine it appropriate for physicians in a healthcare context to query their patients on the condition of their bodies, but in the workplace context for the boss to do the same thing would usually be inappropriate (an exception could be made for circumstances such as the coach of a professional football team inquiring about a player's heart condition). To friends, we confide details of romantic entanglements (our own and those of others); to the bank and creditors, we disclose details of our financial standing (earnings, loan payments); with professors, students discuss their grades; at work we discuss performance goals and salaries—all generally appropriate attributes in these contexts.

Recognizing the import of information type, some, like theorist Charles Fried, have strung it along a single continuous dimension of more to less intimate, more to less sensitive; others, as mentioned above, have split it into dichotomies of personal versus nonpersonal (or public), highly sensitive versus not sensitive, and so on. In contrast with these approaches, appropriateness is not one-dimensional nor is it binary. For example, it is not simply that one discusses intimate matters with friends and impersonal matters with, say, coworkers, because in many societies it is inappropriate to discuss salaries and financial standing with close friends but appropriate to do so with one's boss and one's banker. The factors determining appropriateness are simultaneously variable. Consider that friends are typically aware of each other's religious affiliations, while such information is off limits in a job interview or workplace (at least, in the United States). Information about an applicant's marital status is inappropriate for a job interview in the present-day United States, but quite appropriate in the context of courtship. Physicians are familiar with medical conditions but would hesitate to delve into either the religious affiliation or financial standing of their patients.[7]

Those who may be expecting a precise definition of information type or attribute will be disappointed, for I rely throughout on an intuitive sense, assuming that it is as adequate for the explication of contextual integrity as for many important practices and policies successfully managed in society with nothing more. One need look no further than the endless forms we complete, the menus we select from, the shopping lists we compile, the genres of music we listen to, the movies we watch, the books we read, and the terms we submit to search engines to grasp how at ease we are with information types and attributes. Our daily lives are organized, and complex political and institutional functions are managed, by means of myriad information schemes that require at least an understanding of spoken language, though obviously there are times when expert or specialized knowledge is important. In highly circumscribed contexts, such as an organization wishing to automate a spectrum of its business processes, a top-down, finite taxonomy of attributes may be useful; for example, the Internal Revenue Service or the U.S. Census Bureau might seek to automate policies for the finite data fields extracted from their forms.[8] In general, this is not only unnecessary but might even be inimical to the idea of contexts as evolving structures and the activities, actors, norms, values, and attributes comprising them evolving simultaneously. In general, attribute schemes will have co-evolved with contexts and not be readily accessible to fixed and finite representations.

Transmission Principles

A transmission principle is a constraint on the flow (distribution, dissemination, transmission) of information from party to party in a context. The transmission principle parameter in informational norms expresses terms and conditions under which such transfers ought (or ought not) to occur. The idea of a transmission principle may be the most distinguishing element of the framework of contextual integrity; although what it denotes is plain to see, it usually goes unnoticed.

How transmission principles function is probably most effectively conveyed through illustrations. One of the most salient is confidentiality, stipulating that the party receiving information is prohibited from sharing it with others. Other familiar instances include reciprocity, by which I mean a principle determining that information flows bidirectionally; dessert, determining that an actor deserves to receive information; entitlement (similar to dessert), determining that one party is entitled to know something; compulsion, determining that one party (often, the information subject himself) is compelled or mandated to reveal information to another; and need, determining that one party needs to know information of a particular kind. A transmission principle might determine that information must be shared voluntarily, or consensually; it may require the knowledge of the subject ("notice"), or only her permission ("consent"), or both. Transmission principles may allow for commercial exchanges of information bought, sold, bartered, or leased in accordance with the rules of a competitive free market. The list is probably indefinite, particularly if we allow for nuanced and complicating variations.

Transmission principles are but one of the parameters embedded in an informational norm, in a given context, covarying with the other parameters of actors and attributes. Imagine these as juggling balls in the air, moving in sync: contexts, subjects, senders, receivers, information types, and transmission principles. Again, examples drawn from familiar experiences might help clarify this. In the context of friendship, we almost always expect information to be shared voluntarily. One chooses to share information with one's friend, though friends often draw conclusions about one another on the basis of what each says and does. Although the type of information shared in friendship is wide-ranging, there are generally certain locally relative (probably also age-relative) prohibitions. Friends share information reciprocally, generally assuming that what they say to each other will be held in confidence. Although, in the context of friendship, some departure from these norms is generally allowable (as when friends coax information from each other), straying too far may be viewed as a breach. Ferreting out information about a friend from third parties, peeking in a diary, or divulging to others information shared in friendship are actions that not only may be judged as betrayals, but call into question the very nature of the relationship.[9]

Contrast the configuration of transmission principles in health care with those of friendship. True, as with friendship, strict confidentiality is thought to govern the flow of information to the physician about past and present physical ailments, but unlike in friendship, the subject's discretion does not reign supreme. Instead, something closer to the physician's mandate determines the flow, in the sense that a physician might reasonably condition care on the fullness of the patient's information disclosure. This does not apply to all information, however, but information the physician deems necessary for delivering a sound diagnosis and competent care by standards of the profession. Another difference is that the flow is unidirectional (i.e., not reciprocal); physicians are not expected to share information about their physical ailments, or much personal information at all, with patients.

A further point of difference between the contexts of friendship and health care is that many of the informational norms in the latter are formally codified, either through law or codes of professional conduct (in the United States and most other countries), and complex rules stipulate such matters as when a patients' explicit consent is required for transmission and how the flow of information is affected by the nature of the ailment in question (for an example, see the Health Insurance Portability and Accountability Act of 1996). Rules also govern the set of appropriate recipients, for example, caregivers are obliged to transmit information about incidents of food poisoning or highly infectious diseases to public health officials; law enforcement agents are entitled to information about gunshot wounds; medical insurance companies, under the current regime, are entitled to know what categories of ailments patients are treated for, and so on. Despite the existence of these complex rules, there are still open and controversial issues; for example, what transmission principles ought to govern the flow of various categories of information to drug companies, and whether people are entitled to know the HIV status of their sexual partners.[10]

A few more illustrations may be useful for filling out and elucidating the range of possible transmission principles and the way they function in familiar scenarios. In transactions between customers and mail-order companies, customers are required to provide, at the very least, information necessary to pay (e.g., credit card information) and to receive the goods (e.g., a shipping address). Although the job of law enforcement might be easier were the investigation of criminal activity allowed to proceed with no restrictions, this context is governed by a rigorous set of rules governing how officers conduct themselves, what they are and are not allowed to ask citizens and suspects, and how they may and may not transmit this information thereafter. Further, although arresting officers are constrained in what they are and are not allowed to ask at various stages, suspects, though compelled to answer certain questions, are free to volunteer information beyond this. The admissibility of information as evidence in court, defining another transmission principle, would need to be addressed on a case-by-case basis guided not only by policy but the discretion of the presiding judge. Courtrooms are generally tightly rule-governed. Even the Fifth Amendment may be understood as defining a transmission principle: suspects themselves may not be forced to provide self-incriminating evidence although this evidence presumably may be obtained by other (legal) means.

Control Versus Access

It is worthwhile revisiting the persistent, irresolvable disagreement discussed in Part II over whether a right to privacy is a right to control versus a right to limit or constrain access to information by others. The framework of contextual integrity reveals why we do not need to choose between them; instead, it recognizes a place for each. The idea that privacy implies a limitation of access by others overlaps, generally, with the idea of an informational norm. The former focuses on diminishment of access; the latter includes diminishment of access as one way information flow might be governed (though it may govern the flow of information in other ways). Informational norms are generally far richer in specifying not only when access is diminished but, as we have seen, allow one to specify about what, about whom, and against whom. Philosopher

Jeffrey Reiman (1995), we recall, offers some of this specificity when he requires that access not be at the discretion of others.

Control, too, remains important in the framework of contextual integrity, as one of the transmission principles. Whereas many dominant accounts of privacy identify the right to privacy as a right to control, in the framework of contextual integrity, as we have seen, it is but one among many possible transmission principles, which in turn are but one of the parameters determining whether informational norms have been respected. Accordingly, whether or not control is appropriate depends on the context, the types of information, the subject, sender, and recipient.

Contextual Integrity as a Decision Heuristic

Motivating this book is the challenge of socio-technical systems and practices that have radically altered the flow of information in societies and thereby affected institutions, power structures, relationships, and more. Conceptions of privacy that have served adequately until now are, in my view, unable to adapt to the new landscape, not quite able to conform to the ebb and flow of anxieties that these systems and practices provoke. In proposing contextual integrity as an alternative conception of information privacy I am not as concerned with capturing the full meaning of privacy but with precisely and systematically characterizing the nature of these radical alterations. Most importantly, I am interested in addressing the question of when and why some of these alterations provoke legitimate anxiety, protest, and resistance. In applying contextual integrity to this question I call on it to serve as a decision heuristic, a framework for determining, detecting, or recognizing when a violation has occurred. Contextual integrity, in this capacity, not only helps predict when an activity or practice is likely to arouse protest, indignation, or resistance, it helps explain and pinpoint the sources of objection.

Before and After Change, Establish and Compare

How does the framework of contextual integrity guide an assessment of, say, a problematic new practice resulting from the deployment of a novel technical device or system? Clearly, the question that needs asking is: Does the practice in question violate context-relative informational norms? Answering it requires that a comparison be drawn between entrenched practice and the novel practice. Although there may, of course, be a host of ways in which novel practices alter the status quo, the framework of contextual integrity focuses our assessment on the key parameters of context, actors, attributes, and transmission principles.

Establish the prevailing context. In order to ascertain what norms prevail, one must determine the prevailing social context. Some cases are clear enough—a grade school in an educational context; a hospital in a healthcare context; a department store in a commercial marketplace. But others might take a little work and even then, the practice under consideration might occupy a zone of overlap or conflict, or might be in zones of a context for which norms are incomplete. These hard cases need not be obscure or mysterious: Should one tell one's friend her spouse is having an affair? Should one tell one's boss her spouse is having an affair? Should a hospital share injury records with police officers? Should a parent read a child's blog postings? Aspects of the framework developed in the next chapter offer ways to address some of these ambiguities but, for now, we merely register them as problematic, not specifically for contextual integrity but for any attempt at modeling social systems and nuances of social experience.

Establish key actors. Ascertain whether the new practice brings about changes in who receives information (recipient), whom the information is about (subject), or who transmits the information (sender). One of the most common, yet under acknowledged changes brought about by newly deployed information systems is an enlarged set of recipients. In the case of the E-ZPass road-toll system, for example, recipients of information may now include system management companies and state departments of motor vehicles.

Ascertain what attributes are affected. Ascertain whether the changes affect the types of information transmitted from senders to recipients. Swipe cards, for example, not only control entry to and egress from many university buildings and residence halls, but also transmit and log the times of entry and egress.

Establish changes in principles of transmission. New practices may entail a revision in the principles governing the transmission of information from one party to another. Currently, in the northeastern United States, drivers are offered a choice between cash and E-ZPass, and thus may choose whether toll passage information is shared with officials. Were cash lanes phased out entirely, the principle would shift to one in which drivers are mandated to transmit information.

Red flag. If the new practice generates changes in actors, attributes, or transmission principles, the practice is flagged as violating entrenched informational norms and constitutes a prima facie violation of contextual integrity.

Descriptive Validity of Contextual Integrity

I have offered the framework of contextual integrity as a model for understanding and predicting reactions to alterations in information practices, particularly those caused by the deployment of information technology. Contextual integrity is offered as a benchmark for privacy, yielding assessments that reflect common sentiment and map well onto judgments that privacy has been violated. Here, and in the two chapters following, I build a case for this claim, arguing not only that contextual integrity is a sound metric for describing and predicting common reactions but that the framework, expanded to include a normative component, serves well as a prescriptive guide. The normative component is developed and discussed in Chapter 8. In the rest of this chapter I offer what I am able to in the form of empirical support—serendipitous controlled studies and surveys. For the most part, however, the clearest support for the framework of contextual integrity, discussed here, in Chapter 8, and mainly in Chapter 9, is its effective analysis of the puzzles and problems discussed in Chapter 6, of the divisive socio-technical systems and practices discussed in Part I, and its general compatibility with a wide range of cases, findings, and progressive privacy regulation.

Empirical Findings: A Study of Privacy Preferences

Most existing privacy surveys and polls are of limited relevance because the way they frame their questions does not allow for a correspondence to be drawn between answers and the key parameters of informational norms. In my view, this is one reason for the discontinuity between people's actions and survey results, not because people do not care about privacy, as privacy skeptics have charged, but because our actions are finely modulated to the variables. Questions in surveys that do not fix these variables explicitly are, thus, highly ambiguous. Although there have, to date, been no empirical studies explicitly guided by the framework of contextual integrity, ideas emerging in the field of human-computer interaction (known also as computer-human interaction) are strongly compatible with it. Dourish and Anderson, for example, conceptualize privacy in terms of what they call "collective information practice ... ways in which social action is sustained and reproduced through the formulation and flow of information," (2006, 323) and assert that "flows of information ... serve as markers of social boundaries, providing a means to negotiate, demonstrate, and sustain patterns of identity, membership, and affiliation in social groups" (p. 322).

There is one controlled study that affirms the complex and sometimes subtle dependencies between privacy judgments and a variety of factors partly corresponding to the variables in informational norms (Olson, Grudin, and Horvitz 2005). The investigators sought to show that people's privacy preferences do not reflect a simple desire to control and withhold information, but rather exhibit shifting and finely tuned tendencies to share and withhold. Conducted in two phases, the study began with a pilot survey of eighty-three subjects who were asked to describe situations in which they had been reluctant to share information and reasons for their reluctance. In the second phase, a different set of subjects were asked to complete a large grid, indicating on a five-point scale how comfortable they were sharing information of a particular type, drawing on findings from the pilot. The matrix did not simply ask how comfortable, but how comfortable to share with specific others, acting in certain roles. This study, therefore, avoided much of the ambiguity rife in privacy surveys.

Respondents were highly discriminating in their reports, and similar to one another in how their judgments were affected by circumstances, types of information, and recipients, affirming that the degree of comfort people experience when sharing information is a function of several factors and not simply one, such as control or sensitivity of information. Information types or attributes included age, marital status, health status, opinions, salary, Social Security numbers, religious affiliations, and phone number; and recipients included family members, telemarketers, and coworkers. Individual variability was overshadowed by striking similarities in the degree to which information types and recipient roles were predictive of the respondents' level of comfort in sharing information. This should put to rest the frequent insinuation that privacy preferences are personal and idiosyncratic. Although explicit mention was not made of contexts and transmission principles, they were implicit in the questionnaires through the presentation of highly scripted recipient types, such as spouse, manager, and corporate lawyer. Differences in reported comfort levels between the case when a manager gains access to information "ex officio" and when the manager receives the same information but this time in trust, suggests that context—workplace versus friendship— also affects judgments (Olson, Grudin, and Horvitz 2004, 2005).

Although most polls do not contextualize their questions, those that implicitly invoke context do reveal sensitivity to it in people's responses. For example, most people consider it legitimate for lending institutions and credit card companies to gain access to applicants' credit histories; for automobile insurance companies to gain access to driving records; and for prospective employers to gain access to an applicant's criminal history (though only in cases where an applicant initiates the transaction) (see Louis Harris & Associates and Westin 1990, 1992).

In the following brief accounts of three well-known events, I demonstrate how the framework of contextual integrity, by enabling structured analysis of information flows, helps to clarify and guide normative evaluations.

Case One: The Clinton-Lewinsky Scandal

During the period from January 1998 through February 1999, lurid details of the Clinton-Lewinsky affair preoccupied the population and the popular media in the United States and beyond. As part of a broader investigation, which need not concern us here, President Clinton came under fire for lying about a sexual liaison with Monica Lewinsky, who had served as a White House intern in 1995. The case stimulated public discussion about what rights to secrecy public figures have in the details of personal intimacies. Neither this, however, nor the primary narrative of the Clinton-Lewinsky affair is our central concern. Instead, we focus attention on the peripheral drama featuring Lewinsky and Linda Tripp. Tripp was a former White House employee who befriended Lewinsky in 1996 while both worked at the Pentagon. Lewinsky confided details of her relationship with President Clinton to Tripp, as well as her feelings for him. For almost three months (October 2 to December 22), Tripp secretly recorded phone conversations with Lewinsky, turning the tapes over both to Kenneth Starr, the independent counsel leading an investigation into Clinton's role in a real estate venture in Arkansas, and to lawyers for Paula Jones, who had accused Clinton of violating her federal civil rights by making crude sexual advances while she was a state employee and he the governor of Arkansas.

The Clinton-Lewinsky case evoked wide-ranging reactions for and against, but the reaction to Linda Tripp was virtually uniform in its distaste. Months after the dust had settled, Tripp made several attempts to restore her reputation, explaining that she had acted in the name of truth, that she had sought to protect her children, and even that she had acted in Lewinsky's best interests. Whether there is truth in these explanations and whether they excuse her behavior are questions open to debate. That she betrayed a friendship seems to be an irrevocable judgment readily modeled in the framework of contextual integrity. Considering the interactions of Tripp with Lewinsky in the context of friendship, Tripp's actions violate at least two informational norms: first, recording intimate phone conversations without asking or even informing Lewinsky and, second, transmitting these recordings to others. Even if, on balance, more good than harm came of Tripp's actions, they violated informational norms of friendship by transgressing transmission principles of knowledge, consent, and confidentiality, and mark her as traitorous to the friendship.[11]

Case Two: The Gramm-Leach-Bliley Act

In 2001 the Individual Reference Services Group, Inc. (IRSG), a nonprofit trade association representing information industry companies, and Trans Union LLC, one of the largest credit reporting agencies, sued the Federal Trade Commission (FTC). IRSG and Trans Union contended that FTC-formulated rules were both unlawful and unconstitutional. Specifically, these rules regulated the status and use of credit headers. The dispute originated with the Gramm-Leach-Bliley Act of 1999 (GLBA), which created a new framework for the financial sector allowing financial service providers (e.g., banks, insurance companies, and securities firms) greater flexibility than existed before in pursuing mergers, affiliations, and competitive offerings. But because such mergers, abetted by powerful computerization and communications technologies, could result in the pooling of vast repositories of customer and consumer information, the GLBA included a proviso to protect the security and confidentiality of what it called "nonpublic personal information." With the stated purpose of guaranteeing more comprehensive financial privacy than had ever before been enacted by Congress, the FTC was charged with implementing this requirement in a set of rules (hereafter Rules), which it did in Spring 2000 (FTC 2000; also see IRSG v. FTC 2001, 11).

The framework of contextual integrity reveals considerable wisdom in several aspects of the court's decision, and by implication, in the relevant FTC

Rules. Here I discuss a few illustrative points, referring interested readers to the full cases (FTC 2000; Trans Union v. FTC 2001; IRSG v. FTC 2001). One major source of contention was how the category of "nonpublic personal information" (NPI), which falls under the purview of the Rules, was to be defined. The FTC determined that this category included any information that a consumer provides to a financial institution to obtain a financial service or product, any information about a consumer that results from a transaction involving a financial product or service, or information the institution obtains about a consumer in connection with providing a financial product or service to that consumer (FTC 2000, 17).

The IRSG and Trans Union faulted the FTC for an overbroad definition, extending well beyond the class of "personally identifiable *financial* information" originally covered by the Fair Credit Reporting Act (FCRA 1992), considered the predecessor of GLBA. They contended that the FTC's definition of information within the scope of the GLBA included not only strictly financial information, but identifying information, such as name, address, Social Security number, and telephone number, which are the items included in credit headers (named so because they are typically printed at the top of a credit report). GLBA rules required financial institutions to provide notice to consumers prior to transmitting covered information to others, and to permit them to opt out (subject to certain exceptions). This meant that credit header information, which previously had been freely sold (for such purposes as target marketing), was now subject to GLBA requirements. Trans Union and the IRSG argued, among other things, that financial privacy rules should govern only *intrinsically financial* information, which, according to standard usage, is information pertaining to matters of money, credit, and monetary receipts and expenditures (IRSG v. FTC 2001, 26). They also argued that the FTC Rules amounted to a violation of their First Amendment rights to free speech.

The court decided in favor of the FTC that its Rules neither contravened the meaning of the GLBA nor abridged First Amendment rights of free speech. For our purposes, however, the punch line is in the court's reasoning. By refusing to base the way information is treated on its being *intrinsically* anything—financial versus merely identifying—the court was not swayed by arguments on the other side that sought to measure the potential harms of freely transmitting NPI. It focused, rather, on the FTC's rationale that "any information should be considered financial information if it is requested by a financial institution for the purpose of providing a financial service or product"

(FTC 2000). The court ruled that even when the information in question is "otherwise publicly available," restriction should apply because,

> in drafting the GLB Act, Congress recognized that the status of particular types of information may vary according to the context in which it is used. Information used in or derived from a financial context is nonpublic personal information under (number) 6809(4)(C)(i); the same information in another context, however, may not be NPI. Thus, it is the context in which information is disclosed—rather than the intrinsic nature of the information itself—that determines whether information falls within the GLB Act. (IRSG v. FTC 2001, 27)

A ringing endorsement of contextual integrity, although the court was not to know.

Without striving, the court followed some of the steps of the decision heuristic for contextual integrity, stressing that the self-same information warrants divergent treatment, depending on context and the roles of subjects transmitting and receiving this information. Expressing this in the language of contextual integrity, the court effectively decided that in a financial context all information about clients (subjects) emerging from a financial transaction (information type), transmitted to agents of the relevant financial firm (recipients and senders) or to third parties (recipients), is subject to the transmission principles prescribed in the GLBA (confidentiality, notice, consent, etc.) as interpreted by the FTC in its Rules (informational norms). I would quibble only with a small detail of the court's analysis. For the court to arrive at its decision—in my view, the correct one—it needed to focus on the type of information in question. In the framework of contextual integrity, the result falls out more easily because the framework includes the additional dimension of transmission principle. Name and address are still name and address. The difference is that in a financial context, the transmission of name and address from financial firms to others is governed by FTC Rules.

The worldview of contextual integrity is also strongly compatible with a particular fragment of the court's reasoning dealing with free speech. The court's first step was to relegate credit headers to the category of commercial speech, warranting weaker First Amendment protection. Second, it determined, contrary to the plaintiffs' challenge, that the FTC Rules do serve a public interest in preventing harm. The twist here is what the court regards as *harm*: interestingly, a harm does not require evidence of familiar consequences of use and disclosure such as identity theft, but "use and disclosure of that information without the consent of the consumer" (IRSG v. FTC 2001, 55). In the language of contextual integrity, the court has recognized that information subjects in financial contexts have a right emanating from informational norms embodied in valid FTC Rules. In particular, these Rules prescribe an obligation on financial institutions to obtain express consent from subjects, in order for them to disclose NPI to third parties. Accordingly, if a financial institution transmits information in violation of this norm, no matter what other consequences may flow, the court recognizes the harm to subjects of having had this right violated (IRSG v. FTC 2001).

Case Three: PIPEDA and Privacy of Medical Prescriptions
Whereas the court's defense of FTC Rules demonstrated an impressive sensitivity to the effects of contexts on the meaning and significance of information, the Privacy Commissioner of Canada seemed stifled by a rigid dichotomy in his reasoning about physicians' privacy in relation to prescriptions. In June 2001, physicians in Canada filed a complaint with the Privacy Commissioner, George Radwanski, against IMS Health Canada charging that it violated section 12 of the Personal Information Protection and Electronic Documents Act (PIPEDA) by selling information about their prescribing habits and disclosing information across borders without their consent.[12] IMS gathers detailed information about individual prescriptions from pharmacies, matching it with the prescribing physicians' names, although gathering only basic demographics about patients. IMS transmits this information to its data processing center in Philadelphia where it produces various customized information products for pharmaceutical companies, including ProMap, which tracks monthly prescribing activities of physicians who have attended events sponsored by participating pharmaceutical companies.

Radwanski did not support the physicians' complaint. Reasoning that because prescription-writing habits do not constitute information *about* a physician but merely information *associated* with the physician, they do not constitute personal information and are not, therefore, covered by PIPEDA. Radwanski concludes, "Accordingly, I find that prescription information— whether in the form of an individual prescription or in the form of patterns discerned from a number of prescriptions—is not personal information about the physician" (Radwanski 2003). If not question-begging, this reasoning is quite bizarre, asking readers to go along with the notion that "it (prescription writing habits) discloses little or nothing about the physician as an individual" but something "once removed." Because I know too little about the details of PIPEDA and of this case, my comments about Radwanski's analysis and conclusion do not question his competence. It is quite possible Radwanski's argument was forced by highly specific definitions of "personal information."

The problem I see stems from a framework of reasoning that builds a complex set of rules atop the highly dubious distinction between personal information and information "once removed" when there is so much more we can draw from in this case, for example, what we know about the role and responsibility of physicians in society; the system of prescriptions for certain families of drugs; and the intricate interdependencies that exist among physicians, patients, pharmacies, and pharmaceutical companies. The framework of contextual integrity invites this type of analysis. It is quite possible that the conclusion reached would be the same as Radwanski's, but it would be grounded in a solid grasp of what is at stake in this case, not on an artificial distinction between information *about* a person and information *associated with* a person.

In the next two chapters I will elaborate on the rich dependencies that exist between expectations about the flow of information and details of social systems in which these flows occur.

8   Breaking Rules for Good

CONTEXTUAL INTEGRITY HAS BEEN PROPOSED AS A JUSTIFICATORY framework for evaluating in moral and political terms the myriad new technology-based systems and practices radically affecting the flow of personal information. Despite the proliferation and virtual ubiquity of these technologies, systems, and practices and the institutions that have grown around them, the preeminent legal and moral conceptions of privacy seem out of step with the contours of public reaction, either by underplaying certain anxieties or exaggerating them. One important approach, discussed in Chapter 5, which has sought to delineate a coherent but more limited conception of privacy by planting theoretical and normative roots of privacy in the conceptual apparatus of the public/private dichotomy, dismisses many of the complaints as irrelevant to privacy. Another, also discussed in Chapter 5, although revealing deep and subtle connections between privacy and other important moral and political values, rarely gives enough direction on how to respond to challenges posed by countervailing values and interests that have motivated the new information practices in the first place.

Addressing some of these limitations and plumbing the layers of social structure more deeply, the framework of contextual integrity introduced in Chapter 7 holds that context matters to the demands of privacy, as well as a number of critical parameters defining the flow of information. According to the framework, these factors affect our experience of a practice and, consequently, our judgment of whether or not it is morally acceptable. The framework of contextual integrity requires that practices be evaluated in relation to entrenched context-relative informational norms, which in turn requires characterizing them in terms of actors (subjects, senders, receivers), types of information, and principles of transmission. If a novel practice results in a departure from the patterns of flow prescribed by entrenched norms, the novel practice is flagged as a breach and we have prima facie evidence that contextual integrity has been violated. Because it invokes several parameters simultaneously and incorporates conceptual resources for resolving conflicts not found in many other theories, contextual integrity is a more sensitive instrument for identifying privacy breaches. In particular, it avoids the impossible mire into which the overworked public/private dichotomy frequently leads when applied to the messy and contingent realms of privacy. Yet, while it overcomes the shortcomings of predominant approaches, the framework of contextual integrity as described thus far introduces a few problems of its own.

Is Contextual Integrity Conservative?

Opportunity Costs

If conformity with pre-existing informational norms is a measure of contextual integrity, then any new practice that contravenes entrenched norms is flagged as problematic. Because many of the new technologies discussed in Part I fit this pattern, they would be judged problematic (discussed in detail in Chapter 9). This judgment, although apt for some cases, seems to fly in the face of intuition for others, particularly where a technology and associated practices have been introduced precisely with the intention of altering and disrupting entrenched flows of personal information in order to achieve greater good. As many new practices have troubled us because of their threats to privacy, so do many others exist that have offered the promise of public benefit. Examples already mentioned include new, high-quality devices that assist in monitoring patients' vital signs in hospitals and nursing homes and alerting staff to deterioration in their condition. Also in the healthcare context, information service providers offer to supply aggregated information about physicians, usually for a small fee. In the past, people requiring heart surgery may have had to ascertain a surgeon's competence by consulting friends and acquaintances, hearsay, and checking with a family physician.

Not only is such inquiry unsystematic, it places people whose social circles do not include medical professionals at a significant disadvantage. Online public and private databases now enable access to the general public to basic information about degrees earned, malpractice suits, publications, and past employment with far greater ease. Refusing people effective access to information such as this, in the name of privacy, would be depriving them of an important opportunity.

As we have seen, the framework of contextual integrity enables one to register as well as to characterize changes in the flow of information from past to present; in many instances competing approaches see no change at all. This is a good start. At the same time, if the framework implied that flagging a practice because it breaches entrenched informational norms was sufficient grounds for prohibiting it, this would seem to imply enormous opportunity costs.

Tyranny of the Normal

A second challenge is the flip side of the same coin. As it stands, the framework of contextual integrity appears to provide no buffer against insidious shifts in practice that ultimately gain acceptance as "normal." This is illustrated in the case of Florida v. Riley (1989), discussed in Chapter 6, in which the Supreme Court determined that the Fourth Amendment had not been breached by police sightings from a surveillance plane of marijuana plants growing in the suspect's courtyard. The Court reasoned that people have no reasonable expectation of privacy from overhead surveillance because airplane flight is sufficiently commonplace. In Kyllo v. United States (2001), however, the Court reached the opposite conclusion in a case involving technology-enhanced surveillance. In this case, it concluded that the Fourth Amendment had been breached by law enforcement officers when they trained a thermal imaging device on Kyllo's private residence in order to ascertain, from heat patterns, whether Kyllo was cultivating marijuana plants. A major element in the Court's reasoning was that, in contrast with plane flight, thermal imaging was not yet commonly practiced. As a result, it violated a reasonable expectation of privacy, amounting to an unwarranted search. In both of these cases, Justice John Harlan's notion of a "reasonable expectation of privacy" (Katz v. United States 1967) was taken to mean that prescription follows practice, and not vice versa.

The rapid transformations we have witnessed in socio-technical systems brought about by computing and information technologies has often thrust change upon people and societies without a careful evaluation of harms and benefits, perturbations in social and cultural values, and whether and by whom these changes are needed or wanted. Like the movement of the hands of a clock, such changes may be imperceptible moment to moment in real time, yet, as we know, over an extended period, imperceptible change may lead to inexorable ruptures. By the time these ruptures surface in public deliberation, protest, or court cases, the new normal may be comfortably entrenched, but far from comfortably accepted. The case of video surveillance may be one such lost cause, so commonplace now that objections are increasingly difficult to carry against the force of the reasonable expectation, against what I regard as the "tyranny of the normal." As long as contextual integrity is tied solely to actual practice, as long as it merely defines a heuristic for detecting effectively when novel practices deviate from entrenched norms, it can be judged an instrument of this tyranny.

Dilemma

Cognizant of a wider range of pertinent variables, contextual integrity serves as a keener measure of morally relevant change than other predominant approaches to privacy and, for this reason, offers greater descriptive power than the alternatives. Yet, as a normative approach to privacy, contextual integrity seems to have its own blind spots: the problems of opportunity cost and tyranny of the normal. In fact, both these problems are rooted in a single source: conservatism. Contextual integrity, as it has been described thus far, is inherently conservative, flagging as problematic any departure from entrenched practice. This confronts us with a two-part dilemma. One path forgoes any significant role for contextual integrity in the moral evaluation of controversial socio-technical practices. It embraces the framework of contextual integrity for its descriptive accuracy but accepts that it offers only limited help for deciding the moral status of new practices that transgress entrenched norms.[1] A second path leads us to dig in our heels, insisting that contextual integrity carries moral weight, committing us to a justificatory framework with a rigidly conservative bias. Ultimately, a third path which avoids both horns of the dilemma will be hewn that extends the conceptual framework of contextual integrity to incorporate a distinctive moral component. The way through this dilemma for me was to draw guidance from the history of moral and political thought on the virtues and limits of conservatism. This led me to understand conservatism in relation to the privacy threats I have been considering, and to appreciate how to amend the framework of contextual integrity to move beyond it.

The Virtues and Limits of Conservatism

As I have admitted, there is strong kinship between contextual integrity and the concept of a reasonable expectation, which has powerfully served in countless legal disputes about whether a right to privacy has been violated. Both concepts attribute moral authority to entrenched social practice. In deference to greater intellects, consider the reasoning of two historical figures, champions of custom, who have grappled with the virtues and limits of conservatism and have understood why past social practice deserves to be respected.

Conservatism, in the form of one's expectations being fulfilled, contributes to the security of members of a society. This is the simple value to which Jeremy Bentham draws attention when he advises law makers on the importance of custom: "When new laws are made in opposition to a principle established by old ones the stronger that principle is, the more odious will the inconsistency appear. A contradiction of sentiment results from it, and disappointed expectations accuse the legislator of tyranny" (1843, 151). For Bentham, one of the founders of utilitarian moral theory, the fulfillment and disappointment of expectation are forms of pleasure and pain, respectively, unique to human beings and ought to be respected in social policy. Specifically, respect for custom (in this case through law) yields the sense of security that comes from knowing that expectations based on past experience are likely to be met, which in turn links discrete experiences into a continuous sequence. According to Bentham, "This presentiment, which has so marked an influence upon the fate of man, is called expectation. It is hence that we have the power of forming a general plan of conduct; it is hence that the successive instants which compose the duration of life are not like isolated and independent points, but become continuous parts of a whole" (p. 111). In sum, respect for custom leads to greater continuity in life and means that expectations are likely to be met, producing a form of security and pleasure contrasted with the pain of disappointment.[2]

Edmund Burke, a major historical proponent of political conservatism, reasoned further that traditional wisdom is often sounder than contemporary offerings. Writing over 200 years ago, Burke maintained that custom, or "settled principle" (1790, 457) of convention, is the best guide to shaping key institutions of civil society, particularly government, because it constitutes the accumulated wisdom not only of a community but of communities through the ages.

> The science of government being, therefore, so practical in itself, and intended for such practical purposes, a matter which requires experience, and even more experience than any person can gain in his whole life, however sagacious and observing he may be, it is with infinite caution that any man ought to venture upon pulling down an edifice which has answered in any tolerable degree for ages the common purpose of society, or on building it up again without having models and patterns of approved utility before his eyes. (1790, 443)

In his famous repudiation of the French Revolution, Burke wrote, "We are afraid to put men to live and trade each on his own private stock of reason, because we suspect that the stock in each man is small, and that the individuals would do better to avail themselves of the general bank and capital of nations and of ages" (1790, 451).

An implicit conservative bias is also reflected in certain theories of society (discussed in Chapter 7). They are conservative insofar as they claim that the particular arrangement of social systems (fields, institutions, practices) is determined by an internal logic, or settled rationale, in order to achieve a variety of valued social purposes. It is conservative because any initiative to alter the structures would need to reckon with the potential for obstructing the achievement of these purposes.

Even Burke, however, recognized that there are times when traditional wisdom must be challenged. Never a supporter of revolutionary change, Burke accepted that political systems may need reform, albeit measured reform:

> A state without the means of some change is without the means of its conservation. Without such means it might even risk the loss of that part of the Constitution which it wished the most religiously to preserve. The two principles of conservation and correction operated strongly at the two critical periods of the Restoration and Revolution, when England found itself without a king. At both those periods the nation had lost the bond of union in their ancient edifice; they did not, however, dissolve the whole fabric. On the contrary, in both cases they regenerated the deficient part of the old Constitution through the parts which were not impaired. (1790, 424)

Although he reviled the French Revolution, Burke acknowledged that the French nobility missed an opportunity for positive reform when it reserved leadership in the military for men "of family. . . . A permanent Assembly in which the commons had their share of power, would soon abolish whatever was too invidious and insulting in these distinctions; and even the faults in the morals of the nobility would have been probably corrected by the greater varieties of occupation and pursuit to which a constitution by orders would have given rise" (1790, 471). Burke also recognized that received wisdom in one place need not mirror that in another, and that acceptable custom in one place could well be disdained in another. Accordingly, much as he detested the French Revolution, he saw justification in the American bid for independence. Thus, because convention is the bedrock of government, and because different cultures and countries have evolved variously, varieties in mode of governance are to be expected (1791, 485).

Conservatism and Contextual Integrity

What does this all mean for contextual integrity as a moral concept? For reasons of expectation, accumulated wisdom, and settled rationale, a presumption in favor of entrenched, context-relative informational norms makes sense. In recognition of this presumption, if a new practice breaches entrenched informational norms, I will say that there has been a prima facie violation of contextual integrity. At the same time, if a way can be found to demonstrate the moral superiority of new practices, this presumption could be overcome and what was recognized as a prima facie violation may be accepted as morally legitimate. So far, so good, but what might be the proper criteria for comparing entrenched practices with challengers? Burke, for one, provided no general methodology for making the discernment beyond offering this general injunction: "Thus, by preserving the method of Nature in the conduct of the state, in what we improve we are never wholly new, in what we retain we are never wholly obsolete" (1790, 429). In relation to contextual integrity, the equivalent requirement is for systematic criteria to measure the moral standing of established practices against challengers to justify when the latter should be accepted or resisted. Challengers should neither be embraced nor always viewed with suspicion, but evaluated according to these criteria. So doing gives the theory much-needed moral traction.

In sum, contextual integrity explains the complex and subtle variability in people's reactions to the flow of personal information; the indignation roused by certain patterns of flow compared with positive acceptance of other patterns that seem on face to be quite similar. Because it is rooted in convention, habit, and custom, however, more is needed from contextual integrity if it is to serve further as a moral concept. Although contextual integrity refines our ability to identify when custom or expectation has been violated, and to predict potential sources of indignation, more is needed to assess the moral standing of custom in relation to novel practices. If it is to attain moral authority, the framework of contextual integrity should be able to adjudicate the legitimacy of intrusive information gathering, not merely predict that it will be experienced as intrusive. As Barry Bull, a philosopher of education, has elegantly stated, with the framework of contextual integrity we can explain why "not only are many people surprised and irritated by such invasions but [why] they also have a right to object to them" (2006).

Political Morality of Contexts

Let us take stock. In order for contextual integrity to serve usefully not only as an indicator of breaches of entrenched informational norms but as a guide to the moral legitimacy of such breaches, it needs to provide a way to measure that a new practice is not only different from entrenched practice but that it is morally or politically superior (or inferior). The answer to this need is a familiar one, but with a twist. As a first step, we bring to bear general moral and political considerations. In the cases we evaluate, particularly relevant are insights drawn from the works discussed in Chapter 4 that link privacy with critical individual and social values, including security against harms such as identity theft and stalking; protection of individual freedom and autonomy; promotion of fairness, justice, and equality; nourishment of human and social relations; and support of democratic institutions and publics (Reiman 1976; Gavison 1980; Regan 1995; Cohen 1996; van den Hoven 2001). This is the range of criteria one would need to bring to bear in judgments on a case-by-case basis. But if that is the strategy, there seems to be no significant role for contexts and contextual integrity. If one is able to discern moral and political superiority among competing scenarios on the basis of general moral considerations, why do we need the mediation of a context-relative analysis at all in establishing the moral legitimacy of new versus entrenched practices?

The answer to this question is already embedded in contexts themselves. Recall the key elements of social contexts from the previous chapter. Among them is a teleological element that is almost always factored into the theoretical accounts of social structure, identified variously as values, ends, purposes, or goals. This element was included in my account of contexts, along with the thesis proffered by other theories that norms of a context, field, system, or institution are importantly related to values (ends, purposes, etc.). After all, in the absence of purpose and drained of teleology, normative practices are little more than empty rituals; purpose is what the extraterrestrial anthropologists from Mars must grasp in order to make sense of what they have observed on Planet Earth. These purposes are not merely important properties of contexts, they are partly constitutive of them. Informational norms, just like other norms, support or promote the attainment of the background contexts. One makes sense of and evaluates informational norms (i.e., the norms governing the flow of prescribed types of personal information [attributes] from senders to receivers and about subjects [actors] according to prescribed constraints on flows [principles of transmission]) just as one evaluates other norms: according to their function in relation to a context's purposes.

The challenge to contextual integrity, as it is to any conservative theory for which moral legitimacy is important, is how to allow for at least some departures from entrenched normative practice. The approach I recommend here is to compare entrenched normative practices against novel alternatives or competing practices on the basis of how effective each is in supporting, achieving, or promoting relevant contextual values. If the practices prescribed by entrenched informational norms are found to be less effective in this regard than challengers, or, in the cases of particular interest here, less effective than novel practices resulting from newly deployed sociotechnical devices and systems, this constitutes a moral justification for replacing entrenched practices with novel challengers. I will elaborate considerably on this recommendation but before doing so will draw parallels to similar ideas in other works that have influenced my own. These works also contribute to some of the conceptual apparatus that has been useful for this purpose.

Walzer's Spheres of Justice

In political philosopher Michael Walzer's pluralistic account of distributive justice as complex equality, a just society is one in which social life is made up of autonomous spheres defined by their ideologies and social goods (1984).[3] Social goods are distributed not according to a single criterion, or principle, or a single set of criteria across all spheres, but according to different criteria within each of the distinctive spheres. Spheres, ideologies, goods, and criteria of distribution are not independent, objective elements but are mutually constitutive. Accordingly, goods acquire their meaning from the spheres and ideologies of the spheres in which they operate, and the criteria, or principles of distribution according to which goods are distributed, are derived from this meaning of particular goods within respective spheres. Walzer describes the interrelatedness of these elements: "goods with their meanings—because of their meanings—are the crucial medium of social relations; they come into people's minds before they come into their hands; distributions are patterned in accordance with shared conceptions of what the goods are and what they are for" (1984, 7). Walzer offers education, the marketplace, politics, established religion, health care, and the workplace as examples of spheres in which clusters of different social goods operate and are distributed according to different criteria. Money and commodities are key social goods operating in the marketplace, distributed according to principles of the competitive free market (at least in countries with capitalist economies). In the sphere of education, for example, some of the goods are teaching positions, instruction, and scholarships, distributed according to criteria, for example, of qualifications, possibly residency (K–12 in the United States), and talent (merit or performance), respectively.[4] The principles of distribution—marketplace for commodities and money, talent and academic achievement for grades and spots at top universities—are derived from the meaning attributed to these goods in the spheres.

A just society is one in which complex equality prevails. Complex equality requires that the social goods in a particular sphere be distributed in accordance with the principles of distribution that are appropriate to the meaning of those social goods within that sphere. This pluralistic vision of justice holds that "different social goods ought to be distributed for different reasons, in accordance with different procedures, by different agents . . . these differences derive from different understandings of the social goods themselves—the inevitable product of historical and cultural particularism" (Walzer 1984, 6).

Defined this way, justice allows for social goods to be distributed in unequal measure within particular spheres as long as "no citizen's standing in one sphere or with regard to one social good can be undercut by his standing in some other sphere, with regard to some other good" (Walzer 1984, 19). Injustice arises when social goods in one sphere are distributed according to the principles of another sphere as when, for example, political office is bought and sold with money, university professorships are granted on the basis of birthright, and commodities are distributed in accordance with political power. When the possession of a social good within one sphere is allowed to promote interests of its possessors in another, invading "the sphere where another company of men and women properly rules" (p. 19), according to Walzer the result is tyranny. When such tyranny is extensive, when a particular social good becomes currency across many or all spheres, the result is domination: "The critique of dominance and domination points toward an open-ended distributive principle. *No social good x should be distributed to men and women who possess some other good y merely because they posses y and without regard to the meaning of x*" (p. 20).

There are important structural similarities between Walzer's account of complex equality and the augmented account of contextual integrity I am building here. Both conceive of social life as comprised of autonomous social spheres and both assert the existence of a multiplicity of distributive criteria that justice (or in my case, integrity) requires be appropriately matched with goods and spheres. However, the third aspect of Walzer's account, of particular relevance to the present task of augmenting contextual integrity with a normative component, is the question of what principles bind these distributive criteria with particular goods in particular spheres. Walzer's answer, as I noted, is that distributive principles are inferred from the meanings of social goods. Or, more specifically, that justice requires that the principles operating in all spheres be inferred from the meanings of the relevant social goods, and that tyranny and possibly domination result when this is not so, when principles attaching to social goods in one sphere intrude into the distribution of goods in another.

If one asks why we should not distribute grades on the basis of votes, or political office on the basis of lineage, or workplace promotions on the basis of sexual favors, Walzer would answer that this is because of what education, or democratic politics, or the workplace is. To say that spheres, social goods, and their distributive principles are co-constitutive is to agree that goods have meanings in relation to spheres and these meanings dictate, or at least imply, what form the distribution principles ought to take. I do not believe there is a fleshed out general theory on how best to match principles to goods within spheres; instead, each sphere demands focused investigation to draw out the connection. We need only consider a few illustrations to accept, for example, that majority vote, not the highest monetary bid, is the soundest principle for distributing political office in a democratic political sphere; that grades should be assigned on the basis of the quality of work in the educational sphere and not the popular vote of classmates; and so forth.

The Context of Education

Returning to contextual integrity, I am like a traveler returning home from a foreign country with a souvenir—in this case, Walzer's idea of the meaning of a social good—and finding it surprisingly serviceable even in relation to local needs. As an illustration, consider the case of a conscientious high school administrator deciding on features for a new computerized student record system. Mindful both of functional needs and privacy concerns, the administrator must decide what information to store in the system, for how long, to whom access should be granted, and under what terms. The administrator must also decide what analytical tools to integrate into the system; for example, longitudinal compilation of records, aggregation into dossiers for individual students, the capacity to mine the data for attribute clusters and assign students to certain profile groups on the basis of these findings, and so forth. The administrator, well-versed in the descriptive components of the framework of contextual integrity, immediately flags the system as a prima facie threat because it is obvious that in a number of ways it will result in information flows that breach entrenched norms of information flow. A strictly conservative approach would flag such changes as problematic; an augmented approach helps to guide an evaluation of such changes.

For a start, an evaluation would prescribe that the system be judged in terms of what we have called general moral considerations, such as whether any harms might follow the selection of a particular feature (e.g., harm that may follow exposure of information about students to anyone besides their teachers). One may also ask whether there is any unfairness involved in a system that "remembers" so well, and as a consequence requires students to carry the "baggage" of past years' performance and bad behavior, or includes prejudicial information about their troubled households as part of an electronic dossier that all teachers receive. The administrator might consider whether the awareness of stricter surveillance might cause students to behave with greater caution and fear than before; in other words, have a chilling effect on behavior. These and other general considerations may weigh in favor as well as against potential utilities offered by such a system. We have, thus far, invoked liberty, autonomy, fairness, and harm as cautions against lessening constraints on flows. There may also be considerations weighing in the opposite direction; for example, efficiency and cost effectiveness, potential income for schools willing to sell information about students for marketing and employment recruiting purposes, potential to increase security in high-risk neighborhoods by keeping closer track of social and religious groups within schools, past associations, and so on. All these factors may support adopting a system that opens up the flow of information, expands the list of recipients, and is more liberal with the transmission principles it endorses.

So far, so good. But, having decided that all these considerations are worthy, how does the administrator resolve the clear conflicts among them? Does one go for compromise? How effective will redesign be? Or if one pursues trade-offs, what should these be? The values of a context can help steer a course through many conflicts. How much we know about these values is a function of how much we know about the contexts themselves, not about the framework of contextual integrity itself; establishing what these are might be neither easy nor uncontroversial. For an account that goes beyond an academic demonstration, one really needs a well developed background theory; for now, I rely on a robust, relatively uncontroversial subset to demonstrate how to use this component of the framework to address difficult questions about legitimate patterns of information flows. Accordingly, for the case of the high school record-keeping system, I take into consideration the purposes of an educational context. Drawing on Walzer's (1984, chap. 8) and others' discussion of the educational sphere, I take these to include transmission of knowledge, traditions, and rituals from one generation to the next; enhancement of critical faculties of the intellect and understanding; discovery and cultivation of talent (particularly those talents deemed socially, economically, or culturally beneficial); and development of character, social discipline, and citizenship. It is worth noting that the values of educational contexts include those accruing not only to individuals but also to surrounding societies as students are educated in the virtues of democratic citizenship (Gutmann 1987).

In an initial assessment of the proposed information system, aggregation and data-mining features would be flagged because they deviate from entrenched practices by enlarging the set of attributes and, possibly, the recipients of aggregated information. If effective, they could have significant impacts on the attainment of educational values, such as detecting patterns of decline in students' performance and responding with early intervention and remediation. Likewise, configurations of special talents might emerge and be nourished earlier; teachers could become acquainted more quickly with students' needs and enter new classrooms with greater ease. Regarding access criteria, educational goals could be consulted to consider whether, under what conditions, and to what types of information access should be given to teachers, parents, other staff, regional administrators, political representatives, reporters, advertisers, and potential employees. Each disclosure would need to be considered on its own merits, on the basis not only of moral and political principles, but on factual knowledge of systematic mutual effects on students and those seeking access. Both general effects and those pertaining to the goals of an educational context should be considered.

Taking a specific case, consider whether a local company should have access to student records for hiring purposes on the grounds that this benefits the company as well as the students. A critic resisting this move need not dispute the general on balance benefits, but may raise concerns about the effects on internal purposes of education. Intellectual experimentation might be inhibited as the practical orientation of the company punctures the relative safety of a school to try out ideas. Further, there is the potential that the school might adapt its curriculum to pander to the needs of the local business at the expense of other educational goals. To the extent that schools are training grounds for democratic citizenship, scrutiny by external parties might stunt development of critical skills. The balance is obviously a delicate one, between the accountability of educators to specific actors and society at large on the one hand, and professional autonomy on the other. In general, however, the balancing and trading off is not to be performed "at large," but against the backdrop of the specific ends, goals, purposes, and values of an educational context.

The Context of Health Care
What I have termed context-relative purposes played an important rhetorical role in recent rule making on privacy in U.S. health care. When Congress failed to meet its deadline for developing privacy rules in accordance with

conditions laid out by the Health Insurance Portability and Accountability Act, the task was assigned to the Department of Health and Human Services (DHHS). In the intervening years (1996–1999), key stakeholders—including medical professionals, insurance and pharmaceutical companies, healthcare organizations, and patient advocacy groups—argued their cases in all kinds of public forums. Those arguing on behalf of strict privacy constraints high-lighted the great sensitivity of medical information and its potential to cause direct harm to patients, including unfair discrimination. An alternative tack, cogently articulated by health-privacy advocate Janlori Goldman, pointed out that unrestricted information flows could undercut the core mission of health care itself. In self-defense, people might engage in strategies such as "doctor-hopping," withholding crucial but damning information, or simply not seek-ing help at all. These strategies, when used by people with stigmatized and easily transmitted diseases, could jeopardize the health of the individuals in question, others with whom they have contact, and even the general public. Lax privacy rules, in other words, place in jeopardy the very purposes of health care.

Within the healthcare setting, consider two situations: one, a company's claims to access employee medical records; another, a person's claim to access their lovers' medical records. In the first case, even if a general cost-benefit analysis or a comparison and trade-off of interests indicates in favor of employers, the analysis via contextual integrity would most likely prohibit release of medical information to employers under the assumption that ben-efits accrued by employers are irrelevant to the attainment of healthcare goals. In the case of lovers, however, what is known of sexually transmitted diseases suggests there might be conditions under which sexual partners may have a right to limited access to each other's medical records even without permis-sion from the subject.

Many experts attribute this wave of attention to health-related personal information to important social and technological developments, including the reconfiguration of healthcare delivery and institutional support struc-tures hand-in-hand with development and deployment of computerized, net-worked systems for patient health records (Committee on Maintaining 1997; Waldo, Lin, and Millett 2007). These shifts, in one way or another, have threatened the norms of strict confidentiality that have been entrenched in the medical profession since at least the fourth century BCE, and make up the eighth principle of the Hippocratic Oath: "And about whatever I may see or hear in treatment, or even without treatment, in the life of human beings—things that should not ever be blurted out outside—I will remain silent, holding such things to be unutterable [sacred not to be divulged]" (von Staden 1996, 407). This commitment has held throughout the ages and across geographic regions. In the tenth century, the Holy Abbas Ahwazi (n.d.) advised physicians: "A physician should respect confidence and protect the patient's secrets. In protecting a patient's secrets, he must be more insistent than the patient himself." Similar commitments are reflected in contemporary professional codes that have been adopted by physicians across the globe. Although many considered it a breakthrough to finally have federal rules protecting patient privacy, when compared to confidentiality requirements that have evolved through the ages, the DHHS rules might be seen in several ways as reducing patient privacy by explicitly sanctioning the flow of information to public health agencies, insurance companies, accounting firms, and law enforcement.

Under the decision heuristic of contextual integrity, DHHS rules reveal many significant departures when compared with, say, rules deriving from the eighth Hippocratic principle. Thus, they would be flagged as prima facie breaches of contextual integrity. While a thorough evaluation of DHHS rules could, itself, fill a book, I can afford only a few sentences here to highlight how the augmented conception of contextual integrity would guide it. The requirement that physicians inform public health officials in cases of specific diseases is flagged as an instance of a departure from absolute patient confidentiality. Upon further evaluation this departure seems acceptable not because of a general trade-off of patients' interests against those of others, but because it supports values of the healthcare context. From what contemporary science and medicine has revealed about how infection is spread and the impact of health threats in the environment and toxic contaminants in food and water, the understanding and treatment of an individual's medical conditions can no longer be pursued in isolation from those nearby, or the public at large. Knowing that an individual's health condition might seriously affect and be affected by the health of others, or could signal a larger threat to the health of a community (as in the case of an environmental hazard), requires a deliberate expansion of information sharing in order to promote important values of the healthcare context. New norms are required not because physicians today care less about confidentiality than they did in the times of Hippocrates, but because of the changing landscape in knowledge and population contingencies linking information flow and healthcare values.[5]

A final remark about the flow of individual health information concerns transmission principles. This analysis suggests to me that adjustments to healthcare context informational norms include not only an expansion of the legitimate recipients of medical information, but of attributes (i.e., a list of specific diseases) and transmission principles governing the flow from party to party. Instead of confidentiality as the principle governing the flow from patient to physician, I propose that the most apt principle is fiduciary because, ideally, we would want and expect physicians to act in the best interests of their patients even if this involves sharing information with others, such as public health officials or fellow physicians. In general, the fiduciary principle is one that bears far more extensive study both in the healthcare context and others.

The Context of Psychoanalysis
The impacts of transgressive practices on purposes or values can vary in their degree of acuteness. In the context of psychoanalysis, which could be considered a subcontext of health care, patient (or client) confidentiality is not only important, it is, some would argue, critical. Whatever interests might be served by sharing information about patients, such as in a court of law or in a case study presented at a research conference, might cause harm or severe embarrassment to patients themselves. At some level, this can be framed as a typical conflict of interests. But in this case, confidentiality is of greater significance because within the context itself it is considered "an essential prerequisite of psychoanalytic psychotherapy" (Levin and Ury 2003, 62). Expert practitioners agree that the process "can only develop in private" (Mauger 2003, 54). Because progress is achieved in talk-based psychotherapies by drawing out deeply held beliefs and memories, the possibility of a breach in confidentiality undermines the possibility of progress. The psychoanalyst asks a patient

> to suspend their rational, moral, or social inhibitions so as to say whatever comes to mind, be it true or false, silly or serious, lurid or laudable. Within the limits of the therapeutic hour, we promote irresponsibility in speech, the very opposite of what is exhorted on the witness stand. Patients are encouraged to engage in experimental thought and to postpone critical

judgment. By this stratagem, the murky and poorly understood parts of our inner life eventually find expression in words allowing them to be contended with. . . .

The object is not just to permit the patient to unburden him- or herself of socially unacceptable thoughts, whether it be, for example, that of a man's wish to violently possess a woman, or a woman's wish to be violently possessed. The object is also to permit for the first time a space and a time for thinking these thoughts out loud and exploring their significance and signification for self-concept and self-esteem. (Furlong 2003 13, 18)

As before, the framework of contextual integrity guides a comparison between competing practices by requiring that one study and demonstrate what contextual values are at stake in a move from entrenched to novel information flows, rather than stopping at the point of observing and weighing conflicting interests and values. In the healthcare context, generally, the upshot is sometimes to favor novel practices and flows over those guided by entrenched informational norms. These can cover certain types of information about patients, recipients, and transmission principles, but may also extend to changes in the flow of information about physicians where greater access to credentials and past records caused breaches in entrenched flows, all in the name of improved healthcare delivery and medical outcomes. Yet the case of psychoanalysis raises another layer of concerns. Even if the revocation of confidentiality is shown to serve certain general interests and values, its destructive potential for the very enterprise of psychoanalysis is so great—existential, in fact—that little besides the direst need seems able to justify it.

The directness of the relationship between particular informational norms and particular contextual values can be quite varied. In some instances particular informational norms might demonstrably support particular values, while in others—in practice, probably most—norms acquire moral standing as components in systems of norms. An instance of this noted in the previous chapter are traffic rules such as "go on green; stop on red" which do not have inherent moral import individually but acquire it as components of a system of rules designed to promote road safety and physical well-being (Raz 1975). This complicates the task of evaluating entrenched normative practice in light of novel challenges because it requires a more global understanding of the purposes achieved by the entrenched practices. One needs to understand first how a particular information norm functions in relation to the system of norms; second, how the system as a whole is affected by the challenge; and, finally, how a perturbation of the system affects the attainment of values. The effects of norms on the attainment of values, ends, and purposes are often mediated by systems. This explains why contexts might use distinctive systems of norms to achieve their respective ends equally effectively, even across historical periods, cultures, and societies. This applies even to contexts with similar sets of values, ends, and purposes. The directives "drive on left" in the United Kingdom and "drive on right" in the United States may achieve traffic safety goals equally effectively as long as the rest of the respective normative systems are adjusted accordingly.

Voting

The context of democratic politics is rife with informational norms and systems of norms, including, as a case in point, the highly regulated setting of a polling station during popular elections. Specifically, the drama of enforced privacy—the curtained voting booth—signals to voters that they are alone and free to make their selections. Interestingly, these elaborate rituals not only deny a voter from accessing another's help on the ballots voters are casting, but deny to voters themselves control over verifiable information about their ballots. Although control over information has been traditionally proffered as the basic requirement of autonomy, in this instance the intricate system of norms regulating popular elections paradoxically denies control to individuals, with the express purpose of protecting them from having to kowtow to external pressure. In an interesting way, this constraint on control indirectly protects autonomy in voting.[6]

The controversies surrounding electronic voting reveal how intricately interwoven normative practices and values are, as new voting technologies are found to excel in supporting one value, such as convenience and efficiency, but found wanting with respect to others, such as accountability, anonymity, verifiability, or security (Rubin 2006). Attempts to interject such technologies, to *improve* the process, have shown how past practices, now entrenched, have achieved a delicate balance. Albeit imperfectly, these practices have more or less succeeded in maintaining utmost confidentiality for individual voters while maintaining reliability and accountability, and achieving an accurate count while protecting voters against coercion and (the harm of) retaliation. (There is much here to recommend the Burkean faith in wisdom of the ages!) Consider the scenario in which a voting technology is proposed that achieves efficiency, accuracy, and verifiability but is a risk to this enforced confidentiality; how might we reason about it? I am not sure any exponent of democracy would accept the trade-off of voter autonomy for these other values and that is because of the meaning— appealing to Walzer's notion—of voter autonomy in the context of popular elections. The premise of democracy is that the ideal of popular election is achieved when each citizen of the state votes in accordance with his or her autonomous preference. Although the autonomy of citizens, in general, is a factor worthy of consideration in a given trade-off, in the context of popular democratic elections it assumes a particular significance in relation to the contextual values at stake. Accordingly, any move to alter information flows— technological, or any other kind—needs to reckon not only with possible injustices or harms to individuals but with the threat to this fundamental commitment of the context.

To underscore that the issue at stake is not individual autonomy, generally, but the meaning of autonomy for particular actors in a given context, in relation to specific attributes, notice that the demands of secrecy do not extend to all voters in the context of democratic politics. In the assemblies in which elected officials cast votes, such as Congress or Parliament, citizens expect these votes to be open; we expect officials to be accountable for these votes even if this means that their choices are constrained and influenced by the attention of others (media, voters, watchdog groups). Citizens are not held to answer in this way; elected officials are. If this impinges on the autonomy of officials, this is an acceptable consequence in light of the role elected officials play as representatives of a constituency in a democracy and the way settled informational norms in parliament serve the values of democratic politics.[7]

Employment

In the context of employment, the hiring juncture involves a particularly rich information exchange that is not always harmonious. For the typical scenario in which applicants submit resumes (or curriculum vitas) and are called in for job interviews, there may be numerous conflicting claims supporting various values and rights. For purposes of illustration, I focus on one in particular companies' freedom to pursue information about applicants and applicants' capacity to control access to this information. In the language of contextual integrity, at issue is not only the conditions under which information about applicants flows to companies (what transmission principles govern flow), but also the types of information appropriate for this interaction. Investing applicants with control (some would call it respecting applicants' privacy) supports their autonomy, in particular, the aspect of autonomy identified in Chapter 4 as "self-presentation." It is clear why presentation of self would be important for applicants, but just as clear why companies might resist applicants' claims trumping their own.

The practice with which many readers of this volume are likely to be familiar is a telling compromise between these incompatible inclinations. To the extent that it does work, it is not because it represents the results of direct balancing and trading off of these inclinations, but a balancing and trading off in light of the ends, purposes, and values of a labor and employment context. The practice itself generally allows applicants to present themselves through such means as resumes and portfolios while it allows companies to go some distance outside these bounds by requiring references, transcripts, and test scores. The interview is an interesting, if sometimes fraught, site of contestation, allowing both actors a degree of leeway. And all of this takes place within a framework of laws and regulations that set in place certain boundary constraints. Entrenched informational norms prescribing full control by subjects over the flow of information might give rise to suboptimal hiring, bad not only for companies but for productivity and labor generally. By contrast, norms that impose no restrictions on companies might drive away competent but timid applicants, or competent and willful applicants, generally resulting in a suboptimal match between competencies and workplace needs. Although a lot more could be said about this context, the main point I wish to convey is that while self-presentation is an important reason for supporting subjects' control over personal information, there are important contexts in which, because it may hinder the attainment of goals, purposes, and values, it must give way to alternative principles of information transmission.

Legal Integrity

With the brief references to Bentham and Burke in the opening sections of this chapter, I wanted to show the structural similarities between the rationale I had offered for according special moral standing to entrenched informational norms and how, in general, political theorists have addressed the age-old issue recognizing the moral suasion of entrenched systems of rules in the face of novel, transgressive practices. In *Law's Empire* (1986), the contemporary legal and political philosopher Ronald Dworkin addresses a similar question about the moral legitimacy of a society's legal system: What underwrites the moral authority of a community's rules such that its members are obligated and may even be coerced to obey even those rules with which they personally may disagree? Dworkin resists the answers of both legal conventionalists, who consider the conventional standing of existing rules as carrying sufficient weight to support legitimacy, and legal pragmatists, who consider existing rules as merely a transitory "compromise between antagonistic interests" (1986, 210), which may be readily dispensed in light of conflicting cost-benefit calculations. Instead, he posits legal integrity as the source of moral legitimacy. A system of law has legal integrity if its rules flow or are derived from a coherent scheme of principles that have been adopted by a properly constituted political community (elaborated in the next section).[8] From those empowered with rule making and rule changing, such as judges and legislators, legal integrity demands not that they slavishly and literally follow existing rules and past rulings, or ignore them and issue rulings on instrumental grounds alone, but that they seek consistency with what they adduce to be the moral and political principles animating existing rules and rulings (pp. 94–96).

The analogy with contextual integrity is this:[9] to establish whether a practice that results in novel information flows is problematic, the decision heuristic outlined in Chapter 7 directs one to assess whether the novel flows comply with or violate entrenched context-relative informational norms. If they violate any norms, the counterpart of a strict conventionalist endorses entrenched norms and rules against the practice. The counterpart to the pragmatist does not set much store by what happens to be entrenched, but recommends judging each new practice on its individual merits; in comparing it with entrenched practice it merely requires better performance on a cost-benefit analysis. The aspiration of contextual integrity is similar to that of legal integrity: there is a presumption in favor of entrenched rules rather than strict adherence to the letter that can be overridden if new practices are demonstrably more effective at achieving contextual values, ends, and purposes or the equivalent; in the case of legal integrity, more effectively satisfying or promoting a duly constituted political community's scheme of principles.

Contextual Values Versus the Value of Contexts

This is as far as I take the account of contextual integrity in this book, recognizing that there are numerous unexplored avenues and unanswered questions that are not unimportant but open up vistas that extend beyond those I am able to assimilate here. One, in particular, bears mention. As we have seen, the augmented account of contextual integrity given in this chapter requires that practices affecting information flows be assessed in terms of their compliance with context-relative informational norms. Context-relative norms themselves may be evaluated in terms of values, purposes, and goals, and overridden, at times, when novel practices are shown to be comparatively more effective at achieving these values, ends, and purposes. There the analysis has stopped. However, as we only briefly hinted above, Dworkin does more than this, providing an approach to evaluating principles themselves within his theory, requiring that they emanate from what he deems a truly or genuinely associative community. It does not matter for our purposes what the criteria are for such a community, only that Dworkin does not believe that any principles whatsoever may serve as the foundation for moral legitimacy.

Likewise, we may question the conditions under which contextual values, ends, and purposes are themselves sound or might turn out to be legitimately challenged by transgressive practices that run afoul not only of norms but of these values. Right now, the theory takes the respective arrays of contextual values as a given: for example, it may simply accept that physical well-being is a goal of healthcare contexts; material well-being is a constitutive value of economic contexts; efficient trading is a value in commercial contexts; personal fulfillment, procreation, and the care of children are values in marriage; intellectual development, training, and sorting are for a purpose in education; and so on (see Miller 2001). Even if we assume that a society's commitment to a particular configuration of contexts and values is relatively stable, a theoretical account of social contexts ought to leave room for the possibility that a society may, on occasion, revisit and scrutinize contexts and their respective values, potentially concluding they are unsound or unworthy. One possible consequence of such judgments is for the values to be jettisoned and, in turn, the context itself redrawn or even jettisoned, due to the co-constitutive relationship between particular contexts and respective values (an insight drawn from Walzer's conception of the relationship between spheres and social goods). Sometimes, pressures to reconfigure might come from extreme external contingencies such as war, famine, or radical political changes.

Let us pause a moment to pull together some of the disparate strands. In Chapter 7 I introduced contextual integrity as an indicator or metric for privacy, arguing that it models intuitive judgments better than existing predominant theories and approaches to privacy, particularly in light of challenges from radical alterations of information flows due to socio-technical systems. According to the framework, a practice under investigation is judged a violation of contextual integrity if it runs afoul of context-relative informational norms, which are specified in terms of contexts, actors, attributes, and transmission principles. The framework was augmented with a normative component, asserting that entrenched norms do not merely indicate when novel practices contravene traditional practices, but can be generally justified on moral grounds insofar as they support the attainment of general as well as context-based values, ends, and purposes. This opens up the way for challenges to entrenched practice from nonconforming practices, when the latter are shown more effective in supporting or promoting respective values, ends, and purposes. In evaluating a challenge, however, a presumption in favor of entrenched norms recognizes that these norms are likely to reflect the settled rationale of a given context. But we embraced the possibility that challenges might outperform entrenched practices; in this event, entrenched norms legitimately give way to new practices.

Augmented Contextual Integrity Decision Heuristic

Before considering applications of the framework to some of the cases of socio-technical systems and practices introduced in Part I, this is a good place to review the contextual integrity decision heuristic, the original heuristic derived from the descriptive component alone, augmented by prescriptive elements developed in this chapter.

The point of departure is a controversial system or practice that may be under consideration or already in place, yet drawing protest. The decision heuristic provides an approach to understanding the source or sources of trouble as well as an approach to evaluating the system or practice in question.

1. Describe the new practice in terms of information flows.

2. Identify the prevailing context. Establish context at a familiar level of generality (e.g., "health care") and identify potential impacts from contexts nested within it, such as "teaching hospital."

3. Identify information subjects, senders, and recipients.

4. Identify transmission principles.

5. Locate applicable entrenched informational norms and identify significant points of departure.

6. Prima facie assessment: There may be various ways a system or practice defies entrenched norms. One common source is a discrepancy in one or more of the key parameters. Another is that the existing normative structure for the context in question might be "incomplete" in relation to the activities in question. Although I have not discussed such scenarios in any detail, it is quite possible that new technologies enable actions and practices for which no norms have yet developed. A breach of informational norms yields a prima facie judgment that contextual integrity has been violated because presumption favors the entrenched practice.

7. Evaluation I: Consider moral and political factors affected by the practice in question. What might be the harms, the threats to autonomy and freedom? What might be the effects on power structures, implications for justice, fairness, equality, social hierarchy, democracy, and so on? In some instances the results may overwhelmingly favor either accepting or rejecting the system or practice under study; in most of the controversial cases an array of factors emerge requiring further consideration.

8. Evaluation II: Ask how the system or practices directly impinge on values, goals, and ends of the context. In addition, consider the meaning or significance of moral and political factors in light of contextual values, ends, purposes, and goals. In other words, what do harms, or threats to autonomy and freedom, or perturbations in power structures and justice *mean* in relation to this context?

9. On the basis of these findings, contextual integrity recommends in favor of or against systems or practices under study. (In rare circumstances, there might be cases that are sustained in spite of these findings,

accepting resulting threats to the continuing existence of the context itself as a viable social unit.)

Two Illustrations

I offer two illustrations to demonstrate how one might follow the suggested analysis.

CASSIE

A number of public libraries in the United States recently adopted Computer Access Software Solution (CASSIE) for managing library computers and information systems. Although it offers an array of administrative functions, the one that has drawn the most public attention and protest is the capability it offers librarians to remotely view the contents of patrons' computer screens (Librarica 2007). Employing the contextual integrity framework highlights at least one departure from entrenched practice (the access CASSIE gives librarians to patrons' exploration of the online catalog). Prior to CASSIE, librarians typically would have access to patrons' records of items actually borrowed; now they may also know what patrons are considering, exploring, and looking up. That is, CASSIE expands the types of information that librarians may have about patrons. Following the decision paradigm, CASSIE is flagged as a prima facie violation.

A fully fleshed out evaluation, which I will not pursue here, would involve taking an array of values into consideration in the context of public libraries. Drawing on received views on the potential chilling effects on behavior of surveillance, CASSIE would result in a potential conflict between patrons' freedom and autonomy, on the one hand, and institutional efficiency, on the other. It is also possible that CASSIE might be called on under provisions of the USA PATRIOT Act in investigations of particular patrons to support the ends of national security. To work toward a resolution of these conflicts, the contextual integrity framework prescribes a closer examination of the purposes and values of public libraries. Finding that these include the edification of citizens through untrammeled access to books (and, increasingly, media of other types) and, generally, unconstrained intellectual exploration implies that what is at stake is not merely the autonomy of patrons. We must also take into account the *meaning* of autonomy in relation to the institutional values, ends, and purposes of public libraries. In light of these, contextual integrity suggests librarians ought to reject the monitoring capabilities of CASSIE, except if it is clear that monitoring can directly abet dire national security needs.

Caller ID

The case of Caller ID illustrates how even small modifications in technology can raise vexing privacy issues. Around 1988, when telephone companies announced this new feature, a lively public debate ensued (Rotenberg 1992; Wikipedia 2007b). Supporters argued that having callers identified by number and possibly name would allow call recipients to screen calls, anticipate the needs of specific callers, and gauge interest in their businesses; detractors worried that the feature violated caller privacy, would discourage the use of hotlines, and might result in the capture of caller names for intrusive "junk" calls. Analyzing caller ID in terms of information flows is relatively straightforward: an attribute, that is a phone number and name of the subscriber, are transmitted automatically to the call recipient before the call is taken. Previously, the caller could choose whether or not to announce his identity after the recipient answered the call. Thus, there are alterations in both attributes and transmission principles, warranting that the feature be flagged for further assessment. Accepting claims made on both sides about potential effects, values at stake may include harm, autonomy, and equality affecting both the caller and the call recipient.

Moving beyond this point, however, is not straightforward in ways we might expect. Why? In my view, this is because a social context has not been uniquely specified. Consequently, factors that are needed for a sound evaluation of the relative merits of Caller ID are not available. This ambiguity was reflected in public debates as views on the moral standing of Caller ID varied according to the respective contexts (e.g., family and social, commercial marketplace, and social services) that proponents read into their analyses, and, accordingly, the factors they found salient to their findings. I will leave matters here.

It is worth stressing that contextual integrity is not a function of technical systems alone, but technical systems as they function in social contexts. Telecommunications systems affect a variety of contexts in various ways depending on a host of factors, and the same holds true for other technologies, including databases, data mining, closed-circuit television, and more. For such technologies, the ideal is flexibility in how they are adapted to particular contexts so the flows of information may be tailored according to the requirements of entrenched informational norms. Interestingly, some semblance of precisely this has emerged in the case of Caller ID, as, sensitive to the demands of various contexts, telephone companies have designed into their systems a number of settings that enable fine if not perfect tuning of systems to the contexts of social life.

9 Privacy Rights in Context: Applying the Framework

THE CENTRAL THESIS OF THE FRAMEWORK OF CONTEXTUAL integrity is that what bothers people, what we see as dangerous, threatening, disturbing, and annoying, what makes us indignant, resistant, unsettled, and outraged in our experience of contemporary systems and practices of information gathering, aggregation, analysis, and dissemination is not that they diminish our control and pierce our secrecy, but that they transgress context-relative informational norms. These norms preserve the integrity of the social contexts in which we live our lives, and they support and promote the ends, purposes, and values around which these contexts are oriented. In this chapter I discuss whether and how well contextual integrity addresses issues that other theories cannot, whether it avoids some of their pitfalls and blind alleys, whether it allays some of the cynic's jibes, and, most importantly, whether it sheds light on daily encounters with systems and practices that individually diminish privacy and, considered in aggregate, imply that privacy might be a quaintly old-fashioned value with no place in this so-called information age.

Puzzles, Paradoxes, and Trade-Offs

Privacy skeptics' arguments, reviewed in Chapter 6, questioned the seriousness of people's commitment to privacy when their observed behaviors regularly contradict expressed concerns and give little evidence that they share the advocate's position on privacy as among the rarefied class of fundamental human values. Although several plausible rebuttals considered in that chapter undermine the skeptic's argument, the framework of contextual integrity also challenges it. If a right to privacy is a right to *context-appropriate* flows, and not to secrecy or to control over information about oneself, there is no paradox in caring deeply about privacy and, at the same time, eagerly sharing information as long as the sharing and withholding conform with the principled conditions prescribed by governing contextual norms. With this conception in mind, one can simply pick through and explain most, if not all, of the skeptics' examples of actions that purportedly contradict people's expressed preferences for privacy.

In a similar way, historical and cultural variability is no longer a puzzle requiring explanation, but an expected consequence of general cultural and historical variation due to internal factors and the imprints left from external contingencies. Unsurprisingly, equivalent social contexts may have evolved along different paths, and may have assumed diverse characteristics in their basic institutions, functions, and practices, even if they subscribe to a similar cluster of values, ends, and purposes. Such diversity is clear, for example, in family, child rearing, education, employment, religion, commerce, and health care. Norms supporting these patterns, including informational norms, reflect this diversity accordingly. For example, the absolute prohibition on disclosure of medical information, embodied in the Hippocratic Oath, undergoes transformation in present day medical contexts governed by science-based medicine and third-party payment schemes; in cultures with strong extended family or clan ties, informational norms governing family contexts may be different from those in cultures with nuclear family structures; and salaries are less guarded from friends and colleagues in socialist leaning countries such as Sweden. Entrenched informational norms reveal not only the activities and practices that are likely to provoke privacy concerns but potentially may constitute a rich source of insight into the social and political archeology (Introna 2000) of particular social contexts in particular societies.

The framework of contextual integrity also provides a way through many of the intractable trade-offs that appeared an inevitable outcome of the functional approaches discussed in chapters 4 and 6. Because the point of departure is a commitment to appropriate flow and not to secrecy and control over information, many of the conflicts simply do not materialize. Consider, for instance, the scrutiny of air travelers that has become routine, including back-room profiling, close monitoring, and tracking as travelers pass through various airport checkpoints. One way to describe these sorts of situations is as a trade-off between privacy and some other value; in this case, safety or security. Built into such descriptions, however, is an assumption that privacy means secrecy or control, which must be partially relinquished in favor of the other value or values. With the requirement of privacy as contextual integrity, the right in question is appropriate flow; that is, norm-governed flow of information that has been calibrated with features of the surrounding social landscape, including important moral, political, and context-based ends, purposes, and values, as discussed in the previous two chapters.

The escalating level of scrutiny for travelers, though it increases the flow of certain types of information to various officials, does not necessarily constitute a violation of privacy understood as contextual integrity. Following the steps of the contextual integrity (CI) decision heuristic, the new flows of information effected by new regimes of airport security may, indeed, lead to a prima facie judgment that contextual integrity has been violated. In pursuing the analysis further, however, it is possible that these new flows are embraced as preferable to the old if they are seen as more effective at achieving values, such as safety, security, and efficient movement through the system, that might credibly be high among the aims of a transportation context. If the opposite determination is reached—that the values, ends, and purposes are less effectively achieved by the new systems and practices—then we may truly say that the new system violates contextual integrity, but we will have learned quite a lot about what is at stake in pushing forward with the systems and practices in question.

The case of increased scrutiny at airports turns out to be particularly interesting in light of results from the "International Surveillance and Privacy Opinion Survey," a nine-country, comprehensive survey of peoples' views on and understanding of surveillance and global information sharing. The study, which spanned four years and included almost 10,000 respondents, incorporated results from public opinion polls, questionnaires, and qualitative focus groups on a range of topics from national identification cards to closed-circuit television (CCTV), terrorism, and control over personal information (Zureik 2006; Zureik et al. 2008). One particularly interesting finding was how respondents answered one of the questions in the section of the survey devoted to air travel. To the question, "To what extent is your privacy respected by airport and customs officials when traveling by airplane?" the majority of respondents reported feeling that their privacy is "completely," "a lot," or "somewhat" respected by airport officials, with only between 2 and 18 percent (varying according to country) feeling that it is not respected at all. Under the conception of privacy as control over information or degree of access to it, this is a curious finding. In an environment where we identify ourselves several times, have our luggage X-rayed, have the contents of our purses scrutinized, are forced to remove jackets, shoes, and belts, and have our bodies examined and patted down, the answer to this question should be a resounding "not respected!" In light of contextual integrity, however, the finding is not in the least surprising.[1]

Finally, privacy in public, a problem for a justificatory framework that presumes a private/public dichotomy, poses no particular difficulty for the framework of contextual integrity. As discussed in Chapter 6, the problem arises when policies governing systems and practices assume that only the private warrants privacy protection and for the rest, anything goes. According to the contextual integrity framework, because all information flows are norm-governed in some way, there simply is no setting in which a blanket "anything goes" prevails.

Reevaluating Socio-technical Systems and Practices in Light of Contextual Integrity

The framework of contextual integrity is intended as a descriptive tool, systematically accounting for people's reactions to the myriad technical systems radically affecting the flows of personal information. But it is also intended as a framework for evaluating these systems from a moral and political point of view. It is time to circle back to the systems introduced in Part I to see contextual integrity in action. After all, the impetus behind its development was the innumerable technology-based systems and practices in which privacy appears to be a casualty, yet cannot easily be analyzed by preeminent accounts of privacy. I have argued that this failure is not so much because these theories fail to recognize its importance, but because they do not recognize the crucial social determinants—embracing or resisting these systems and practices—of people's reactions. The framework of contextual integrity is an account of these social determinants (not a full-blown theory of privacy) used to explain when and why people resist and react with anxiety to certain systems and practices and why these reactions are justified in a subset of these situations.

The three key elements of the framework—explanation, evaluation, and prescription—are recapped below.

Explanation. Contextual integrity functions as a metric that is sensitive to meaningful changes affecting people's reactions to new systems or practices. Merely revealing these changes can constitute a decisive rebuttal to an initial response frequently offered by those seeking to justify the system, namely, that no significant change relevant to privacy has occurred. By contrast, I have suggested that a new system or practice should be examined in light of context-relative informational norms that might have been breached. Doing so requires ascertaining the governing context, whether key roles (sender, recipient, subject) have been affected, whether there have been changes in the types of information or attributes transmitted, and whether the terms under which information flows violate relevant transmission principles. Any of these would be sufficient to trigger resistance, and, conversely, protest and resistance are often reliable indicators that informational norms have been breached.

Evaluation. In some instances, recognizing that change has occurred and pinpointing its source might be all that is needed to resolve a controversy, or at least to clarify what is at stake. In others, however, revealing that practices violate entrenched norms serves mainly to sharpen the sources of controversy. An evaluation is then required, comparing altered flows in relation to those that were previously entrenched. Although there is no simple recipe, the framework of contextual integrity, as developed in this book, attributes an important role to contextual values (goals or purposes). In some cases, when attainment of contextual values is obstructed or diminished by an alteration in flow, the alteration is judged problematic against alternatives that do not have the same deleterious effects. Other systems that create conflicts among general moral or political values, including informational harms, justice, security, trust, unfair discrimination, threats to autonomy and liberty, reconfigurations of power, efficiency, security, and speech, may need to be confronted and settled in light of contextual values. Confronting and settling conflicts involves (borrowing terminology from Walzer 1984) establishing the meaning or significance of respective values in light of contextual ends and purposes. A possibility that I mentioned only in passing in Chapter 8 bears repetition. New flows of information might not register with any of the entrenched informational norms because the context into which they are introduced might be incomplete (i.e., have no pre-existing guiding norms in relation to the new practices; see the discussion in Chapter 7). When new technologies are the enablers of such systems and practices, they may facilitate activities that were previously inconceivable. In such cases, the strategies developed to comparatively evaluate new with entrenched practices can also guide an evaluation of new systems and practices.

Prescription. In light of contextual integrity, an evaluation that finds a given system or practice to be morally or politically problematic, in my view, is grounds for resistance and protest, for challenge, and for advocating redesign or even abandonment. If special circumstances are so compelling as to override this prescription, the burden of proof falls heavily upon the shoulders of proponents. These broader considerations of practice fall outside this book's purview, though some attention will be paid to them in the Conclusion.

Monitoring and Tracking

A common justification of technology-based monitoring and tracking systems is that they are both more efficient and efficacious without an added cost to privacy. Justifications of these kinds have been offered for CCTV video surveillance of public parks, vehicle safety communications systems that include identifiers, roadside license-plate recognition systems, radio frequency identification (RFID)–enabled passports, and, no doubt, many other technologies. Their proponents claim that these systems do not increase privacy incursions because these are public places and no new information is involved, and pointing out the sharp increases in the number of such systems (e.g., surveillance cameras covering public spaces in London or New York [Farmer and Mann 2003]) is powerless against such defenses because numbers, in themselves, do not count (Taurek 1977).

The CI heuristic, however, reveals additional dimensions of change, enabling the discovery of innumerable alterations in information flows, including some that violate entrenched practices in ways that matter to contextual integrity. Such alterations are unsurprising, as monitoring and tracking systems excel at capturing information in real time with increasingly sophisticated lenses and microphones, have vast storage and processing capacities enhanced by the adoption of standardized formats, and are continuously improving their communications media, all of which enable accessibility to a broad array of recipients for a broad array of uses. These affordances (Norman 2002) of advanced systems draw attention to some of the ways in which we might expect informational norms to be transgressed. A few of these are highlighted below in regard to the examples discussed in Part I.

CCTV. In the familiar instance of a typical city park fitted out with CCTV, one immediate casualty is reciprocity, a transmission principle generally governing visual access. In CCTV setups, even when the cameras are fairly evident, not only are the viewers of video feeds invisible to surveillance subjects, the subjects are generally ignorant of whether live feeds are being viewed at all. Furthermore, depending on the details of the setup, the images gathered by CCTV systems may be easily transmitted elsewhere and widely distributed, certainly well beyond the immediate passersby we expect to see and notice us in a public park.

Some CCTV systems may alter the type of information transmitted to recipients by allowing authorities to string together images captured across time and space. Information types could be further affected by biometrically enhanced CCTV, such as a system with facial recognition capability. Such enhancements raise similar worries to those characterized by critics of license plate recognition systems as a "stalker effect" (Evans-Pugh 2006). These variations amount to alterations in the type of information flowing to the authorities staffing the CCTV systems in question because authorities now have continuous image feeds of potentially identifiable individuals rather than momentary glances they may have had in situ. Another aspect of a CCTV setup that may result in further breaches of entrenched norms is not informing people about its presence; hidden cameras mean that the transmission principle of notice (subjects normally are aware when others see them) is no longer in play. There are many other details of a setup that may have correspondingly diverse effects on contextual integrity, such as whether images are stored and for how long, and whether they are freely distributed among government offices and under what conditions.

The CI heuristic also highlights why neither the descriptive defense (asserting that the system brings about no significant change) nor the normative defense (that there is no expectation not to be seen when one is out and about on a public street) of the Street View utility in Google Maps are sound. In this case, breaches of informational norms include almost all those mentioned above in relation to video surveillance (types of information, recipients, and transmission principles) as well as the posting to a new venue, the Internet. Accordingly, Street View clearly transgresses reasonable expectations of people on public sidewalks if one understands *reasonable expectations* to be defined as expectations shaped by entrenched informational norms.

RFID.   The framework of contextual integrity raises many of the same concerns in commentaries on RFID technologies. It also highlights a point made earlier in our discussions of caller ID and data mining, that violations resulting from its uses are not inherent in the general technology itself, but depend on the context of use and to what extent its deployment affects the range of information recipients, the types of information transmitted, and the principles governing transmission. Problems anticipated by advocacy organizations and individual analysts include the possibility of covert or hidden transceivers, long-term tracking, and unauthorized interception of signals between tag and authorized readers. Even when systems are functioning normally, as stated and intended, the resulting alterations in information flows may transgress entrenched norms. Familiar arguments that nothing has changed, or nothing relevant to privacy has changed, are as hollow sounding here as elsewhere.

These general observations indicate likely trouble spots but in my view, action or policy guiding evaluation needs to be ultimately grounded in particular contexts. When evaluating the E-ZPass system, for example, the context has altered from the entrenched information flows involving a human toll operator glancing at a car or even a car's license plate as it drives by to signals from transponders attached to vehicle windshields picked up by transceivers at RFID-enabled toll plazas. It is worth stressing that the constellation of departures from entrenched flows is as much a function of the overarching socio-technical system as it is of the RFID technology, as it is of the system that determines whether RFID-enabled toll plazas are linked with a cash-based or anonymized back end, rather than with identifiable credit card payment schemes, and can be tailored to mitigate many flow patterns judged undesirable.

In commercial marketing contexts, critics have been able to rouse attention and worry among consumers over the prospect of RFID tags embedded in consumer items by pointing out the potential for merchants and third parties to monitor consumers not only at point of sale but beyond, both outside their premises and within, as in repeat visits to the same store or cooperating branches. They have suggested a set of principles of fair information practices for RFID systems, building upon the positive consensus surrounding those introduced in the historic 1973 report, *Records, Computers, and the Rights of Citizens* (U.S. Department of Health, Education and Welfare 1973; Garfinkel 2002b; Consumers Against Supermarket Privacy Invasion and Numbering, et al. 2003). These principles refer to requirements of transparency and openness to let people know when RFID tags are embedded in products; purpose specification to let people know how they are used; a right to have embedded chips removed, deactivated, or destroyed; a right to know what information is stored in a chip and associated databases; and requirements of adequate security measures.

Although these principles, in their own right, are worthy of a full discussion, I will stay true to my course and discuss them in light of the requirements of contextual integrity with which they overlap in telling ways. Take, for instance, the conditions of transparency and openness. Expressed in terms of the framework, they are principles of transmission required for any deployment of RFID in the commercial marketplace, blocking, for one, the surreptitious capture of information. Insisting that people have a right to destroy and deactivate RFID tags is another instance of preserving an entrenched transmission principle governing the flow of information beyond an initial purchasing transaction. Performing a fully fleshed out evaluation of an actual deployment of RFID would require an audit of all changes in flow as well as an evaluation of these changes in light of relevant values, ends, and purposes. In the context of a commercial marketplace, an evaluation would require answers to a series of questions about how the new patterns of information flow reconfigure critical aspects of the relationship between consumer and merchant: Does it, for example, give unfair advantage to one or the other of the parties? Does this redrawn relationship undermine the values, ends, and purposes of the context itself? Do altered flows result in efficiencies for merchants and if so, are they beneficial to consumers as well? Is the increased scrutiny likely to lead to a chilling of consumer behaviors? Answering these questions will inform prescribed norms for the design and deployment of RFID systems, a worthy undertaking requiring substantive expertise in commerce, marketing, and economics.

Online.   There is no doubt that transactions mediated by the Internet and, most commonly, the Web involve significantly different flows of personal information in all the dimensions covered by informational norms from their counterparts conducted in physical space. In some cases, the networked environment has diminished information flow, enabling many actions and transactions without simultaneously conveying many physical attributes conveyed in equivalent face-to-face actions and transactions. (With cameras and microphones more commonly bundled with computer apparatus and integrated into operating systems, this might change.) In other ways, the amount and types of personal information transmitted online exceeds that conveyed in equivalent interactions in physical, unmediated environments. Characterizing the flow of information both off- and online in terms of informational norms and the respective parameters of context, roles, attributes, and transmission principles usefully reveals some of the texture of these shifts. The framework, generally, can help explain why Amazon.com's ability to recommend books to their customers based on their buying habits may cause mild queasiness but cross-site tracking and targeted advertising by companies such as DoubleClick provoke an extended spell of indignation (Hoofnagle 2004; National Association of State Chief Information Officers 2004). The nature of alterations varies across systems and practices as each affects, in different ways, the range of recipients, the types of information, and conditions under which information is transmitted from one party to another. Whether the alterations amount to transgressions, and whether these transgressions are morally and politically legitimate depends, of course, on the contexts in which they transpire and how they bear on relevant values, ends, and purposes.

Controversy surrounding the monitoring and tracking of individuals' Web searches by Web search companies, described in Chapter 1, provides a useful though complex illustration of how the CI heuristic may be applied to a real-world conundrum. Perusal of library catalogs and reference books as well as library borrowing records serve as a plausible if not complete comparison point for a Web search, since the Web has emerged as a preeminent public repository of knowledge and information. Accordingly, it makes sense to compare the practices of search companies in relation to search query logs with entrenched informational norms governing patrons' uses of library and reference resources. Generally, these norms are guided by professional codes of conduct for the librarians, who usually are the direct recipients of information about patrons' catalog searches as well as records of their reading and borrowing activities. Historically, these codes govern the transmission with principles of strict confidentiality, recommending that records of patrons' reading and borrowing activities be maintained only for purposes of monitoring the whereabouts of holdings and shared with no third parties (Zimmer 2007).[2] As direct recipients of search queries, search companies appear to fill a similar role to that of a librarian, at least in this regard, and as such, would appear bound by similar obligations of strict confidentiality; Web search information should be shared with no third parties whether private or governmental.

Let us consider how the CI decision heuristic might guide a decision by search companies on whether to share information about Web searches with government actors or with private, corporate actors. In drawing comparisons with the context of a library, the descriptive component of the heuristic establishes that such sharing constitutes a transgression of the principle of confidentiality and a breach of informational norms and, consequently, a prima facie violation of contextual integrity. (As an aside, a principle of confidentiality is breached no matter what principle governs the transmission of query log data from search companies to third parties, whether compelled by government or bought by private third parties.) The prima facie finding, in my view, accounts for virtually universal resistance to the maintenance and dissemination of search query logs. However, a further step assessing the legitimacy of search query sharing is required by the heuristic.[3] As noted earlier, this step requires a comparison between old and new practices in terms of their respective impacts on the configuration of values in the context of a Web search. Weighing in favor of more open sharing practices, government actors cite the benefit of reduced availability of child pornography[4] and improved capacities to identify and diminish national security threats. Knowing what individuals are searching for and what links they clicked from query results pages are believed to be valuable indicators of people's proclivities, commercially valuable not only to advertisers and merchants but also to search companies who stand to profit from the sale of search query logs to third parties. In addition, the commercial interests of Web search companies may be served by strict confidentiality if it sustains user confidence and loyalty.[5] Strict confidentiality is also important for individuals using search engines, as it supports an assortment of freedoms and interests associated with inquiry, education, and expression.

The function of the Web as a venue for commercial transactions, forming and maintaining associations, socializing, participating in political activities, and finding community with others, including a religious community, continues to increase dramatically. In relation to all these activities, common sense, endorsed by claims and findings of a vast literature on surveillance, affirms a connection between confidentiality and freedom. Specifically, the freedom to inquire, associate, and express, mediated in large measure by Web search engines, flourishes in an environment insulated from external scrutiny, secure against reprisal, interference, intimidation, influence, control, and even embarrassment. So, should strict confidentiality prevail, or give way to alternative principles?

Having considered the purposes and values served by these alternatives, what steps help determine whether any one of them is better than the others on moral or political grounds? The CI decision heuristic recommends assessing their respective merits as a function of their meaning or significance in relation to the aims, purposes, and values of the context of Web search. In other words, moving beyond a direct weighing against one another of the values and purposes served by the respective alternatives to considering them all in light of their importance for the context of Web search; that is, asking what becomes of the aims, purposes, and values of Web search under one or another regime of norms. In my view, strict confidentiality—in this case conservatism—wins.

The Web has assumed a central role as a repository of information, a site of education, and a source of research; it is a social and political environment as well as a place of commerce, finance, communication, broadcast, and entertainment. We use search engines to find people, organizations, information, and communities; to satisfy curiosity, answer questions, conduct business, protest, and simply to surf. We do much more, in fact, because the Web is in constant flux both in what it contains and in the roles it plays in people's lives. None of this should be novel, surprising, or controversial to anyone who has used the Web and followed its trajectory of development; it is drawn from common experience and echoes what has been said in innumerable popular articles and as many learned ones. The freedoms required to pursue these activities include many of the venerated political freedoms of speech, association, communication, conscience, and religious affiliation, warranting the highest levels of protection. These freedoms in turn enable and promote inquiry, formation of community, development and pursuit of interests and passions, and, for that matter, even whims. They are the bedrock of an educated, informed, autonomous citizenry; integral to social and political life, and the basis of law and other political institutions of liberal democracies.

Search engines mediate access to content, to connections, to communities, to entertainment, to religious practice, and more; they are not the only access points but they are predominant (Hargittai 2007). As long as search engines serve a critical function of finding information, people, and communities on the Web, and as long as the Web continues to function as a critical repository for information, a venue for self-development, inquiry, expression, association, and so forth, confidentiality is a necessary principle for informational norms governing search query logs. The point I am asserting is not that when you add up the freedoms and interests weighing on the side of confidentiality and compare them with those on the side of supporting open sharing at the discretion of search companies, the former generally outweighs the latter. It is that these freedoms and interests prevail in light of key values, aims, and purposes in the context of the Web, and by implication of Web search. The same freedoms do not prevail in the context, say, of an airport (in the twenty-first century) where people, as evidenced in the findings from Zureik and colleagues' (2008) Globalization of Personal Information survey, tend to accept monitoring and tracking in the name of security, to the extent of having our bodies and effects scrutinized by natural and X-ray vision. These practices, even though highly intrusive, are not objectionable because, arguably, they support the aims, purposes, and values of the airport context.[6]

Spheres of Mobility, Spheres of Trust

In an effort to capture key dimensions of difference between contexts such as the Web (and Web search) and those, say, of airports, information and media studies scholar Michael Zimmer proposed the concept of "spheres of mobility" (2007). In spheres of mobility individual autonomy is dominant; Web search is one such sphere according to Zimmer, and navigating public roadways for automobile drivers, at least as conceived in popular culture, is another. In spheres of mobility individuals are generally permitted to act at their own discretion, to be answerable and accountable to no one.[7]

A similar claim may be defended against the use of digital rights management systems, which breach anonymity, in contexts of reading, selecting music, and viewing images and videos occurring in the home and other private places of association and socializing.[8] Because these contexts and paradigmatic activities serve a cluster of ends including personal development, education, and inquiry, it makes sense to characterize them as spheres of mobility. Conceiving of Web search as a sphere of mobility suggests an even stronger obligation for search engine companies than strict confidentiality; it places search logs in the special category of information over which individuals are entitled to complete control, consequently placing Web search companies in a fiduciary role in relation to them—caretakers of this information who may use the information subject only to the desires and preferences of individual searchers (Zimmer 2007, 2008a, 2008b). Although this does not necessarily prevent Web search companies from using search query logs and selections from results to improve security and to better serve respective users, it requires search companies to demonstrate that whatever ways this information is transmitted or used are connected in credible ways to users' desires and preferences. The idea that companies holding information about online explorations and transactions might have a fiduciary duty to information subjects has also been proposed by legal scholar Ian Kerr (2001) regarding the duties Internet service providers have to their customers.

A general point worth repeating in the context of this analysis is that in assessments of contextual integrity, the challenges to entrenched informational norms may stem from any of the key parameters. While many familiar arguments supporting privacy of information like video rental records and reading and listening habits are regularly expressed in terms of fundamental human rights over particular types of information (against the world), assessments of contextual integrity force greater fastidiousness with respect to the recipients of information, as well as to principles of transmission. There is no need here to list in detail all the reasons why, for instance, agents of government should not have access to what people are reading, what videos they are watching, what religions they practice, and so forth. Yet these types of information are readily, even eagerly, shared with and among friends, family, and fellow congregants. Indeed, odd would be the person who was not prepared to tell friends and family what movie he watched or to discuss a book he was reading. Although we expect to share such information with friends and family, and have it reciprocally shared with us, we would most likely protest were even these same individuals to seek this information from the video rental company or book vendor, because this would violate the governing principle of transmission of subject control, which in turn, is partly constitutive of what, in contrast with spheres of mobility, we might call spheres of trust, and so on, with other spheres characterized by distinctive familes of norms.

Before moving to the next section, let us review some of the lessons learned about the approach from this cluster of applications. One is that the measure of context-relative informational norms is ultimately taken in its relation to the context itself. General assessments of alternatives in terms of familiar rights, values, freedoms, interests, and claims are not final, but must be stacked up against ends, purposes, and values of the contexts in which practices are being evaluated. A second is that the framework does not support substantive prescriptions for general families of technologies, such as RFID systems, data mining, or even biometrically enhanced video surveillance systems, although they ought to be carefully analyzed in terms of the types of powers they offer for affecting (sometimes in extreme ways) the flow of information. Rather, the most fruitful assessments take place within particular contexts; for these it is indeed possible, even mandatory, to prescribe design constraints based on context-relative informational norms. A third is that a full-blown analysis and evaluation of informational norms in relation to the challenges posed by novel practices often requires substantive, sometimes expert acquaintance with the contexts in question. Although some assertions can be accepted as common knowledge, such as the causal impact on behavior of close monitoring, others might demand dedicated study, such as the importance of search engines for all forms of participation and inquiry online. Finally, the lens of contextual integrity may also be useful for seeing where commitment and advocacy on behalf of certain values, ends, and purposes might be needed. In the context of Web search, for example, people might consider it reasonable for dominant search companies, after concluding a careful cost-benefit analysis, neither to guarantee confidentiality for search-query logs nor user control over them. In one view, the slight disadvantage to individual searchers would be considered a relatively benign one, particularly in liberal democratic states, because there are unlikely to be egregious implications for human rights. This misses the point. It misses the opportunity costs, the foregone ends, purpose, and values that might be achieved in a Web understood and protected as a zone of inquiry, association, and so forth. A Web in which search records are up for grabs might continue to be active and useful for some purposes, but severely limited for these others. A fully developed analysis in terms of contextual integrity draws attention to these interdependencies and may help to guide intervention and advocacy.

Aggregation and Analysis

As with systems that monitor and track and systems that aggregate and analyze, the lens of contextual integrity reveals sources of indignation not always evident when viewed from the perspectives of other approaches. Here too the contours of underlying technologies may point us to potential sources of trouble, but the underlying technologies neither correspond to breaches of informational norms feature-by-feature nor are alone able to serve as organizing principles for policy and prescription. As was the case with systems that monitor and track, detecting and identifying breaches of informational norms by systems that accumulate and analyze information, and prescribing responses to such breaches, requires a rich elaboration of the surrounding context as well as an account of key parameters. In Chapter 2 I provided an overview of ubiquitous technology-based systems and practices that aggregate information from primary sources, passing it onward to secondary aggregation points and beyond. As reported in the established literature on the subject, although these widespread systems and practices are not necessarily hidden from data subjects, they are usually not advertised nor transparent (Gandy 1993; Cohen 2000; Solove and Rotenberg 2003; Solove 2004; Lyon 2007).

To demonstrate how the framework of contextual integrity and the decision heuristic may be applied to these practices in both general and in specific cases, I have organized my discussion around the parameters of context-relative informational norms—actors, transmission principles, and attributes—to show how they may be affected by the practices of aggregation and analysis. Upon concluding this discussion, I tackle the thornier and more complex task of evaluating particular cases, focusing on those introduced in Part I.

Actors and Transmission Principles

Demonstrating that these flows of information from primary to secondary recipients breach entrenched informational norms is not difficult. In healthcare contexts, for example, entrenched norms are breached when an explicit principle of confidentiality governing the flow of information from patient to physician is disregarded by practices allowing (even mandating) such information to be forwarded to insurance companies or public health agencies. Norms are breached not only because transmission principles are disregarded, but because the set of actors receiving information has been changed. The nature of a breach depends on the details of specific instances; for example, when consumers complete warranty forms after purchasing household appliances, they do not see it as a breach of informational norms if information about their purchase is shared with local repair service providers because this flow of information is functionally necessary for provision of services. But if the company sells the information to an information broker like ChoicePoint, it breaches informational norms by extending the set of recipients and violating a transmission principle.

Disregard for entrenched transmission principles and expansion of the set of information recipients are characteristic of many of the transactions constituting aggregation and analysis, particularly prevalent in the commercial marketplace and financial sectors. When information about the contents of a shopping basket, readily inspected by fellow shoppers and registered at a supermarket cashier, unbeknown to the shopper, flows to information brokers, the set of recipients is expanded and transmission principles are violated. Online and offline vendors of books (e.g., Amazon.com, Barnes and Noble), magazines, consumer products, travel services, hotel accommodations, and telecommunications services (typically telephone and cable companies) regularly barter, exchange, and sell customer information individually or in aggregated form to other industry incumbents, information brokers, and government actors, who, in turn, barter, exchange, and sell this information to others, and so on. Of course, customers realize that merchants maintain records of their purchases and transactions. They are, however, frequently surprised and indignant when they learn about breaches of notice and confidentiality, as this information moves beyond the merchants with whom they transacted to others one, two, or several removes beyond. Although systems and practices of aggregation and analysis may cause clear and extensive alterations in the actors receiving information and the principles under which information flows, their effects on the types of information, discussed in the next section, are less obvious but, to my mind, more insidious.

Aggregations and Attributes

One of the most common defenses of aggregation practices is that they merely pool that which is already freely available in repositories of public records of government actors, or freely shared by data subjects in the course of transactions with private actors, rather than tapping into any sources of sensitive and personal information, or, in fact, any new sources of information at all. Extensive dossiers are created by combining information from these far-flung sources, including demographic data, occupation, phone number, birthplace, political affiliations, purchasing activity, property holdings, and much more (described in detail in Chapter 2). The defensive rhetoric seems unassailable: assemble innocuous bits of information and you will have an innocuous assemblage; databases of non-sensitive information are non-sensitive databases. Another line of defense likens information service providers to community gossips who gather "juicy" bits of information about people, processing it particularly for its scandalous interest, and passing it along to others (Barlow 1994; Volokh 2000a). The implication here is twofold: first, gossip is inherent to social life and might even serve useful purposes, and second, the best way to stay out of a gossip's line of sight is to refrain from scandalous activity, or, at least, hide it well (Goodman and Ben-Ze'ev 1994).

Setting aside the question whether these third parties are legitimate recipients of this information, this defensive rhetoric is, at best, disingenuous. Data subjects and third-party harvesters alike are keenly aware of qualitative shifts that can occur when bits of data are combined into collages. This is, surely, one of the most alluring transformations yielded by information sciences and technologies. It is anything but the case that an assemblage of bland bits yields a bland assemblage. The isolated bits may not be particularly revealing, but the assemblages may expose people quite profoundly. It is not merely that one actor, one set of eyes, can now view the entire assemblage but that the assemblage adds up to more than the sum of the parts. One source of surplus is new information that may be inferred from the combined bits—triangulation. Although such inferences are probabilistic, the story Ruth Gavison (1980) relates about a man who introduces himself to a third person as a priest's first confessor, when, unbeknown to him, the priest has just revealed to that third person that his first confessor confessed to a murder, illustrates that such inference can even be deductive. Know a person's profession, zip code, political party registration, level of education, and where he earned his undergraduate degree and one can infer with a high degree of certainty his income and views on a range of social issues. Learn that a woman of a certain age purchased a home pregnancy test and infer activities in which she recently engaged. Combine the information that a person watched *Psycho* with information that he watched *The Omen 666*, *Halloween*, and *Dawn of the Dead* within the past six months and infer that he is a fan of horror movies.

To liken the activities of omnibus providers to community gossips is to liken a flood to drizzle. The quantity of information residing in databases versus in a gossip's head, the scope of its transmission, the terms under which it is transmitted (for sale or lease), and the transparency of the gossip's activities all distinguish present-day aggregation and analysis from the ages old, if slightly dubious, community gossip. Once and for all, we must lay this specious parallel to rest!

The illustrations I have drawn above are trivial in comparison with what more can be and actually is extracted from information aggregates; they are not mere aggregations but fertile grounds for the generation of more information, more and different information. Therein lies both their power and their threat. It is what Sherlock Holmes (and a real world counterpart) does when he pins the crime on the criminal, what a physician does when she diagnoses a disease from the symptoms, what we all do when we predict the future from the past or see the forest for the trees. ChoicePoint, Acxiom, First Advantage, and other omnibus information providers open such opportunities on an unprecedented scale not by providing larger databases of the same information, but by inferring, inducing, and disseminating new information.

To sum up the central claim of this and the previous section, I have observed that runaway practices of aggregation and analysis, powered by incumbents of the information industry and tuned to a fine art by developing sciences and engineering of information, may cause significant breaches of entrenched information flows. No longer is it plausible to claim that nothing significant has changed and no reasonable expectations violated, because, depending on the context and particular applications, these practices almost always alter and usually expand the normal set of recipients, breach governing principles of transmission, and augment the types of information flowing from one actor to another. The moral legitimacy of such practices, therefore, rests not upon finding that nothing important has changed but that novel patterns of information flow initiated by those who amass personal information, those who give or sell information, or those who buy or otherwise gain access to it, are promoting social goals, ends, and values more effectively than traditional patterns of flows regulated by entrenched norms.

Aggregation and Analysis Evaluated

I have offered contextual integrity as a refined metric for characterizing changes in the flows of information likely to provoke the feeling that privacy has been threatened or violated. Merely pointing out these changes is sometimes sufficient to divert or halt the practices in question, as occurs, for example, when a court decides that a given activity must cease because it violates a reasonable expectation of privacy.[9] Nevertheless, the framework allows for the possibility that overturning entrenched norms and embracing novel flows induced by new systems and practices, in this case, data aggregation and analysis, might not only be morally defensible but even prescribed.[10] Prescribed not only because the practices in question improve decision-making capacities of government officials and corporate executives and yield greater efficiency in administering the allocation of goods and services and even producing general welfare, but because they support the attainment of context-relative ends, goals, and values better than entrenched practices. To the extent that aggregation and analysis of health information provides, for example, improved diagnostic tools for individual and community health, assists physicians in making sense of puzzling symptoms, and enables public health officials to detect patterns of illness pointing to environmental hazards, they may constitute a welcome change in flow even if they violate entrenched norms of confidentiality. Whereas flatly ruling out change merely because it violates entrenched normative flows may be morally problematic, unconditionally accepting it is equally so. Instead it needs to be carefully considered and evaluated as prescribed by the CI decision heuristic.

Omnibus Information Providers.   Evaluation strategies of the framework of contextual integrity may be usefully applied to omnibus information providers. Because information providers gather information from diverse sources and actors and service diverse needs of diverse actors with diverse products and services, the framework requires that evaluation be localized within recognizable contexts. This approach might seem overly cautious and piecemeal, but it allows for the reasonable possibility that while certain interventions are deemed morally problematic, others are unassailable. It is not necessary, however, to construct contexts from the ground up, because the information service providers, in their marketing strategies, target their information products and service to specific contexts, recognizing the utility of embracing important pre-existing organizing principles that contexts (not labeled thus, of course) provide, which, in turn, help to pinpoint the likely needs providers might fill in relation to them. In my discussion, I too will follow these pre-existing contours as they are adopted in the marketing blurbs of information broker Web sites.

A final caveat is that my conclusions must be regarded as somewhat tentative because factual details needed for more definitive conclusions are not readily available, partly because omnibus information providers are generally not transparent about crucial aspects of their practices (e.g., holding back a full account of precise sources, database content, customers, and details of their analytics) presumably for competitive business reasons.[11]

Commercial Marketplace.   Among the most commonly advertised products and services are those catering to the needs of the commercial marketplace. Generally, these are generated by the providers from large warehouses of information that they have aggregated from a huge array of sources including consumer purchasing records, online activities and transactions, magazine subscriptions, book purchases, air travel and frequent flyer memberships, hotel stays, professional affiliations, education level, and employment, combined with information harvested from public and court records, as well as from databases of data-holding companies they have acquired.[12] These warehouses may provide a gold mine of opportunities yielding to sophisticated tools of analysis. One commonly cited is the creation of dossiers that associate identifiable individuals with enumerable data points (including, increasingly, geographic location). The information may also be mined for emergent categories or organized according to predefined attributes into classes, or profiles, believed to be useful for marketing as individuals determined to fit certain profiles or to fall in certain emergent categories are considered good targets for particular treatments (Ellis-Smith 1980; Rule et al. 1983; Gandy 1993, 1996; Cohen 2000; Garfinkel 2000; Swire 2002; Reidenberg 2003; Schwartz 2004; Solove 2004; Lyon 2007).

There are contributors and participants who have good reasons to vaunt the novel flows these systems have yielded all along the production line that leads to these data warehouses and the services and products derived from them. To begin, those who garner information in the course of direct transactions with consumers, customers, or citizens may extract incremental value from these transactions by profitably selling this information.[13] The end users of processed information (i.e., retailers, advertisers, and marketers) who purchase these products and services may claim it improves business efficiency by enabling more precise tailoring of marketing efforts and sales strategies and enabling them to identify and cultivate a more reliable, generally desirable customer base.[14] Government users might offer similar goals of efficiency in addition to goals of improved efficacy in law enforcement and national security. And, of course, one must assume that the information middlemen themselves are keenly interested in and benefit from these activities. Some have defended these practices not only because they serve important ends and purposes such as business efficiency or law enforcement, but because they constitute the exercise of important rights and liberties including speech (Volokh 2000a).

Others, defending these practices, have included information subjects among the beneficiaries, claiming they are less likely to be bothered by unsuitable offers (Direct Marketing Association 1999) and more likely to enjoy the more relevant, cheaper goods and services that flow from more efficient business practices. Much of the commentary published in academic and consumer advocacy circles, however, has focused on the negative potential of consumer profiling. Following the CI heuristic, this might include the risks of informational harms, two in particular. One is the risk of security breaches whether by break-in,[15] loss,[16] or inadvertent disclosure to bad actors.[17] These increased risks are a direct consequence of huge, valuable assemblages of individually identifiable dossiers held centrally and vulnerable to attack.[18] The second risk is aptly captured by humorist Dave Barry:

> Every day, in every town, there are heartwarming stories like this one: A 53-year-old man suddenly starts experiencing severe chest pains and shortness of breath. An ambulance rushes him to a hospital where, as his condition worsens, doctors administer a series of tests, the results of which are instantaneously transmitted via a special fiber-optic telephone cable to a giant medical database computer a thousand miles away. Almost instantaneously an electronic message comes back, informing the doctors that the patient—whom the computer has mistaken for another man, with a similar name who actually died thirty-eight months earlier—has fallen behind in his car payments and should be denied credit at the hospital. The computer then—*without even having to be asked*—disconnects the patient's electrical and phone services and cancels every one of his credit cards. All of this is accomplished in less time than it takes you to burp. (1996, 8–9)

This risk, of course, is harm due to the high incidence of error and inaccuracy routinely present in large assemblages, for example, the finding of errors in 100 percent of personal records, including error rates of 60 to 70 percent for basic biographical information, in a study of aggregators Choice-Point and Acxiom (Pierce and Ackerman 2005). One can imagine the impacts such errors may have on the quality of life in contemporary society, from insurance rates to issuance of credit cards to approval of mortgages.

Another powerful critique, famously developed by media and communications scholar Oscar Gandy (1993, 1996, 2000, 2003) and extended by sociologist David Lyon (2003, 2007), cites discrimination, or "social sorting," as a sinister consequence of the machinations of aggregation and analysis of information, and, ultimately, profiling and differential treatment based on its results.[19] This critique substantiates the connections frequently claimed between privacy and equality, revealing many ways that analytical tools applied to aggregated databases of personal information generate systems of profiles into which individuals are slotted, eventually leading to a segmented society. According to people's assignments to these segments, they receive differential treatment of one kind or another. Giving short shrift to this critique, legal scholar Lior Strahilevitz warns that if the urgings of Gandy, Lyons, and others were heeded and privacy protection allowed to obstruct social sorting, discrimination would not cease. Instead, it would merely shift "from unproblematic criteria like purchasing patterns, social affiliations, criminal histories, insolvency records, and Internet browsing behavior back toward the old standbys—race, gender, and age" (Strahilevitz 2007, 11).

The argument from discrimination against social sorting is not a general argument against differential treatment for different people in diverse conditions. It is also not a general argument against holding people to account for past actions. This would not make sense. It is an argument against *unfair* discrimination and *unreasonable* accountability. While Strahilevitz and other proponents of aggregation and profiling presume that the logic of reputation is unproblematic, Lyon, Gandy, and others think otherwise. Whether people receive a loan, a credit card, banking services, or insurance and the rate at which they receive them, whether they are added or dropped as recipients of certain kinds of consumer offers or even merely information, and the treatment they generally receive in the commercial marketplace are part of what Lyon calls a person's "life chances" (2007, 186), meaning significant determinants of a person's prospects and quality of life. With this much at stake for individuals, the design of a fair system of decision making would be one that balances the interests of commercial actors with the interests of individuals, giving consideration to such features as assuring non-arbitrary grounds for exclusion, transparency of principles determining inclusion and exclusion, and the relevance of decision criteria to particular decisions. For assurances such as these to be meaningful, they need to be firmly grounded in something, whether theory or clear empirical evidence. It is worth noting that aggregates and profiles obtained from information service providers extend across a wide range of information types, not necessarily limited to purchasing histories within the pertinent sectors. In order to shake off the charge of unfair discrimination, the assurances Lyon and others recommend should be included among the operational criteria shaping the products and services end-users acquire from ChoicePoint, First Advantage, Acxiom, and other omnibus information providers.

Strahilevitz's claim that the criteria he lists are relatively "unproblematic" is radically incomplete. Decision criteria are not fair or unfair in themselves but in relation to the goods being distributed according to them. Breaking with the long and dishonorable practice of using race, gender, and ethnicity as decision criteria may constitute progress, but not if we uncritically embrace decision criteria embedded in the "Panoptic sort," even if their history is relatively brief. The fairness of these criteria must be demonstrated by showing, attribute by attribute, how they are relevant to the decision at hand. Beyond assurances that a system is internally sound, justifying operational decisions is at least as important since the best for which one can hope are recommendations that are correct much or most of the time. If there are no clear ways to support statistical correlations with underlying theories of causation, individuals who are denied a good based on them have suffered arbitrary discrimination that is no better than what Strahilevitz calls the "old standbys."

While the form of discrimination that worries Gandy and others is exclusion from access to commercial and financial goods, others worry about personalized pricing of goods and services; that is, price discrimination based not on the goods and services but on the identities or profiles of customers. The idea of price discrimination has previously been associated with deregulated airline ticket pricing and increasingly with online distribution of music and other content, typically referring to differential pricing based on terms and conditions of purchase or access; for example, booking an airline ticket two weeks in advance or agreeing to a fixed number of viewings of a movie. According to mathematician Andrew Odlyzko, the logic of price discrimination based on personal information would lead to an "Orwellian economy"

(2003, 4) in which sellers charge different prices to different buyers. In this scenario, dynamic pricing responds to personal characteristics such as wealth (ability to pay), urgency of need, vulnerability to certain enticements, or marketing approaches. At the back end, sellers secure their prices by means of nontransferable contracts with identifiable buyers in order to control arbitrage, or buying from intermediaries who have acquired the goods and services at a lower price.

Citing both anecdotal and historical evidence that people dislike price discrimination and find it disreputable, Odlyzko admits, nevertheless, that general issues of harm and benefit are notoriously difficult to settle and presumably depend on many circumstantial factors. Some of the unseemly hypothetical forms of price discrimination, however, draw attention to another problem identified by critics of aggregation and profiling. Certain forms of price discrimination strike us as reasonable, even shrewd business practices, such as airlines charging premiums on the last few available seats, merchants offering discounts to entice early shopping in their stores, or even scalpers charging high prices for tickets to sold-out performances. Other forms of price discrimination, however, seem distasteful, such as charging more to buyers whose needs are greater, such as an airline raising the price of a ticket for a customer desperate to reach a dying parent or drugstores charging customers known to suffer chronic pain more for analgesics. (An interesting and ancient illustration is the Qur'anic prohibition on riba (usury) which typically covers interest charged on loans. Similarly, and frequently cited as particularly pernicious, is the boatman who charges more to rescue a drowning victim than he normally charges to ferry people across a river.)

Although a sentence or two will not do justice to the complexity of these cases, there seems to be a line, however fuzzy, between entrepreneurial salesmanship and unethical manipulation. Forms of consumer profiling and targeted marketing are already part of our common experience, such as baby product offers sent unbidden to parents of newborns, AARP membership solicitations to people nearing retirement age, and ads alongside e-mail windows driven by message content. How far, how personal, does personalization have to go before it shifts from being clever and efficient to being sinister and manipulative? What if marketers, adducing people's vulnerabilities from past purchases, club memberships, arrest records, and professional affiliations, target them with special offers for alcohol, cigarettes, and free rides to Atlantic City? Critics of consumer profiling warn that sellers taking advantage of personal conditions of buyers and possibly driving unfair bargains compromise buyers' freedom and autonomy (Cohen 2000), whether it is charging higher prices to those known to be in dire need or catering to known vulnerabilities, such as sending coupons for free cigarettes to people who have recently completed smoking cessation programs or purchased nicotine patches (Zarsky 2002). In other words, the problem is not that assemblages are used at all, but that they are assembled in a particular manner for purposes that are manipulative and paternalistic and not transparently evident to the consumers who are the subjects of these personalized treatments.

Anticipating a rebuttal to these arguments, it is worth paying heed to the role that uneven power and wealth can play in these general settings. A defiant line of response to technology-mediated information practices is to eschew restrictive inclinations of privacy advocates and embrace what novelist David Brin (1998) calls "the transparent society," in which we no longer fight the practices but work to ensure that all are watched and watching equally. The problem is not that information is being gathered, hoarded, and disseminated, but that it is done so unevenly. Despite the liberating ring of this argument, it is misguided for two reasons, both having to do with a world in which power, as well as information, are unevenly distributed. One, for which I will offer no further argument, is that information is a more effective tool in the hands of the strong than in those of the weak. The other is that in a free market of personal information, characterized by omnibus providers, the needs of wealthy government actors and business enterprises are far more salient drivers of their information offerings, resulting in a playing field that is far from even.

My goal has been to demonstrate how contextual integrity may be applied to troubling but ubiquitous practices in the commercial marketplace of aggregating far flung information, developing identifiable dossiers, classifying consumers on the basis of information profiles, and targeting them for particular treatment on the basis of these chains of analysis. Focusing on omnibus information providers as a case study demonstrated the significant alternations in flows of information caused by these practices, thus contradicting at least one common justification. More than this demonstration is needed to satisfy the persistent supporter, however, who admits that changes are radical but resists uncritical loyalty to entrenched norms. In other words, having established that these practices run afoul of entrenched informational norms, how might they be adjudicated as matters of ethics and political morality?

To address concerns of this interlocutor, the theory of contextual integrity calls for evaluation in two modes. One is to assess the full range of diverse, morally relevant harms and benefits accrued by key actors. Synthesizing familiar commentaries, both favorable and critical, allowed acknowledgment of potential gains, such as increased profit, efficiency, and efficacy for merchants, marketers, and service providers, potentially trickling down to information subjects in the form of well-targeted promotions and potentially cheaper goods and services. Potential losses included informational harms, unfair discrimination, threats to freedom and autonomy of consumers, and a widening of the power differential between individual consumers and commercial actors.

The other mode evaluates entrenched norms and novel practices comparatively, in light of ends, purposes, or values of the relevant context, which in this case is the commercial marketplace. My reasoning here is necessarily incomplete, mainly because a fully worked out analysis lies not only outside the scope of this book but beyond my expertise. In previous applications of contextual integrity to confidentiality of health information, an important consideration was the effect of weakening confidentiality constraints on health itself. Likewise, we must ask how novel information flows mesh with principles of a competitive, free market.

In Odlyzko's discussion of price discrimination, he draws a parallel to pervasive price discrimination for both passengers and freight practiced in the nineteenth century by rail companies. Public antipathy was so great that legislated restraints on discriminatory pricing schemes were included in the Interstate Commerce Act of 1887 and strengthened in the Elkins Act of 1903. Beyond the details, which are not relevant here, of interest is some of the rationale provided in support of these legislated restrictions. In particular, price discrimination as practiced by railroads was deemed "unequal treatment in an opaque environment" (Odlyzko 2003, 12). That average prices were lower under the existing schemes of price discrimination was less important to the public, which expressed a clear preference for fairness, predictability, and transparency. Proponents of restrictions on discrimination argued that it undermined the "moral legitimacy of capitalism" (p. 12).

Ideals of a competitive free market are realized to the extent that buyers and sellers are well informed and free to choose among marketplace offerings. Manipulative marketing challenges the assumption that buyers are free and informed. Once it becomes known that different services and prices are triggered by the personal characteristics of buyers, the stage is set for adversarial and resentful engagement where buyers might have to initiate defensive investigations of their own, spending resources to discover prices, services, and products not offered to them. Depending on how difficult and expensive these efforts are, so too is the degree of inefficiency introduced into the market. Finally, as consumers become aware of no-holds-barred sharing of details about their purchases, with potential for broad and long-lasting consequences, they may seek evasive actions, adopt adversarial strategies (swapping frequent buyers cards is one example), and, in some instances, simply refrain from buying (Cranor 2003, 2007; Swire 2003). To the extent that mutual trust is important for a market, an adversarial stance is likely to have deleterious consequences.

These claims are made tentatively, mainly with the intent of demonstrating how constraints on information flows may be linked to purposes of a context, in this instance a free, competitive marketplace. General considerations of ethics and political morality require that we make general assessments of competing, legitimate claims and interests against one another. In some cases, the claims might be so strong, and offenses so egregious, as to trump all others. In many cases, however, where controversial information practices result in deadlock, the further step of understanding the significance of respective interest claims in light of contextual ends becomes an important tie-breaker. This stage of analysis is sorely needed to gain a better and deeper understanding of diverse morally and politically important consequences of omnibus information middlemen. My remarks above and below are the mere beginnings of such investigations; conclusive evaluations are likely to rely on knowledge drawn from economic theory and the premises of a well functioning competitive free market as well as empirical findings (where such exist) comparing consumer behaviors in markets where prices are more or less stable with those where goods are not marked but prices vary, often according to personal assessments of buyers, such as flea markets or used-car sales lots.

Other Contexts.   Equivalent analyses could be applied to other contexts currently served by omnibus information providers, including finance, insurance, employment, housing, political participation, law enforcement, and national security. These would run a similar course, initially exposing deviations from entrenched norms in proposed or newly instituted practices; the potential impacts these discrepancies might have on the attainment of ends, purposes, and values of contexts; structures of benefits and costs; and, ultimately, the significance of these benefits and costs for respective contexts. In the case of employment, for example, it is not sufficient to argue that a given company can minimize its risks in hiring by seeking the services of a Choice-Point, but that doing so serves a society's needs for a robust, well-functioning sphere of labor and employment. A system that places no restrictions on what information companies can access and use in their employment decisions (e.g., enabling prejudicial exclusion of certain applicants, such as married women, those with particular religious affiliations, or ethnic backgrounds) might serve the interests of that company very well, or at least not harm them, but could also result in suboptimal development of its human resource potential.

In the context of political participation, political campaigns increasingly employ services of companies that offer "high quality voter data for political organizations" (Aristotle, Inc. 2007). Although segmentation by district or by other traditional groupings, such as race, gender, or socioeconomic level, has always occurred, the idea here is to personalize down to the individual. Segmenting voters according to aggregated personal attributes, campaigns engage in triage, tailoring messages and deciding how much attention and effort to allocate to constituencies based on personal profiles. One might defend the practices of going after highly detailed profiles of identifiable voters on grounds that parties and candidates should be allowed to seek a competitive edge over their opponents, or one might worry more about how these practices might distort decision making by voters (by individualized, highly targeted messages on the one hand, or simple neglect on the other; Johnson 2007). How does one resolve a resulting conflict between the liberties and interests of candidates and parties on the one hand against the autonomy of voters on the other? According to the augmented CI decision heuristic, it is premature to balance and trade off at this stage. Rather, one must take into consideration the significance of these findings for the context of political participation in democratic societies. An argument can be made that personalizing the messages that individual voters receive may bankrupt the public sphere, diminishing opportunities for political campaigns to distinguish candidates through open debate of a common set of controversial issues. This would require that citizens across the board be exposed to a common set of messages and themes. Tailoring campaign messages to individuals also may involve withholding crucial information from them. Whatever the shortfall of democracy in practice from the ideal of autonomous citizens casting votes on the basis of informed preferences, personalized messaging based on voter profiling tugs us even farther from this. Ultimately, then, the trade-off between conflicting values and interests is only one component to be factored into a policy decision about voter targeting through aggregation and profiling; the other is the effects of these practices on the values, ends, and purpose of the context itself.

Personal information is integral to the pursuits of law enforcement and national security. Precisely because it is so important and so alluring, citizen watchdog groups, government agencies, political representatives, public advocacy organizations, the media, pundits, and academics are unceasingly preoccupied with establishing ideal limits on its collection and use (Birnhack and Elkin-Koren 2003; Rubinstein, Lee, and Schwartz 2008). In pursuing their ends, agencies of law enforcement and national security have constantly looked to the cutting edge of promising information technologies, including systems and devices for monitoring, aggregation, data mining, and profiling the general citizenry as well as suspects. In the past decade alone, intensive public discussion has focused on Admiral John Poindexter's infamous Total Information Awareness program (later dubbed "Terrorism Information Awareness"), the close collaboration of security agencies with private sector omnibus information providers, and the emergence of state-based, so-called information fusion centers.

These areas of public and political life, although regulated by complex and long-standing Constitutional and other principles and policies, may nevertheless be shaken by extraordinary events such as the attacks of September 11, 2001. Democratic societies strike a delicate balance between the functions of security and law enforcement and citizens' freedoms, and the norms embodying this, usually enshrined in law, may need to be recalibrated in the wake of these and sometimes even less dramatic events. When such events happen, scholars and public interest advocacy organizations (e.g., the Electronic Privacy Information Center) perform an essential function of spelling out, in detail, the connections between highly specific policy proposals and principles of liberal democratic governance. By so doing, they place the connections between these policy proposals and ultimately the values, ends, and purposes of the political context in the public eye. In the United States, debates over practices such as wiretapping of citizens' phone calls by the National Security Administration and massive aggregation of personal information into fusion centers by state law enforcement agencies correctly address not only whether these practices violate entrenched norms but also how they affect the distribution of various harms and benefits. The framework of contextual integrity, however, supports further crucial questions asked by public interest advocates: Are these practices likely to lead to a different kind of society? If so, is this the kind of society in which we want to live?[20]

One of the most important contributions contextual integrity can make is to debunk the logic once and for all in the claim that information shared with *anyone* (any *one*) is, consequently, "up for grabs," and because of this the activities of information middlemen, such as omnibus providers is, at worst, morally and politically no more problematic than those of the community gossip. What this reasoning fails to recognize is how critical it is to spell out the actual and potential recipients of information. Whether the information is transmitted in raw form or assembled, digested, and mined, it makes an enormous difference whether the recipient of this information is your neighbor, your boss, a potential employer, an insurance company, a law enforcement officer, your spouse, or your business competitor. Obvious power and other qualitative discrepancies mean that the same information carries significantly different potency in the hands of respective actors; some hold the keys to important life opportunities, some the power to inflict harm, others mere inconvenience, embarrassment, or disapprobation. Sensitivity to these differences means resisting, once and for all, the idea of public information; that is, resisting the idea that recipients do not need to be explicitly spelled out.

Contextual Integrity, Publication, and Dissemination

The prodigious capacity of information technology and digital networks to publish and disseminate information has given rise to a host of privacy problems and puzzles. Except for cases in which the positions of winners and losers clearly line up with their interests, the roots of dispute and disagreement over what is and is not acceptable practice are often elusive. To see how the framework of contextual integrity helps to cut through some of the muddle, let us briefly return to two of the cases sketched in Chapter 3, Google Maps' Street View and online access to public court records.

With Street View, critics expressed indignation over online placement and universal accessibility of identifiable images of faces, places, and objects that are included in photographic images of highly specific geographic locations. Responding to the requirements of national laws in Canada and Australia, Street View blurs images of faces and license plates, but in its growing coverage of cities in the United States no such measures are taken.[21] To individuals who believe that images of them appearing in Street View are somehow problematic, Google offers a protocol for removal.[22] Although rumor has it that the process is tedious and requires a great deal of personal information from the requestor, this author initially failed to locate the protocol after quite a number of clicks on promising-looking links.[23] Details of the case are less important for this discussion than the way Google justified its initial refusal to take down identifiable images. In a familiar move, it denied that there was problem at all because their images capture people in public places and are captured from public places. In the case of online placement of public and court records, there is a similar configuration of arguments both for and against, though tailored to the specifics of the case at hand.

I will assume that readers who have stayed with me to this point need no further convincing that "public" is not synonymous with "up for grabs," that even if something occurs in a public space or is inscribed in a public record there may still be powerful moral reasons for constraining its flow. Although this debunks frequently heard arguments about expectations in public places such as those defending Street View and analogous, categorical support for global, unrestricted access to public records, there is still a need to account systematically for the sources and specifications of legitimate restrictions, in particular cases. And this is what I claim the framework of contextual integrity is able to offer.

Violations of context-relative informational norms in the case of Street View are similar to those resulting from CCTV in public streets, parks, malls, and so forth, except magnified by the potentially countless users of Street View who gain access to these images. Further, to say that people walking the streets or visible from public places have implicitly consented to anything more than being seen from a reasonable distance by others generally visible themselves is to indulge in obvious equivocation, or at least, to beg the question, simply asserting that they have consented to being seen by anyone and everyone and not adding anything new.

Recipients and Transmission Principles

With public and court records, the picture is more complex because records, jurisdictions, and patterns of access are diverse, established not only through explicit regulations at national, state, and local levels, but, in the past, through a variety of material constraints ranging from technical affordances of the medium to mundane constraints such as the hours of operation of responsible offices. However, the shift to online posting (usually via the Web) potentially affects all three parameters of informational norms: the set of recipients, transmission principles, and attributes. Traditionally, the recipients of public records include fellow residents or those with direct and specific interests in the information in question, such as fellow residents wanting to identify the owner of derelict property or sex offenders in nearby neighborhoods, reporters following a story, or realtors assessing property prices or wishing to contact a property's owner. On the Web, there are no interest-based or geography-based limitations of any kind. Anyone with access to the Web has easy, instantaneous access to these records. A shift in recipients is related in obvious ways to a shift in transmission principles but it is important not to confuse or conflate the two.[24] Although public records held in courthouses or government buildings are publicly available, access to the buildings or to the records themselves might be conditioned upon identification. Even if one is not required to authenticate one's identity (e.g., by presenting a driver's license), the in-person transaction involves self-authenticating transmission of information such as appearance, voice, and accent. With records online, these no longer govern transmission.

Attributes

If records are placed on the Web and accessible with no authorization requirements, the set of recipients may be radically altered but so are the access conditions. The circumstances allow for stealthy access to particular records and what might be called "fishing expeditions" facilitated by Web-based search mechanisms. Records placed on the Web may easily be harvested en masse by institutional information aggregators that facilitate grand sweeps of public records databases for inclusion in data warehouses. As a result, information drawn from the vast network of public and court records features significantly in the offerings of omnibus information providers, as shown in Chapter 2. The finding in Chapter 3 that aggregation and analysis may yield new types of information applies here too. One particularly noteworthy instance is due to the drastic improvement these practices offer in the capacity to target particular individuals for investigation. Whereas public records have always allowed for the discovery of information like the owner of a particular property or vehicle, or the names of people arrested on particular dates in particular places, online records allow in-depth targeting of particular individuals, with the possibility of short-circuiting much effort if one is willing to pay the fee charged by information providers for dossiers of interest. (This is akin to the reverse phone directory, which clearly is different in functionality from the traditional directory, even though under some descriptions one can argue that there is no new information in it.)

Evaluation

At this point, according to the steps of the CI decision heuristic, utilities such as Street View and placement of public records online constitute prima facie violations of contextual integrity. The question remains whether the changes they have effected are justifiable in moral and political terms. The evaluation requires assessing relevant claims and interests affected by placement of materials online, as well as its impacts on context relevant ends, purposes, and values. Critics of unregulated online access to public and court records warn of threats of harm to subjects, such as vulnerability to harassment, danger from abusive spouses, threats to jurors, and identity theft. There is also the potential for less concrete but still serious harm to reputation and embarrassment.[25] Although the interests of omnibus information providers and those who use them are well served by unrestricted online access to digitized, searchable public and court records, these interests may also be served by access that is restricted in various ways, though admittedly direct and indirect costs for such access might increase. For individual actors, the mixed opportunities and costs have been elaborated thoughtfully in a variety of works. In the case of Street View, individuals are concerned about embarrassment, loss of control over information about their activities and whereabouts, and possible harmful consequences such as ridicule or sanction. The benefits for private users have less to do with acquiring information about identifiable individuals than with visualizing particular locales. For many, this utility is a boon.

Just as there is no "one-size-fits-all" solution corresponding to broad classes of technology such as RFID, video surveillance, and telephony, the same holds for Web-based dissemination of personal information. Once again, context matters. Context-based logic suggests we stop looking for a sweeping solution to all types of public records but tailor policies to particular types of records within the relevant contexts.[26] In my view, there is no shortcut past painstaking study of records in relation to new flows enabled by network-based dissemination, in relation to background contexts served by them. In a case like the 1994 Drivers Privacy Protection Act, restrictions were placed on access to drivers' records that were previously public. Accordingly, although state departments of motor vehicles are prohibited from no-holds-barred dissemination of personal information in motor vehicle records, the act allows a number of exceptions, the most salient being unconstrained access to information that contributes to the well functioning of roadways. This class generally includes any information pertaining to motor vehicle and driver safety, theft, performance monitoring of vehicles, emissions, information needed to notify owners of towed vehicles, and so on. Despite complaints that these exceptions leave gaping holes in privacy protection, the focus on ends, purpose, and values in the context of the public roadways is precisely the direction the CI heuristic prescribes.[27]

The case of court records has attracted much study and attention resulting in informative commentary and clear-sighted suggestions (Center for Democracy and Technology 2002; Winn 2004, 2008; Gomez-Velez 2005; Jones 2006). As with other cases, although consideration of harms and benefits are important, their significance must be understood in light of the ways that entrenched and novel information flows contribute to the realization of the ends, purposes, and values of the justice system. Observers have noted that one key purpose served by open access to court records is transparency in the operations of the justice system, which in turn promotes accountability of judges and other court personnel to citizens, a ready entry point for citizens wishing to understand how the justice system functions, and, in general, a system that effectively metes out justice. Watchdog groups, including journalists and public advocacy organizations, can take advantage of open access to court records to mediate between citizens and the justice system, promoting similar ends of transparency, accessibility, accountability, and efficacy.

The issue, then, is whether the same balance of interests and values can be struck for court records posted online and how to achieve it. One concern is that if information about jurors is published online via search engines and traceable, with no audit trail, there might be greater reluctance on the part of citizens to serve this important function. Another is that individuals (e.g., abused spouses) who have been wronged would be reluctant to seek intervention and redress through the courts for fear that online posting of personal information might prove risky. A third concern, similar to the previous, is that individuals in a relatively weak position might agree to settle cases rather than pursue them in the courts for fear that information posted online, particularly if taken out of a local context, may be embarrassing or cause them harm. Concerns such as these illustrate ways that harms and risks of harms could be assessed, not simply placed on a scale and weighed against the benefits, but interpreted in light of their meaning or significance for the context of the justice system. Crucial considerations weighing in favor of constraints on access include a decrease in willing jurors and a justice system that does not adequately serve those who need and deserve it and is depleted of potentially precedent-setting cases as citizens choose to settle disputes outside of the courts (Winn 2004, 2008 discusses some of these approaches).

My intention here has been to demonstrate the line of reasoning prescribed by the CI heuristic to resolve problems and puzzles specifically relating to open, online access to public records. Although the recommendation for actual cases is likely to require fine-tuning based on specific characteristics of those cases, the general conclusion suggested by the heuristic is for constraints on access to be introduced either by obfuscating some of the information in the records or by means of certain, limited access control or authorization mechanisms. In the case of Street View, I can think of no ends and purposes likely to be negatively affected by de-identifying all images (as required by Australian and Canadian law). By contrast, even the remotest chance of a chilling effect on behavior otherwise permitted on public thoroughfares contravenes purposes and values of these open spaces. Together, these considerations weigh against displaying any personally identifiable images.

Social Networking Sites.   One of the most intriguing cases is that of social networking sites. There is a tendency not to recognize at least two distinct privacy issues facing participants in online social networking sites. As discussed in Chapter 3, the more widely publicized issue is the apparent abandon with which participants confide their inner thoughts and post personal information and photographs of themselves and others to their profiles. This leads many people, experts and non-experts alike, to assert categorically that "the youth of today" do not care about privacy.[28] The second privacy issue, more insidious if less brazen, concerns unilateral policy setting by social media companies (the owners of social networking sites) for gathering, using, and the onward distribution of information, whether posted by users, by others about users, or harvested in the process of users' interactions with the social networking site and other sites.

This issue raises questions intersecting with those discussed earlier in connection with controversial practices by business entities of monitoring, aggregating, analyzing, and disseminating information about clients, customers, and users, online and off. The practices of social networking site operators do not, however, fit tidily into the three analytical categories framed in Part I but, generally, involve all three. Although there seems to be overall agreement that networking site operators harvest information from user profiles, the precise nature of these practices is not known, nor is it easy to glean such information from publicly available sources. Privacy policies provide a decent entry point, but a careful reading of even Facebook's privacy policy, which is one of the most clearly written I have encountered, is likely to leave one hard-pressed to map accurately and fully the flows of personal information allowed by these policies. To offer just a few examples, although Facebook asserts a commitment to "fair information practices," its policies inform us that information (attributes) collected include what the individual explicitly enters, what Facebook is able to learn from monitoring their actions on Facebook, plus information on its users that Facebook routinely collects from third parties (not fully specified). Identifiable profiles are not shared with third parties, but access to users is provided to third-party advertisers who may place cookies and harvest Internet Protocol addresses, and information about users is shared with business partners providing services to Facebook. What does this mean for individual users? While expert readers of such policies might grasp the subtleties, most other careful readers would be struck by these apparent contradictions and be left to wonder what exactly Facebook's practices are with respect to information about participants. To be sure, Facebook is not unique in this regard, and indeed has demonstrated a degree of public awareness of privacy concerns.

I will not repeat the full argument developed earlier in this chapter pointing out, for example, that business owners who monitor, track, record, and sell personal information to others are frequently acting in violation of entrenched informational norms and in ways that cannot be justified on general grounds. When Beacon, an advertising system developed by Facebook, surfaced in November 2007 and users of Facebook began receiving news feeds about transactions in which their Facebook friends engaged with participating third-party merchants and services, they were experiencing the tip of the iceberg that comprises Facebook's use policy for personal information. The indignant outcry that Beacon provoked clearly signaled that Beacon violated users' expectations of acceptable behavior; it did not matter much to vehement critics if Beacon was or was not allowable under Facebook's privacy policies. Whether users cotton on to the other 90 percent of the information flows a system like Beacon needs to function, and realize that Beacon not only transmitted information to friends but to the profile Facebook maintains on its users, is unclear. Users were not mollified by adjustments to Beacon that allowed easier opt-out; the feature is now entirely opt-in.[29] It is possible, however, that the practice of harvesting, aggregating, mining, and selling information by social networking site operators is easier to justify than those same activities practiced by other businesses. First, one could argue that there are no entrenched context relative informational norms to violate because the context of social networking sites is new. Second, since online social network participants are, themselves, posting information in public view, they are clearly indicating no interest in constraining access to it. In my view, both claims are problematic. However, they suggest the need for a theory of how social life operates on online social networking sites and how these sites mediate social interactions, or at least a core set of assumptions and ideas in order to articulate a credible vision of what privacy means in the context of social network sites. Although this is a fertile area of academic research with many scholars and social critics contending for leadership (Boyd and Ellison 2007), there is as yet no full-blown theory that can be considered canonical (and certainly not in purview of this discussion to push further into this territory). However, an analysis of systems and practices driven by the CI framework (and heuristic) must be grounded in substantive assumptions of sufficient richness to answer key questions. In what follows, therefore, I will fill in some of these in ways that are not too distractingly controversial.

To begin, I reject the idea that social networking sites define a newly emergent, sui generis social context with its own internal rules and, accordingly, deny the first of the above two claims—that there are no entrenched norms with which we need to contend. What seems to make more sense is a conception of these sites as a medium of interaction, transaction, information exchange, communication, and much more, serving and extending the transactional range of a diverse variety of social contexts. In a similar vein, one might conceive of the telephone system not as constituting a distinctive context, but as a medium for interactions occurring within diverse distinctive contexts, such as family, workplace, and medical. Although of course the medium of social networking sites, generally, and design characteristics (configurations) of specific sites shape the nature of interactions to some degree, these interactions are also governed by norms of respective social contexts and acquire significance from their occurrences within them. The same, of course, may be said about constraints imposed by material characteristics of a telephone connection and other media. The contexts these sites serve are as variable as the available sites themselves, of which there are at least 350 (Sharma 2007), and some of the variation is likely to correlate with the particular demographic that specific sites have historically served. For example, at one time MySpace characterized itself as "an online community that lets you meet your friends' friends" (http://www.myspace.com) but now serves predominantly teens, while Facebook originally served college students but now describes itself as "a social utility that connects you with the people around you" (http://www .facebook.com); and Blackplanet (http://www.blackplanet.com) aims to let the user "connect with African Americans around the country." (I should clarify that contexts are not to be conflated, for example, with interest or issues groups; these are distinct organizing schemata. Interest and issue groups might exist within contexts, such as patients in a medical context, or might cut across, such as consumers in both commercial and financial contexts.[30]) The explicit purposes expressed by sites that have garnered the most public attention are framed quite generally, while other sites frame their purposes quite specifically; for example, Linked In "brings together your professional network" (http://www.linkedin.com). Commentators have also observed that social networking sites may change over time, starting out as purely social sites for friends and evolving into sites for professional, work-related, sales, and marketing communications as well as political campaigning and activism.

Let us revisit some of the controversial privacy concerns I associated with social networking activities in Part I. These included third-party harvesting of information included by users in their personal profiles (e.g., Rapleaf), opportunities for professional advancement foreclosed when comments and images posted to profile pages displeased decision-making officials, personal information about people posted on other people's profile pages (such as tagged photographs on a Flickr page), and services such as Facebook's News Feed and Beacon. Most justifications of these disputed practices seem to hinge on the idea of a privacy right based in the public/private dichotomy: either something is private and off limits or it is public and up for grabs. Although I have already devoted considerable space to debunking these claims, it is well to be reminded how long they have held sway. Quoting a court decision from 1769: "It is certain every man has a right to keep his own sentiments, if he pleases. He has certainly a right to judge whether he will make them public, or commit them only to the sight of his friends" (Yates in Millar v. Taylor, 1769, quoted in Warren and Brandeis 1890, 198n.2). Building on this, Warren and Brandeis famously argued in 1890 that it is a right of individuals to withhold (or part) with thoughts, sentiments, emotions, and expressive works, foregone "only when the author himself communicates his production to the public—in other words publishes it" (pp. 199–200). Warren and Brandeis were grappling with the impacts of long-range photography and cheap newspapers; we can only wonder how their proposal might have differed had they reckoned with Facebook and Flickr.

Throughout the book, I have questioned the assumption that there is a useful private/public dichotomy for personal information. Justice Joseph Yates, in 1769, offered a more nuanced view, suggesting, at least, that one withholds, makes public, or "commits" information "only to the sight of his friends." This nuance, I believe, accounts for some of the surprise and indignation these controversial activities stir and can be captured within the analytical framework of contextual integrity. Since none of the empirical work of which I am aware investigates the questions quite in the way it is needed, for now, I put forward this hypothesis. Were we to investigate cases in which people have experienced nasty surprises of discovery, we would find that they have understood themselves to be operating in one context and governed by the norms of that context, only to find that others have taken them to be operating in a different one. In other words, the nasty surprises are evidence of a clash of contexts: participants who consider themselves acting in one capacity in one context are treated as if they are acting in another capacity in a different context. As a result, subjects experience a particular transmission of information as a transgression of context-relative informational norms that may be considered in perfect compliance with the informational norms of a different context. For example, when job applicants or employees have suffered setbacks because lewd, irresponsible, or disrespectful materials posted by their friends were seen by recruiters and bosses, they may believe norms have been violated because recruiters and bosses have not respected transmission principles by scanning materials intended for friends and because inappropriate information (information of the wrong type) has been introduced into the workplace contexts.

Some users experience an unpleasant jolt upon learning of services such as Rapleaf and Upscoop, which generate profiles by harvesting and aggregating information from social network sites, including name, age, college attended, and political affiliations. Customers of these services can access more than 50 million profiles by submitting targets' e-mail addresses (Olsen 2007). I suspect that the source of the jolt here, too, is finding that information one has shared with a social circle of certain types and at one's discretion has flowed to other recipients without either consent or knowledge, lacking these general principles typical of social contexts, causing an understanding that these recipients are transmitting this information onward under whatever terms they (and not you) determine; for example, sale or barter. When friends and acquaintances post information about us on their profiles, the violation may be characterized as a breach of confidentiality. Similarly, people have shared information or attended a party, a ballgame, or a political rally expecting information to flow in one way only to discover it has flowed in unexpected ways.

Indignation directed at Facebook over services like News Feed and Beacon can also be explained in terms of prima facie violations of contextual integrity; but not, this time, in terms of a conflation of multiple contexts and their respective norms. Instead they represent a failure to grasp some of the subtle ways people share and withhold certain types of information in the complex web of their relationships. Commenting on the controversy surrounding News Feed, danah boyd, a researcher on youth and social networks, wrote,

> While Facebook assumes that all Friends are friends, participants have varied reasons for maintaining Friendship ties on the site that have nothing to do with daily upkeep. For example, some users treat the Friends list as an addressbook. They may not wish to keep in contact with the girl that they know from freshman psych, but having that connection may come in handy down the road. Yet, there is a difference between the ever-growing addressbook and the list of people that individuals pay attention to on a daily basis. (Boyd 2006)

The News Feed and Beacon utilities were simply insensitive to the different ways that relationships define flows of information of different types, and, in turn, the ways they are defined by them.

My goal in this chapter has been to demonstrate how the framework of contextual integrity, applied to controversial cases such as those introduced in Part I, can shed light and systematically account for puzzling findings. In the case of social networking sites, what others have seen as evidence that people (particularly "today's youth") do not care about privacy, or are simply illogical in their expectations, is altered by the CI heuristic, which reveals that if researchers and commentators would only acknowledge and pay attention to the complex norms that govern the flow of information in the social, professional, ethnic, age-cohort contexts in which social network sites are embedded, they would discover that participants are anything but illogical (there are exceptions, of course) and anything but indifferent to privacy (exceptions to this, too). Users, believing that the flow of information about them and others posted to their sites (in their profiles) is governed by certain context-relative information norms, are rightly surprised and indignant, when, for whatever reasons, other actors have diverted these flows in unexpected ways that breach informational norms. These diversions challenge understandings of the nature of the context as well as the nature of relationships that online social networks embody and foster. If these observations are granted, the question they stir is: so what? In terms of the CI decision heuristic, having demonstrated that some of the practices performed in social network sites that are considered controversial constitute prima facie violations of contextual integrity, can we further demonstrate that they are morally problematic? Is it, in other words, morally problematic to fire the employee, announce consumer purchases to friends, aggregate and disseminate profile information, or even something seemingly mild, such as extending membership of a social network site from college students to virtually all the world? In these instances should entrenched norms give way to novel practices, or vice versa, and should it hold for all or only certain of such cases? One may say that it is, after all, the nature of the technology to make this information readily available; eventually, we must accept these as natural consequences. Online social network participants who do not adjust, who are continually surprised and remain indignant, are simply naïve and foolish.

The evaluative step required by the augmented CI heuristic, supported by the prescriptive component of the framework, is to compare entrenched and novel flows in terms of values, ends, and purposes of respective contexts. Performing this comparison means asking whether novel flows of information to and among friends, families, and others threaten the quality of basic social ties, of family, friendship, and acquaintance; entrenched norms, after all, have evolved over time to support and define these relationships in all their richness and variability. What of trust, what of the subtle exchanges that are part and parcel of getting to know someone when what matters are not simply the facts but the processes of learning them from friends and family and the processes of sharing them with these others? In social contexts of friendships and family, there is a morally relevant difference between knowing information is available with some effort, having it specifically shared with you by your friend, and having it scroll unavoidably across your screen. Bonds of trust, crucial to the myriad other duties and obligations of kinship and friendship, are one of many values supported by norms of information flow. Understanding the ways that norms of information flows relate to values, ends, and purposes of social contexts is crucial to judgments of whether novel flows are acceptable, and if not, constitute reasons for resisting change and weighing in favor of entrenched norms. The practice of harvesting information from social networking sites by third-party aggregators as well as by social networking site operators, job recruiters, and employers is morally troubling because it threatens to disrupt the delicate web of relationships that constitute the context of social life, injecting into workplace and business contexts information of the wrong type, under inappropriate transmission principles. These comments are merely suggestive of the directions an argument would need to take; for substantive conclusions to be drawn, one would need to elaborate and demonstrate key dependencies.

Facebook, which has confronted protests in reaction to numerous of its innovations has, on many of these occasions, responded by granting—what it claims to be—greater and finer-grain control by users over access to information in their profiles. While this addresses some of the privacy concerns, it does not address others because, as I have argued repeatedly throughout the book but most explicitly in Chapter 7, control is merely one (albeit an important one) transmission principle among many. I am holding out hope that social networks will become sensitized to the nuances that the framework of contextual integrity can model through its norms characterized by multiple parameters. Seeing opportunity in users' dissatisfaction with the overly blunt responses by dominant social networking sites, new operators are beginning to offer more sophisticated models of engagement in an attempt to assuage users' concerns. Moli, for example, recognizing that social networking sites serve as a medium suitable for multiple contexts, offers users multiple networking profiles, thereby allowing them to present appropriate facets of themselves to others, understood as assuming a variety of roles in these respective contexts.[31]

Finally, a word on what is often seen as a tension between entrenched social structures and practices and the forward-pulling forces of technology as it manifests in social networking sites. There is a view that recommends letting go of anachronistic sensibilities, asserting that those participating in novel environments constructed from digital information networks are leading the way to new social forms and embracing new norms. Taking a lead from the affordances of technology, they are constructing new modes of interaction, and unfazed by conservative worries they are content to engage in the full range of social relations out in the open. In support of this view that social and normative change is following technological imperatives, they may cite Facebook's News Feed, pointing out that initial objections have subsided significantly, revealing that they were objections more to the unfamiliar than to anything substantive. Generalizing from this case, experience will show that people will adapt, and have adapted.

Making predictions about the future of technology is notoriously risky, yet the temptation, in this instance, is too great to resist. It is not impossible that people, generally, will make some adjustments in their practices of disseminating personal information as a consequence of design imperatives of online social networking sites and their interest in participating in these sites. My bet on the future, however, is that these adjustments will not be radical and they will be tempered by explicit and implicit respect for those entrenched context-relative informational norms that have been finely calibrated to support goals, purposes, and values of the contexts of social life and kinship, such as trust, accommodation, unconditional regard, and loyalty. I predict, therefore, that participants will react to emergent conflicts between these two commitments neither by eschewing social network sites nor by throwing caution to the wind. Instead, they will forge two paths around them. One is to seek out alternative online social networking initiatives, such as Moji, that are more sensitive to the informational norms of whatever contexts these network sites happen to be serving. Another is to adjust their own patterns of sharing and revelation to the constraints and affordances of design characteristics affecting information flows. After a period of observing and learning from our own and others' experiences and indiscretions, living through feedback loops of actions and their implications, frustrated by the smoke and mirrors of privacy policies and opacity in design configurations and site operators behind-the-scenes of business practice, participants will find workarounds that mimic the constraints of informational norms they seek. Even if not embodied in explicit rules or designed-in features, users will impose discipline on themselves by not pursuing all possible relationships under the conditions of exposure set by respective sites. They will selectively opt for those forms of engagement that are suitable to the given context. Caution will result in less self-revelatory, more stereotypical displays in the vein of personal advertisements, less genuinely communicative. These displays might be compelling as public performances, less the stuff of genuine personal engagement. People will not embrace willy-nilly principles of information flow chosen by site designers and operators. Instead, if we must, we will adjust the terms of engagement with and through these sites until they appropriately match these principles.

Conclusion

WE HAVE A RIGHT TO PRIVACY, BUT IT IS NEITHER A RIGHT TO control personal information nor a right to have access to this information restricted. Instead, it is a right to live in a world in which our expectations about the flow of personal information are, for the most part, met; expectations that are shaped not only by force of habit and convention but a general confidence in the mutual support these flows accord to key organizing principles of social life, including moral and political ones. This is the right I have called contextual integrity, achieved through the harmonious balance of social rules, or norms, with both local and general values, ends, and purposes.

This is never a static harmony, however, because over time, conditions change and contexts and norms evolve along with them. But momentous changes—war, revolution, famine—may cause asynchronicities between present practices newly jarred by such discontinuities and expectations that have been evolving incrementally and not kept apace. We are living through one such discontinuity, neither as cataclysmic nor as stark as war and famine, but disruptive nevertheless. The rapid adoption and infiltration of digital information technologies and technology-based systems and practices into virtually all aspects of life, to my mind, have resulted in a schism, many schisms, between experience and expectation. Where a schism has resulted from radical change in the flows of personal information, it is experienced and protested as a violation of privacy.

Accepting privacy as a moral and political right, the framework of contextual integrity is a model of the structure of people's expectations in relation to the flows of information in society. It builds on the substantive thesis that more-or-less coherent, distinctive systems of norms, which shape the contours of our expectations, evolve within the distinctive contexts that make up the social. These distinctive systems of what I have called context-relative informational norms, governing flows of personal information, are finely tuned to the internal purposes of contexts and also to some degree responsive to fundamental human rights and values. In general, informational norms prescribe the principles under which personal information of certain kinds flow from one point, a sender acting in a certain capacity, to another, a recipient acting in a certain capacity.

In this book I have sought to elaborate a rationale for the framework of contextual integrity by drawing attention to discontinuities generated by technology-based systems and practices and gaps left by predominant approaches to privacy in their attempts to articulate a justificatory framework for adjudicating some of these discontinuities. The framework of contextual integrity rejects the private/public dichotomy as a sound basis for a right to privacy and along with it the attempt to define a category of sensitive information deserving special consideration. It is time for us to lay these two ideas to rest.

Beyond the rationale, my hope has been to articulate the structure of contexts and informational norms, two of the key constructs, and to demonstrate how the framework can be used to account for many systems and practices experienced as persistently threatening to privacy. What I have identified as the descriptive use or function of the framework can account for and predict when people experience systems or practices as privacy violations. But the framework also has a normative or prescriptive dimension. Although there is a presumption in favor of entrenched norms, the framework allows that novel flows of information might trump entrenched flows when these novel flows are more effective in promoting general and context-relative values, ends, and purposes.

What I hope I have accomplished with this book is to lay the foundations for contextual integrity, raise and fill out some of its structure, and show the promise of its explanatory and prescriptive functional capacities. Even at these early stages of construction, there is clear guidance from the framework on a number of long-standing, important issues that have preoccupied privacy scholars and advocates. In what follows I briefly point these out as well as identify directions suggested by the framework of contextual integrity. I also highlight areas of the structure that need to be finished, as well as work that needs to be done to flesh out key areas of application.

Contextual Integrity and the Reasonable Expectation of Privacy

It should be clear that the doctrine of "reasonable expectation of privacy," which has usefully served to adjudicate privacy disputes in countless court cases and policy-making settings, is conceptually closely allied to contextual integrity. As with other "reasonable person" doctrines, it has a built-in but not immediately obvious normative requirement because it calls on judges and other decision makers to determine, factually, not only that there is an expectation but that it is a reasonable one. Because we do not imagine that judges and decision makers will quickly conduct large-scale surveys or observations to determine what is reasonable in each particular case or decision before them, we assume they apply wisdom and discretion to *define* what is reasonable. Although I have not conducted a systematic evaluation of all actual applications of the "reasonable expectation" to privacy cases, nor am I an expert in legal theory, I will put forward a suggestion—reasonable, I hope—of what judges might be striving for and how the framework of contextual integrity is able to help them in this endeavor.

A judge may establish that an expectation in relation to a certain activity or practice is reasonable by pointing out that the activity in question is commonplace. Thus, a plaintiff should not be surprised that a defendant acted in a certain way because such actions are common and the plaintiff had no right to expect otherwise. In the case discussed in Chapter 8 regarding the use of thermal imaging (Kyllo v. United States 2001), since the practice had not entered the common experience (in comparison to overhead flights, which have), the plaintiff's expectation was judged reasonable. In terms of contextual integrity, the use of thermal imaging to detect heat patterns within a private residence violates informational norms in at least two ways: by altering the type of information that flows to law enforcement officers and via the transmission principle that governs the flow of information to law enforcement officers. The suggestive correspondence illustrated in the case of thermal imaging is that actions and practices seen to violate a reasonable expectation of privacy correspond to those judged to be violations of context-relative informational norms. Readers ought not to be surprised by this finding even though I am leaving out several steps and caveats in order to jump to the next point, which is how the framework of contextual integrity may help to inform and sharpen the bases for determining reasonable expectations of privacy.

To say that an expectation of privacy is reasonable if the practice in question is commonplace, of course, is to hide at least two of the determinations, requiring wisdom and discretion, that judges (or other decision makers) must make. One is normative, for surely no matter how common certain actions or practices are, one should be able to depend on judges not to blindly sanction them if they are morally or legally questionable. I will not say much more about this point although it could easily lead to a lengthy discussion. It is on the second of the two that I wish to focus: judges must make the determination that the actions or practices in question are analogous or similar enough to previous actions or practices for these predecessors to inform their assessments of reasonable expectation. There is nothing profoundly different here from the type of reasoning inherent in the practice of law, such as arguing that a prior decision should count as a precedent for a case in question.

To determine that an action under consideration violated a person's reasonable expectation of privacy, a judge must be satisfied that the action is similar enough to, or of the same type as, or analogous to, other actions that society deems a violation of privacy. Invoking terminology from the framework of contextual integrity, the judge determines that an action in question violates standing informational norms, or that the action in question is of the same type as actions deemed to violate standing informational norms. In formulating the reasonable expectation requirement in his concurring opinion in Katz v. United States, Justice Harlan argued that a phone call, even though conducted in a telephone booth, was similar enough to phone calls conducted in private residences to be governed—in terms of contextual integrity—by the same informational norms. In my view it is not philosophically obvious even in cases like this, which most people accept as clear and obvious, when such generalizing inferences are (and are not) sound. Although the framework of contextual integrity does not provide an easy formula to transform philosophically demanding questions into straightforwardly simple ones, it does offer a potentially significant resource for answering them and, at the same time, for avoiding missteps.

Of particular relevance to the central aims of this book are cases in which technical system are employed in a manner people find disturbing, such as closed-circuit television (CCTV) introduced into public spaces, the use of thermal imaging to detect heat patterns emanating from residences, mining of large aggregated databases, and radio frequency identification (RFID) tags installed in consumer items. When the U.S. Supreme Court deemed the use of thermal imaging an unreasonable search, one might wonder at what point a court will find that uses of thermal imaging have become common enough to make *Kyllo*'s expectation unreasonable, comparing this to the case in which the marijuana grower was not protected from a search of his courtyard conducted by a surveillance airplane (Florida v. Riley, 1989). For thermal imaging, one can imagine a standard progression of development where the technology is improved, production costs decrease, and (possibly) it enters the consumer market embedded in numerous handy devices. In this scenario, a judge might find a similar case does not have the same understanding of reasonable expectation as *Kyllo*.

The framework of contextual integrity, however, would caution *against* drawing this conclusion. What matters is not merely that a particular technical device or system is not overly unusual, but that its use in a particular *context*, in a particular *way* is not overly unusual. One cannot generalize from the observation that certain installations in certain contexts are commonplace, accepted, and supported to the conclusion that all installations irrespective of contexts will not violate expectations of privacy. A judge deciding whether a particular use of thermal imaging, CCTV, or facial recognition software violates expectations of privacy should not merely assess how common the technologies and how familiar people are with them, but how common and how familiar they are in context, and if this is known, whether the particular application in question violates or conforms to relevant context-relative informational norms. This conclusion follows directly from discussions earlier in the book that caution against applying moral categories to categories of technology, whether they are caller ID, RFID, data aggregation, or mining. Depending on the co-constitutive systems in which they are embedded, and the in-context flows they enable, they may be sinister or a force for good.

Incorporating key steps from the contextual integrity (CI) decision heuristic promises an approach to assessing reasonable expectations of privacy that may be less arbitrary. Judges (and other decision makers) will still need to draw on discretion and wisdom, but contextual integrity suggests where they should be looking for relevant norms, which similar cases constitute reasonable analogies and which do not. Clearly, it would be of great benefit for purposes of practical application to see these ideas developed in greater detail, particularly by reinterpreting more of the well-known cases in which establishing a reasonable privacy expectation was decisive in the outcome of a case.

Contextual Integrity, Privacy Law, and Regulation

The framework of contextual integrity is a justificatory framework for establishing whether socio-technical devices, systems, and practices affecting the flow of personal information in society are morally and politically legitimate. Although, as such, it is neither a theory of a legal right to privacy nor a definition of a legal concept of privacy, it can serve as a foundation for law and regulation by providing a standard against which legislation (existing or proposed) and detailed rules are tested. Contextual integrity, in my view, could serve well as a necessary condition for law and regulation, even if not as a sufficient condition. There seems to be no inherent problem with context-specific legal regulation, which we might think of as blocked exchanges in Michael Walzer's (1984) terms (i.e., distribution principles of one sphere being prohibited in others in order to prohibit or limit tyrannies of one group over others). In our own society we experience such safeguards in laws that prohibit monetary exchanges for certain types of goods (e.g., votes, babies, organs, and sex), those invalidating kinship as a basis for handing down political office, and those rejecting political office as a sound basis for favorable decisions in court. And, as we have seen, we already have laws aimed at constraining information flows of specific types in specific contexts, such as the Video Privacy Protection Act and the Drivers Privacy Protection Act. There are also more far-reaching cases, such as the privacy rules emanating from U.S. laws like the Health Insurance Portability and Accountability Act and the Gramm-Leach-Bliley Act, which prescribe a remarkable fidelity to informational norms that one might expect for respective contexts.

Of course, many informational norms are unsuitable for expression and enforcement in law or public policy, and in liberal democracies, certain contexts, such as friendship, courtship, kinship, marriage, and religion, as rich and important as they are, tend for the most part to be generally off-limits to regulation by law and public policy. Whether and when moral and political norms warrant protection through law and public regulation (and the converse, when law and public policy are grounded in morality) are general questions that are probably as old as law itself and definitive of long-standing traditions in the philosophy of law. To address these concerns here is neither possible nor directly relevant. In considering, specifically, conditions under which informational norms may warrant explicit expression and enforcement through law and public policy, I would suggest those in which violations are widespread and systematic, when the parties involved perpetrating the violations are overwhelmingly more powerful or wealthy and moved by pure self-interest. In such situations, the violations take on public significance and call for public response.

There are, as we know, other ways to codify and enforce norms, including informational norms, whether in the contexts of friendship, education, professional relationships, or religious communities, such as through the codes and sanctions of professional societies and the bylaws of religious organizations and clubs. Another approach is in specifying design characteristics of the technical systems that mediate flows of personal information. Indeed, this was the very starting place for this book: that many technical systems contributing to key infrastructures of society and its contexts run roughshod over entrenched informational norms that, in turn, support the fundamental values, ends, and purposes of these contexts. System designers, as much as judges, legislators, and public interest advocates, have an important role in seeking to embody appropriate norms in technical design. The effort to express contextual integrity in formal terms is a first step toward implementing informational norms in software systems (Barth et al. 2006).

Omnibus Versus Sectoral Approaches to Regulating Privacy

In comparative studies of U.S. privacy law and regulation with other countries, particularly those belonging to the European Union (EU), one key difference that seems generally accepted is that the U.S. approach is "sectoral," while the EU's is an "omnibus" approach. Advocates of privacy tend to prefer the omnibus approach because it is seen as recognizing privacy as a fundamental human right not lightly traded off against other moral and political rights and, in particular, not treated as a preference that may be bought and sold according to norms governing competitive free markets. Because recognition of this fundamental right, sometimes even expressed in national constitutions,[1] is taken to be the common starting place for all privacy law and regulation, this approach is called *omnibus*, suggesting that an overarching commitment to privacy guides all detailed legislation and rule making

(Rotenberg 1998; Schwartz 1999, 1632; Bygrave 2002). The U.S. approach to informational privacy law, by contrast, is described as *sectoral* because there is no explicit right to privacy expressed in the Constitution and legislation has tended to develop somewhat independently sector by sector. Thus, distinct bodies of law are created for distinctive zones, including health care, finance, commerce, communications, and law enforcement.

The framework of contextual integrity suggests that the U.S. approach to privacy legislation, generally disfavored by privacy advocates, may be the more promising one as, at its best, it embodies informational norms relevant to specific sectors, or contexts, in the law. For a credible commitment to privacy, this general approach would need just one "omnibus" principle: the right to contextual integrity from which the appropriate context-relative rights would be derived on a sector-by-sector basis. Such an approach would also be spared the task—impossible, we have seen—of attempting to provide a universally applicable definition of *sensitive information*, a distinct subset of the general class of personal information (i.e., personally identifying information). Instead, the sectoral approach, informed by the framework of contextual integrity, would need to define constraints on all parameters of context-relative informational norms, which, of course, includes information types.

Directions for Future Work

There are many ways the framework and decision heuristic of contextual integrity can be extended and developed. Although they shed light on existing puzzles, paradoxes, and conflicts, and provide guidance on countless challenges posed by technology-based systems and practices, they also raise new and different questions that need answering and details that need to be worked out. In the following sections I list a few that I have encountered as I developed the idea of contextual integrity and wished I would have had the time and, more importantly, the knowledge and expertise to address. I am convinced that the framework would be strengthened, broadened, and made more versatile by attention to them.

Conflicts All the Way Down

As we have seen, the layer of the social—social contexts—brings to the framework of contextual integrity a richer conceptual toolkit with which to analyze values conflicts that inevitably confront all approaches to privacy set within a generally pluralistic framework. Privacy advocates have worried that when privacy collides with other values, more often than not, it is the casualty. By specifying relevant conditions on information flow (e.g., flow restricted by certain transmission principles, in these contexts, regarding those attributes, and in relation to those actors), the structure of context-relative informational norms may reveal that what at first appears as a conflict turns out not to be one on further analysis. This is because respecting privacy is not merely restricting access to information but appropriate flow and, ideally, one would expect the informational norms within a given context to evolve in ways that inherently promote and support important values of the context.

Having neutralized conflicts within contexts, however, does not mean that conflicts have been vanquished everywhere. Indeed, they may surface at a different layer of the analysis, between or among contexts themselves. This possibility was noted in Chapter 7 when I allowed that as people negotiate in and around the many contexts of social life, there are times when they face simultaneous but different demands from these many contexts. The illustration I offered was the dilemma faced by an employer when his nephew is not the best job applicant, or the person who is both friend and physician deciding whether to assume a paternalistic sternness in chiding her patient and friend over lifestyle choices. Potential conflicts of this kind in relation to information flows can easily arise in collisions between library and law enforcement contexts, between healthcare and commercial contexts, and between healthcare and kinship contexts. I can think of no other way to deal with these except case-by-case, optimistic that some of these conflicts will be neutralized within the warring contexts themselves, a challenge for the future.

Fleshing Out Contexts, Norms, and Values

In cases discussed throughout the book, the CI decision heuristic was effective at honing in on significant alterations in the flow of information not readily apparent to alternative framings; for example, those due to deployment of CCTV in certain circumstances and those brought about by the harvesting, aggregating, and mining of information from online public records. The step beyond recognizing change, in which alternative flows are evaluated and compared with one another in terms of values, ends, and purposes, is generally more demanding. As illustrated in the case of aggregation and profiling of individual consumers, it may require expert and non-obvious knowledge of a context, such as, in this instance, the relevant case studies and factors influencing consumer behavior and trust. Even when deep expertise is not necessary, evaluations stand to benefit from an appreciation of the historical origins of entrenched informational norms. To grasp, fully, important causal relationships, an analysis calls for detailed, grounded knowledge of a context in question, including all relevant constitutive elements (as discussed in Chapter 7).

What I have offered here are mere sketches and fragments of what might be considered an ideal, fleshed out analysis. Given the wave after wave of important and controversial questions before us, there is need for energetic study of key contexts of social life in these ways. For some areas that have already been well studied, such as health care, law enforcement, the judicial system, and democratic politics, we have a rich store of knowledge that can be invoked to establish the requirements of contextual integrity. For others, say friendship and kinship, we can draw on direct personal experience as well as the equally rich, astutely observed insights of novels, movies, and poems to draw connections between information flows and internal values and purposes. In many cases, sound laws and rules are exemplary in capturing these connections.

Cross-Cutting Concepts

Throughout the book, analysis, for the most part, has been conceptually organized around contexts. Contexts have served as the organizing principle for considering clusters of informational norms—context-relative informational norms—constraining information flows in various ways. It is possible to follow other organizing principles in systematically investigating contexts and their informational norms. In Chapter 9, for example, I briefly embarked in this direction by considering concepts that cut across contexts, such as spheres of trust and Zimmer's spheres of mobility (2007). Upon being identified as spheres of trust, certain patterns of information flow might follow for such contexts as friendship, family (or kinship), and possibly others.

Spheres of trust might be those with relatively flat power hierarchies, where actors typically share certain types of information with one another on a voluntary basis only. In contexts such as these, the parent chooses not to read the child's journal, even though he knows where the journal is kept, as this would not only violate a principle of transmission but would undermine the bonds of trust. In contexts characterized as spheres of trust, trust serves as the basis of interaction and the fulfillment of mutual obligations, in contrast to contractual or legal obligations that characterize employment or financial contexts. A defining aspect of what Zimmer has called spheres of mobility is that the autonomy of information subjects is paramount. In the case of intellectual inquiry, for example, individuals should not have to account to others for the choices they make, and should be free to pursue their interests. Certain configurations of informational norms are believed ideal to sustain this possibility. Voting in democratic elections might be another sphere of mobility; while driving on the public roadways might once have been conceived as one, it is increasingly constrained in various ways for a variety of reasons.

There are other regularities that might usefully be studied across spheres, as opposed to within. Certain transmission principles might be studied as they manifest in different contexts, such as consent and control. Given the prominence of control in so many definitions of privacy, it would be worthwhile to study the configurations of contexts, conditions, and norms under which control is the prescribed transmission principle. It might also be worthwhile to mark for special attention those challenges to the status quo that involve a relaxation of constraints on information flow; that is, alterations in flows that result in more information being released, to greater numbers of recipients, under fewer or more lenient conditions, and potentially detrimental to information subjects. Although the premise of the framework of contextual integrity is that presumption favors entrenched norms in the face of all challenges, perhaps we will find it useful to devise a cross-cutting measure of "more and less" information, "greater and fewer" numbers of recipients, "stricter or more lenient" constraints, and "beneficial or harmful" to information subjects. And, if we do, it might turn out that some function of these factors models an important dimension of the concept of privacy.

Moral Mathematics: The Whole Is More than the Sum of the Parts

The philosopher Derek Parfit, in his book, *Reasons and Persons* (1986), discusses "five mistakes in moral mathematics," among them, mistakes people make in reasoning about the moral status of actions by themselves causing minor, or even imperceptible, harms (or benefits) but great harm (or benefit) when aggregated with similar actions by others. Another common way Parfit characterizes these problems is under the rubric of collective action (chap. 3). Although his intention in constructing his elaborate schema of hypothetical scenarios is to address perennial disputes internal to ethical theory, the types of concerns he addresses strongly resemble a challenge we face in securing adequate privacy policies.

It is not difficult to see that the assault on privacy (Miller 1972) is generally not due to any one single action, practice, or system. Indeed, it is rare to find any single one among the myriad technology-based systems or practices discussed in Part I that in itself warrants the degree of outrage, protest, and resistance with which it might be received by privacy advocates, the media, or the population at large. Because there are so many instances, people rightly experience each incursion as a step down the slippery slope and, in my view, rightly object to it. If so many of the individual incursions, taken by themselves, cause only tiny, even imperceptible breaches—a camera here, a tagged image there, one's clickstream sold to an ad agency—how is it possible to address the big, truly worrisome totality with policies targeted to any one of these?

Parfit's conclusion to his chapter on mistakes in moral mathematics holds promise as an approach to the analogous problem for privacy:

> It is not enough to ask, "Will my act harm other people?" Even if the answer is *no*, my act may still be wrong because of its effects. The effects that it will have when it is considered on its own may not be its only relevant effects. I should ask, "Will my act be one of a set of acts that will *together* harm other people?" The answer may be Yes. And the harm to others may be great. If this is so, I may be acting very wrongly. (1986, 86)

The difficulty, however, is how to situate a particular practice or system within the "set of acts" that together engender the nightmare conceived by novelists and academics. With collective action problems such as litter and pollution we can see single acts of littering or dumping contaminants in a river as elements of a set of acts that together cause real harm. This has proven challenging in the case of single breaches of privacy. This problem is addressed in the framework of contextual integrity by contexts themselves. Entrenched informational norms generally embody a scheme of settled informational practices roughly oriented around the values, ends, and purposes of a context; contexts generally are the structured social systems that have evolved to manage and accomplish aspects of social life recognized as fundamental in a given society. This scheme imbues each questionable action and system with a meaning that extends far beyond its immediate reach, its direct impact, taken alone. It is the robustness of the social structure of contexts and the efficacy of their respective informational norms that stop the slide down the slope and prevent a society from throwing away privacy in tiny bits.

Notes

Introduction

1. See Judith DeCew's *In Pursuit of Privacy: Law, Ethics, and the Rise of Technology* (1997) for one such admirable attempt.

2. Theorists who have taken this path include Ruth Gavison (1980), Tom Gerety (1997), Charles Fried (1968), and William Parent (1983).

3. See for example works by Cynthia Dwork et al. (Dwork 2006; Dwork et al. 2006) and Rebecca Wright (Wright 2008; Wright, Yang, and Zhong 2005).

4. For the full text, see European Parliament and Council of the European Union (1995), specifically chapter 1, article 2, at http://www.cdt.org/privacy/eudirective/EU_Directive_.html#HD_NM_28.

Part I

1. The choice of these terms was influenced by Lester (2001, 28), in turn influenced by privacy activist Richard M. Smith.

Chapter 1

1. By *public venue*, I mean publicly accessible, not necessarily publicly owned. This includes shopping malls and many retail spaces, but rules out military bases, the White House, and so forth.

2. Although facial recognition systems are not yet sufficiently advanced to reliably pick out "the face in the crowd," improved video-recording technologies ultimately

will contribute toward more successful pairings of image monitoring and biometric identification through facial recognition. This is likely to raise anxieties an additional notch.

3. Michael Zimmer (2007) has developed this idea in some detail.

4. I frequently joke with my students that I can share with their worried parents the odd hours they keep by taking note of their postings to classroom bulletin boards, as the system reveals their precise dates and times.

5. A fascinating account of creeping surveillance through telephone systems and directories can be found in Curry, Phillips, and Regan (2004); also see Phillips (2003).

6. Turning the tables on typical agents of surveillance is sometimes called "sousveillance," meaning "watchful vigilance from underneath." In this context, the term is generally attributed to Steve Mann, an electrical engineer at the University of Toronto. See Mann (2004).

7. Electronic toll collection is in place in more than thirty countries worldwide, including the E-ZPass system in the northeastern region of the United States, Auto-PASS in Norway, Videomaut in Austria, Autotoll and Autopass in Hong Kong, and TollTrax in India (Smith and Benko 2007; Wikipedia Contributors 2007a).

8. At the time of writing, the Vehicle Safety Communication Consortium, consisting of seven of the largest automobile manufacturers, was working on standards for the protocols underlying this dedicated short-range communications systems for the spectrum range near 5.9Ghz allocated to them by the FCC.

9. A detailed discussion about privacy on the roadways and the DOT Vehicle Safety Communications Systems project can be found in Zimmer (2005).

10. The literature on DRM technologies and TPMs is vast. DRM and TPMs are also an active topic in regulatory circles and in the courts. Although most of the attention focuses on how these systems interact with intellectual property regimes, privacy implications have been carefully studied in works by Vora et al. (2001); Cohen (2003); Mulligan, Han, and Burstein (2003); and many others.

11. There are also variations on these two standards, including semi-passive RFID systems, in which transponders are battery powered but yield information only when activated by transceivers.

12. An important discussion of issues relating to RFID focusing on e-Passports can be found in Meingast, King, and Mulligan (2007).

13. One of the security flaws claimed by researchers was that RFID systems could become hosts for computer viruses that could pass from tags to readers and on to middleware applications; see Sullivan (2006). Other possible problems include counterfeit tags, the ability to deactivate tags, insufficient user identification, and encryption weaknesses in the U.S. passport tracking system (see Markoff 2006).

14. For details on this case, see Consumers Against Supermarket Privacy Invasion and Numbering, et al. (2003).

15. Garfinkel, Juels, and Pappu call this the "breadcrumb threat" (2005, 38).

Chapter 2

1. It is important to acknowledge that social and technical transformations are a function of innumerable factors, not least of which are economic. For better or for worse, the economic dimension will not be a significant part of the book's account.

2. By now this extensive multidisciplinary effort is covered in a wide-ranging literature and taught in the academy by numerous schools and departments in courses such as Management Information Systems, Information Studies, Information Science, Library and Information Science, and so forth.

3. For the best accounts of this period and these discussions, see Regan (1995), particularly pp. 71–73, and Solove (2002a, 2002b). For a brief historical overview of the advent of systematic record keeping within government in addition to the private sector, individuals, and households, see Curry, Phillips, and Regan (2004).

4. For a useful nontechnical description and discussion of data mining and KDD, see Zarsky (2004). Also see Tavani (1999) and Taipale (2006).

5. Acxiom was acquired in May 2007 by investment firms Silver Lake and Value-Act Capital in a deal estimated at 2.25 billion U.S. dollars ("Acxiom Panel" 2007).

6. "Acxiom provides information and enhanced analytics to help Americans protect themselves, their businesses and their communities from risk. Whether it's the national authorities searching for criminals, skip tracers attempting to locate debtors or banks preventing identity fraud, Acxiom offers comprehensive data and up-to-date technology to help keep America secure. Acxiom is at the forefront of risk mitigation information, scoring and analytics. We offer a suite of enhanced data in an easy-to-use format and provide access to hundreds of national and state-specific databases to authorized professionals in both online and batch mode" (Acxiom Corporation 2006).

7. See Solove (2002a) and Barber (2006).

8. The Privacy Rights Clearinghouse chronological list of data breaches paint a stark picture of the dangers of entrusting so much personal data to such data brokers. See the Privacy Rights Clearinghouse's Chronology of Data Breaches (Privacy Rights Clearinghouse/UCAN 2007a).

9. Experian, Equifax, and other credit reporting agencies have increasingly generalized their offerings to resemble those of omnibus information providers.

10. Information about these practices was provided by Randy Holmes, Choicepoint Director of Data Strategy. Phone conversation conducted June 20, 2005.

11. According to Holmes, phone conversation conducted June 20, 2005.

12. In testimony before the Senate Banking, Finance and Insurance Committee, on March 30, 2005, Don McGuffey, Vice President, Data Acquisition and Strategy, ChoicePoint Services Inc., asserted that ChoicePoint provides services to more than 7,000 federal, state, and local law enforcement agencies; many Fortune 500 companies; over 700 insurance companies; and many large financial companies and nonprofit organizations.

Chapter 3

1. Some might say as a complex jumble.
2. Versions of both laws exist for state and local government agencies.
3. An excellent discussion can be found in Barber (2006), particularly pages 68–72.
4. From here on, the term *public records* covers both public and court records unless otherwise noted.
5. Also called e-Gov, eGovernment, or digital or online government, similar efforts have occurred all over the world and in the United States at the national, state, and local levels. These initiatives involve a commitment to providing government services to individual citizens and to businesses via the Internet, World Wide Web, and other digital electronic channels. As an example, see "Texas Online: Texas at Your Fingertips" at http://www.state.tx.us/ (TexasOnline 2007).
6. When checked in 2006, Wikipedia's list contained ninety-five "notable" social networking sites (Wikipedia Contributors 2006a).
7. For a general discussion on social networking sites, see Vara (2006).
8. Some of these issues arise not only in the context of social network sites but other social software sites as well; blogs are a case in point.

Part II

1. We might, for example, contrast this with policy choices a community might make which, arguably, are appropriately decided on the basis of collective preference.

Chapter 4

1. As sometimes is the case for underdog approaches. See also Powers (1996); Tavani and Moor (2001).
2. See discussions of these points in Fried (1968), Reiman (1976), Gavison (1980), and Tavani and Moor (2001).
3. Reiman's "symbolic risks" derive from an idea he developed in earlier work (1976).
4. Consider John Stuart Mill's classic defense of free speech (1859).
5. First, however, a comment about terminology: van den Hoven frames his purpose in terms of *data protection*, commonly used in the European scholarly and policy environments with roughly similar intent as the use of the term *privacy* in the United States. Accordingly, van Den Hoven's account of moral reasons for data protection can be adapted, with minor adjustment, to the current examination of privacy.
6. *Harm*, as the term is used here, is distinctly normative and not to be confused with harm understood as an outcome contrary to someone's interests, which may or may not carry moral weight. To give an extreme case, lack of privacy exposing a

criminal plan is an unfortunate outcome for the criminal but not a harm in the sense that I use it here.

7. See Rule (1980) and Laudon (1996) for proposals to establish a marketplace in personal information that would allow individuals to sell and hence profit from the distribution of personal information to other parties.

8. Often called "redlining" and politically problematic. Redlining is a metaphorical expression referring to the practice of excluding whole categories of a population from certain benefits (e.g., home mortgages). It refers, specifically, to the drawing of a red line around high-risk, historically non-White, neighborhoods without consideration of the merits of individuals within those neighborhoods.

9. More will be said about Walzer's theory in Chapter 8.

10. Yet another, mentioned earlier, is that privacy is not important because a person with nothing to hide has nothing to fear.

11. As exemplified in the works by Gavison (1980), Reiman (1995), Cohen (2000), and van den Hoven (2001).

12. Strains of this are clearly evident in Cohen (2000).

13. In later work, Fried repudiated his defense of strong legal protection of privacy, arguing for more limited protection. Readers might be interested in Jeffrey Reiman's (1976) convincing challenge to Fried, which does not dispute the importance of privacy but denies the critical role Fried attributes to information in determining the closeness of relationships.

14. See, for example Gavison (1980), Reiman (1995), Allen-Castellitto (1999), and Nehf (2003).

15. James Nehf (2003) argues a similar point.

16. Other prominent privacy scholars such as Colin Bennett (1992, 202) have made the case for treating privacy as a public good on the grounds of how difficult it is for individuals to establish desired levels on their own.

Chapter 5

1. Contemporary analyses revealing complexity in the dichotomy include Stanley J. Benn and Gerald F. Gaus's (1983) argument that although concepts of private and public serve to organize norms of access, agency, and interest, the dichotomy is not as clear and consistent as some would have us believe. It is possible for a space to be conceived as both private and public; for example, a living room in a house is private in relation to the outside world, but public in relation to the bedrooms. A similar point is captured with Susan Gal's (2002) intriguing conception of the private/public dichotomy as fractal.

2. The outrage over the Bush administration's authorization of National Security Agency surveillance of private citizens, including wiretaps and monitoring Internet use, reflects this. See Lichtblau and Risen (2005), Taipale (2006), Wong (2006), and Kerr (2008).

3. I refer very generally to core political works that have shaped contemporary, liberal democracies. See, e.g., Thomas Hobbes, *Leviathan* ([1660] 1981); John Locke, *The Second Treatise of Civil Government* ([1690] 1986); John Stuart Mill, *On Liberty* ([1859] 1978); Jean-Jacques Rousseau, *The Social Contract* ([1762] 1968).

4. U.S. Constitution, amendments I–X.

5. For discussions of the trend toward increasing reliance on computerized record-keeping systems by government and other agencies, see Rule (1973); Flaherty (1979); Burnham (1983); Kusserow (1983); Rule, McAdam, Stearns, and Uglow (1983); Laudon (1986); Marx (1988); Bennett (1992); and Regan (1995).

6. 5 U.S. Code, sec. 552a.

7. See Berman and Goldman (1989) and Regan (1995, 77–85).

8. See e.g., Computer Matching and Privacy Protection Act (CMPPA) (1988); Right to Financial Privacy Act (1978); Electronic Communications Privacy Act (1986) (codified in scattered section of 18 U.S.C.). Readers interested in a complete account of the complex system of privacy laws should refer to the second edition of Solove and Rotenberg's 2003 work *Information Privacy Law* and *The Privacy Law Sourcebook 2004*, edited by Marc Rotenberg (2004).

9. Orwell (1949).

10. For example, recall the popularity of Arthur Koestler's *Darkness at Noon* (1941) and the Broadway stage adaptation by Sidney Kingsley (1951). In popular culture, for example, consider the success of Bob Dylan's song "Subterranean Homesick Blues" (critical of overzealous government); Janis Joplin's backup band Big Brother and the Holding Company; Crosby, Stills, Nash, and Young's song "Ohio" (regarding the Kent State massacre—"tin soldiers and Nixon coming"); and Francis Ford Coppola's movie *The Conversation* (1974). In the news media see, for example, Field (1987). In scholarly literature see, for example, Shattuck (1984). See also Regan (1995, 81), who provides references to Big Brother rhetoric that peppered floor debates over privacy policy in both chambers of Congress.

11. There is no doubt that security worries following the September 11, 2001, attacks have lessened the dominance of public resistance to overly intrusive government agencies in lives of individuals, as seen in general willingness to accept legislation like the USA PATRIOT Act 2001, Pub. L. No. 107-56, 115 Stat. 272.

12. Although the report itself is now dated and has been eclipsed by many subsequent reports of the public and private sectors, the code's five principles remain at the core of much that has followed. For example, see the Organization for Economic Cooperation and Development Guidelines on the Protection of Privacy and Transborder Flows of Personal Data (1980) and the European Union Directive 95/46/EC on the Protection of Individuals with Regard to the Processing of Personal Data and on the Free Movement of Such Data (European Parliament and Council of the European Union 1995).

13. See generally Turkington and Allen (2002) for a discussion that specifically focuses on information and information technology; LaFave (1996) for a general discussion of Fourth Amendment cases; Solove and Rotenberg (2003) for a discussion on

information and information technology; and Kerr (2009) for a discussion about the limits of Fourth Amendment injunctions with regard to information technology.

14. See DeCew (1997) for an excellent discussion. Also, as Tal Zarsky has pointed out in private correspondence (December 23, 2006), in the landmark case Katz v. United States (1967) the Supreme Court emphasized that Fourth Amendment protection is not limited to a particular private space, such as the home, but also to private zones, such as private telephone conversations.

15. This case will be discussed in greater detail in Chapter 7.

16. Such is the case in South Africa where, each year, high school matriculation results are published in local newspapers; in the United Kingdom, local newspapers publish students' names and the subjects they passed.

17. For a comprehensive overview of this area of law and news media, see the Workplace Privacy Web page of the Electronic Privacy Information Center (2007b). See also Introna (2000) and Weckert (2004).

18. Cohen provides a more pessimistic interpretation—that the increased presence of thermal imaging and similar technologies of surveillance augurs the collapse of a protected private sphere.

19. The FBI developed the Carnivore software, which is now typically called DCS 1000. See the FBI's *Carnivore / DCS 1000 Report to Congress* (2003) and the Electronic Privacy Information Center's page on Carnivore (2005).

Chapter 6

1. For a brilliantly insightful discussion of philosophical and psychological reasons to question whether individuals accepting typical offers of goods and services for personal information are truly free, see Barrigar, Burkell, and Kerr (2006).

2. This phenomenon has been well discussed by Anita Allen-Castellitto in "Coercing Privacy," in which she suggests that liberal governments might need to take steps to coerce privacy: "In the near future, liberal government may have to proscribe and regulate disclosures and publications precisely in the interest of preventing cumulatively harmful diminutions of the taste for the expectation of privacy" (1999, 755).

3. One's income or salary, religious affiliation, alcohol consumption, and school performance are a few examples of information freely discussed in some societies but considered off-limits in others.

4. In an interesting variation, Jonathan Grudin has hypothesized that "Privacy is ultimately a psychological construct, with malleable ties to specific objective conditions," ties that are, on the whole, strategic (2001, 279).

5. Unlike many privacy skeptics, however, her solution is not to give way to these trends but to counter them by educational means or even, where necessary, coercive protective measures.

6. See Westin (2003). Westin reviews data from 1978, 1984, and "more than 120 surveys" from 1990 to 2002 showing the degree of concern over privacy in a variety of

contexts, particularly high acceptance of government surveillance of public places, and even traditionally unpopular initiatives such as national identity cards and monitoring of online postings and phone conversations. Support for the latter, however, had dropped considerably by 2002 (p. 448). See also Radin, Chander, and Gellman (2007).

7. Readers interested in the details of Volokh's legal arguments should consult his articles (2000a, 2000b). They will also benefit from a particularly good critique by legal scholar Paul M. Schwartz (2000).

8. The broader debates have been discussed in such works as Yochai Benkler's *The Wealth of Networks* (2006), Jessica Litman's *Digital Copyright: Protecting Intellectual Property on the Internet* (2001), and many others.

9. Richard Posner has been one of the central proponents of this position, invoking his trademark economic cost-benefit style of argument to demonstrate that although strong privacy protections benefit individuals, they are likely to bring about greater harm, overall, because they give cover to deceitful, self-serving practices (1978a, 1978b).

10. For example, see Pepper (1958), Nagel (1979), Richardson (1990), Bentham (1995), and Berlin (1969).

11. Gellman, Chander, and Radin (2007) incorporates many arguments showing the potential compatibilities between privacy and security.

12. Let us assume, for argument's sake, a control definition of privacy.

13. For a more detailed discussion of this case, see Regan (1995, 103) and Barber (2006).

14. See Gurak (1997). Concern and protest have also erupted around online advertising companies like DoubleClick, which monitor online Web-surfing behaviors of millions of users and create profiles by merging online use with other available information about these users. See the Web site of the Electronic Privacy Information Center for a full account of this case at http://www.epic.org. See also Nissenbaum (1998).

15. Some surveys exist (Electronic Privacy Information Center 2007a) as does at least one study—see Olson, Grudin, and Horvitz (2004).

16. The problem is not that of fuzzy borders but of ambiguity—of significantly different meanings of competing conceptions.

17. This use of the term *personal information* here clearly diverges from the generic use adopted in this book where personal information is taken to mean any information about a personally identifiable individual.

Chapter 7

1. I owe thanks to my colleague Rodney Benson for his expert guidance in this area.

2. Relationships and power structures have garnered much of the attention of critical theory and, of course, Bourdieu's field theory.

3. Social theories identified as "functionalist" attribute great, if not paramount, importance to this dimension of social structures, their function, or functions.

4. Thanks to an anonymous reviewer for pointing this example out.

5. There surely are norms of information flow affecting information generally, but here we limit attention to information about persons because we are interested in resolving questions about privacy.

6. I will not be considering the case of group privacy, although others have advocated for such rights. See, for example, Gandy (2000).

7. People's judgments that a privacy violation has occurred are so dependent on the type of information in question that earlier accounts of contextual integrity had posited distinct norms of appropriateness, distinct from norms of transmission. Later efforts to formalize contextual integrity revealed, however, that at a certain level of generality both are simply elements of informational norms (Barth et al. 2006).

8. Automation requiring finite taxonomies is a step away from formalizations of contextual integrity developed in Barth et al. (2006).

9. We may wonder how it would affect a friendship if one party discovers a friend has engaged the help of the much advertised snoop programs that promise the ability to track e-mail correspondence.

10. See the Public Welfare and Human Services Code of Federal Regulations (2003). For a general discussion of the privacy regulations implemented pursuant to the Health Insurance Portability and Accountability Act of 1996 (HIPAA, 1996), see the Health Privacy Project Web site at http://www.healthprivacy.org.

11. In constructing the details of this account, I referred extensively to the Eagleton Digital Archive of American Politics at The Eagleton Institute of Politics at Rutgers, the State University of New Jersey (Eagleton Institute of Politics, 2004).

12. I owe thanks to Lisa Austin for drawing my attention to this case.

Chapter 8

1. Barth et al. (2006) show how contextual integrity may be useful even in its descriptive capacity as it provides the basis for rigorous expression of complex privacy policies.

2. My thanks go to Jeremy Waldron for drawing my attention to these sections of Bentham's work.

3. I am indebted to Jeroen van den Hoven for drawing my attention to the relevance of Walzer's efforts to my own. I have also benefited from conversation with Walzer himself during my stints at the Institute for Advanced Study, Princeton, first as a member and later as a visitor.

4. It is instructive to note that many universities assert the independence of admissions criteria from financial aid, going to great lengths to separate the processes of the two applications, claiming admissions are based on talent, and aid based on need.

5. Under a radically different account of sources and spread of disease, such as the account given by Adam Ashforth (2004) of beliefs in South Africa regarding the role of witchery in the spread of disease, informational norms of healthcare context might be yet different as the culture attributed different social meaning to disease.

6. A delightful article by Katherine Strandburg details instances where norms deny people the freedom to share information, for example, judging it rude to reveal the intricate details of one's latest surgical procedure, particularly over the dinner table (2005).

7. One can extend this line of reasoning to many other contexts where the need for group deliberation and decision making gives rise to a wide variety in open versus closed (secret) ballot conventions.

8. See especially chapter 6 in *Law's Empire* (Dworkin 1986).

9. My use of the term *integrity* is entirely coincidental, though for the purpose it serves, clearly makes sense.

Chapter 9

1. I am grateful to Emily Smith for drawing my attention to this result in her presentation at the Hixon Riggs Forum on Science and Society, "Experiencing Surveillance in the Airport: The Globalization of Personal Data Survey and Traveler Perspectives on Visibility" (2008).

2. Because I am not certain whether similar codes bind librarians in other countries, I intend these remarks to cover the United States alone, also setting aside controversial mandates of the USA PATRIOT Act.

3. For the purposes of this exercise, we must assume that there is no law detailing the precise conditions—warrants, subpoenas, etc.—under which search companies are obligated to hand over logs to government actors. Further, we do not consider the contribution of what might or might not be stated in a privacy policy.

4. I refer here to the actual case, discussed in Chapter 1, that placed Web search privacy on the public agenda.

5. In the case discussed in Chapter 1, this was among the reasons explicitly cited by Google in their resistance to the Department of Justice subpoena.

6. A more complete argument for restricting the flow of information about users' Web search activity has been developed in Howe and Nissenbaum (2009).

7. It is interesting to note, in an article about location tracking of paroled offenders, a similar connection drawn between privacy and heterogeneous accountabilities to exchange information undergirding social participation: "The issue is not where one might be, and when; it is to whom one might be accountable for one's presence, to whom under what circumstances, and how one might be called to account" (Troshynski, Lee, and Dourish 2008, 7).

8. The Video Privacy Protection Act of 1988 suggests similar concerns in related arenas, namely, records of video rentals. For example, see Kerr and Bailey (2004) and Kerr (2005).

9. It turns out that "reasonable expectation of privacy" is in many instances a decent proxy for contextual integrity, except that the latter provides a finer grain account of the nature of the expectation and why it is reasonable, a discussion I continue in the Conclusion of the book.

10. We will not say much about proponents of a practice who are content to defend it in light of its service to special interests they represent.

11. In itself, this lack of transparency is a serious concern. Furthermore, for fear of negative publicity, and somewhat ironically, companies like ChoicePoint carefully control information about themselves in an effort to shape their public image.

12. For example, ChoicePoint's acquisitions include the National Safety Alliance (drug-testing), Informus Corporation (pre-employment screening), i2 (visual and link analysis), Optimal Decisions Group (insurance information), and USCerts (birth, death, marriage, and divorce certificates). See ChoicePoint (2007).

13. Recall van den Hoven's (2001) account of informational inequality.

14. This practice is known as customer relationships management.

15. In 2007, the offices of the Pennsylvania Public Welfare Department were burglarized and computers with more than 300,000 mental health histories were stolen; similarly, a Kaiser Permanente employee's car was broken into and a laptop containing medical information of 39,000 individuals was stolen (Privacy Rights Clearinghouse 2007a).

16. Bank of America lost backup tapes containing the personal information of 1.2 million federal employees, while CitiFinancial lost a backup tape with the information of 3.9 million people (Jones 2006).

17. ChoicePoint sold 145,000 dossiers to a group of criminals engaged in identity theft (Mayer 2005).

18. The sensitivity of such assemblages, containing far fewer fields of information, is recognized in the stringent measure adopted by Title 13 of the U.S. Code governing protocols related to Census data.

19. Other social scientists have written about morally problematic uses of profiling as a means of social sorting, including Gary Marx (1988).

20. See for example, http://epic.org/privacy/fusion for documents, news reports, and policy recommendations pertaining to "fusion centers" (Electronic Privacy Information Center 2008).

21. During the time of writing, starting with Manhattan, Google has gradually implemented a shift in practice, now blurring identifiable faces in its Street View.

22. Not all images, however, are open to negotiation. A Pennsylvania family, upon noticing photos of its suburban home on Street View, sued Google for invasion of privacy. Google removed the images but argued that the family "live in a residential community in the twenty-first-century United States, where every step upon private property is not deemed by law to be an actionable trespass" and that, furthermore, "Today's satellite-image technology means that even in today's desert, complete privacy does not exist. In any event, Plaintiffs live far from the desert and are far from hermits." Google also stated that the family should have requested removal rather than sue the company (Smoking Gun 2008).

23. Eventually the link was located; from Google Maps, find an area with Street View, and click on "Street View Help" in the pop-up overlay. This provides a link that says "report inappropriate image," which directs to the "Report Inappropriate Street View" page.

24. The two are conflated in Court deliberations in the case of Doe v. Poritz (1995).

25. For a full discussion, see Barber (2006).

26. I am aware that the exercise of matching records to contexts is itself a normative exercise and may not be straightforward.

27. For more detailed information, see the full text of the Drivers Privacy Protection Act (1994) at http://www.accessreports.com/statutes/DPPA1.htm and http://www.law.cornell.edu/uscode/18/2721.html.

28. This notion would be instantly dispelled were they to attempt unbidden entry into one of these youth's bedrooms, or to rifle through their belongings.

29. However, critics maintain that the data is still collected by Facebook even if it is not shared with friends. A class-action lawsuit has been filed against video retailer Blockbuster for its participation in Beacon, with the argument that it violates the Video Privacy Protection Act (Davis 2008).

30. I have drawn on boyd and Ellison (2007) for this discussion.

31. See Naone (2008) and Zimmer (2008c, 2008d) for a discussion of Moli.

Conclusion

1. For example, the new South African Constitution.

References

Acquisti, A., and Grossklags, J. 2006. Privacy and Rationality. In *Privacy and Technologies of Identity: A Cross-Disciplinary Conversation*, ed. K. Strandburg and D. S. Raicu. New York: Springer, 15–29.

Acxiom Corporation. 2006. At Acxiom, Our Mission Is to Protect America. *Acxiom Insight*. Accessed September 14, 2006 from http://www.acxiominsight.com/.

Acxiom Corporation. 2007a. InfoBase. *Acxiom: We Make Information Intelligent*. Accessed June 22, 2007 from http://www.acxiom.com/default.aspx?ID=1756& Country_Code=USA.

Acxiom Corporation. 2007b. Personicx. *Acxiom: We Make Information Intelligent*. Accessed June 22, 2007 from http://www.acxiom.com/default.aspx?ID=1766& DisplayID=18.

Acxiom Panel Unanimously Favored Buyout. 2007. Associated Press, June 11. Accessed June 22, 2007 from http://www.forbes.com/feeds/ap/2007/06/11/ap3810278.html.

Ahwazi, A. (n.d.). Advice to a Physician, Advice of Haly Abbas (Ahwazi) [Tenth Century AD]. In *Encyclopedia of Bioethics*, rev. ed., vol. 5, ed. W. T. Reich. New York: Simon & Schuster Macmillan, 1995.

Allen, A. 1998. *Uneasy Access*. Totowa, NJ: Rowman & Littlefield.

Allen, J. 2001. "Ed" of Internet: JenniCAM Going Strong After Three Years. *CNN.com*. Accessed June 23, 2006 from http://www.cnn.com/SHOWBIZ/Movies/9903/26/jennicam/.

Allen-Castellitto, A. 1999. Coercing Privacy. *William and Mary Law Review* 40: 723–757.

Allen-Castellitto, A. 2000. Privacy Versus the Public's Right to Know. In *The Encyclopedia of Ethical Issues in Politics and the Media*, ed. R. Chadwick. San Diego: Academic Press, 251–262.

Aristotle, Inc. 2007. *Aristotle.com*. Accessed February 19, 2007 from http://www .aristotle.com.

Ashforth, A. 2004. *Witchcraft, Violence, and Democracy in South Africa*. Chicago: University of Chicago Press.

Associated Press. 2006. Texas Police Officer Suspended over Graphic MySpace Page Showing Dismembered Bodies. *Boston Herald*, October 13. Accessed October 24, 2006 from http://news.bostonherald.com/national/view.bg?articleid=162149.

Austin, L. 2007. Privacy and Private Law: The Dilemma of Justification. Paper presented at the Colloquium in Legal and Social Philosophy, New York University School of Law, New York, October 18.

Ballard, M. 2006. UK Car Tracking Database Delayed to Boost Capacity. *The Register*, April 18. Accessed August 19, 2008 from http://www.theregister.co.uk/2006/04/18/ anpr_delayed/.

Barber, G. 2006. Personal Information in Government Records: Protecting the Public Interest in Privacy. *St. Louis University Public Law Review* 25: 63–122.

Barlow, J. P. 1994. The Economy of Ideas. *Wired* 2(3): 84.

Barnes, S. 2006. A Privacy Paradox: Social Networking in the United States. *First Monday* 11(9). Accessed May 31, 2009 from http://firstmonday.org/htbin/cgiwrap/ bin/ojs/index.php/fm/article/viewArticle/1394.

Barrigar, J., Burkell, J., and Kerr, I. 2006. Let's Not Get Psyched Out of Privacy: Reflections on Withdrawing Consent to the Collection, Use and Disclosure of Personal Information. *Canadian Business Law Journal* 44: 54.

Barry, D. 1996. *Dave Barry in Cyberspace*. New York: Fawcett Columbine.

Barth, A., Datta, A., Mitchell, J., and Nissenbaum, H. 2006. Privacy and Contextual Integrity: Framework and Applications. In *Proceedings of the 2006 IEEE Symposium on Security and Privacy* (S&P'06). Berkeley, CA: IEEE Computer Society, 184–198.

Benkler, Y. 2006. *The Wealth of Networks: How Social Production Transforms Markets and Freedom*. New Haven, CT: Yale University Press.

Benn, S. 1971. Privacy, Freedom and Respect for Persons. In *Privacy*, ed. J. R. Pennock and J. W. Chapman. New York: Atherton Press, 1–27. Reprinted in *Philosophical Dimensions of Privacy: An Anthology*, ed. F. Schoeman. Cambridge: Cambridge University Press, 1984, 223–244.

Benn, S., and Gaus, G. F. 1983. *Public and Private in Social Life*. London: St. Martin's Press.

Bennett, C. J. 1992. *Regulating Privacy: Data Protection and Public Policy in Europe and the United States*. Ithaca, NY: Cornell University Press.

Bentham, J. 1843. Principles of the Civil Code. In *The Works of Jeremy Bentham*, vol. 1, ed. J. Bowring. London: Simpkin, Marshall, & Co. Reprint, New York: Russell & Russell, 1962.

Bentham, J. 1995. *The Panopticon Writings*. M. Bozovic, ed. London: Verso

Berlin, I. 1969. Two Concepts of Liberty. In *Four Essays on Liberty*, 118–172. Oxford: Oxford University Press.

Berman, J., and Goldman, J. 1989. *A Federal Right of Informational Privacy: The Need for Reform.* Washington, DC: The Benton Foundation.

Bicchieri, C. 2000. Words and Deeds: A Focus Theory of Norms. In *Rationality, Rules, and Structure,* ed. J. Nida-Romelin and W. Spohn. Norwell, MA: Kluwer Academic Publishers, 153–184.

Birnhack, M. D., and Elkin-Koren, N. 2003. The Invisible Handshake: The Reemergence of the State in the Digital Environment. *Virginia Journal of Law & Technology* 6: 1–57.

Bodell, P. 2007. Exploring the Realities of Megapixel Surveillance Technology. *Security InfoWatch.com,* February 22. Accessed March 1, 2007 from http://www.security infowatch.com/article/article.jsp?siteSection=430&id=10557.

Bourdieu, P. 1984. *Distinction: A Social Critique of the Judgement of Taste.* Richard Nice, trans. Cambridge, MA: Harvard University Press.

boyd, d. m. 2006. Facebook's "Privacy Trainwreck": Exposure, Invasion, and Drama. *Apophenia Blog,* September 8. Accessed July 17, 2007 from http://www.danah.org/papers/FacebookAndPrivacy.html.

boyd, d. m., and Ellison, N. B. 2007. Social Network Sites: Definition, History, and Scholarship. *Journal of Computer-Mediated Communication* 13(1), article 11. Accessed January 22, 2008 from http://jcmc.indiana.edu/vol13/issue1/boyd.ellison.html.

Bray, H. 2006. Google Faces Order to Give Up Records. *Boston Globe,* March 15, E1.

Brin, D. 1998. Privacy Under Siege. In *The Transparent Society.* New York: Perseus Books, 3–26.

Bull, B. 2006. Commentary on H. Nissenbaum's "Privacy and Information Technology: The Trouble with the Public/Private Dichotomy." Paper presented at *Privacy in Public: Ethics, Privacy and the Technology of Public Surveillance Workshop,* Poynter Center for the Study of Ethics and American Institutions. Indiana University, Bloomington, IN, October 26.

Burke, E. 1790. *Reflections on the Revolution in France.* In *The Portable Edmund Burke,* ed. I. Kramnick. London: Penguin Books, 1999, 416–473.

Burke, E. 1791. *An Appeal from the New to the Old Whigs.* In *The Portable Edmund Burke,* ed. I. Kramnick. London: Penguin Books, 1999, 474–498.

Burnham, D. 1983. *The Rise of the Computer State.* New York: Random House.

Bygrave, L. A. 2002. *Data Protection Law: Approaching Its Rationale, Logic and Limits.* London: Kluwer Law International.

California v. Greenwood. 1998. 486 U.S. 35.

Cassidy, J. 2006. Me Media. *The New Yorker,* May 15, 50–59.

Center for Democracy and Technology. 2000. Comments of the Center for Democracy and Technology on the Study of Privacy Issues in Bankruptcy Data, September 22. *CDT.org.* Accessed July 12, 2007 from http://www.cdt.org/privacy/financial/000922ftc.shtml.

Center for Democracy and Technology. 2002. A Quiet Revolution in the Courts: Electronic Access to State Court Records. A CDT Survey of State Activity and

Comments on Privacy, Cost, Equity and Accountability. *Center for Democracy and Technology*, August. Accessed September 17, 2006 from http://www.cdt.org/publications/020821courtrecords.shtml.

ChoicePoint. 2006a. AutoTrackXP. *ChoicePoint.com*. Accessed September 17, 2006 from http://www.choicepoint.com/industry/government/public_le_1.html.

ChoicePoint. 2006b. ChoicePoint Authentication Solutions. *ChoicePoint.com*. Accessed September 16, 2006 from http://www.choicepoint.com/authentication/products.html.

ChoicePoint. 2006c. ChoicePoint Precision Marketing. *ChoicePoint.com*. Accessed September 15, 2006 from http://www.choicepoint.com/business/direct/direct.html.

ChoicePoint. 2007. News Releases: Acquisitions. *ChoicePoint.com*. Accessed August 8, 2008 from http://phx.corporate-ir.net/phoenix.zhtml?c=95293&p=irol-news acquisitions.

Clarke, R. 1988. Information Technology and Dataveillance. *Communications of the ACM* 31(5): 498–512.

Cohen, J. 1996. A Right to Read Anonymously: A Closer Look at "Copyright Management" in Cyberspace. *Connecticut Law Review* 28(3): 981–1058.

Cohen, J. 2000. Examined Lives: Informational Privacy and the Subject as Object. *Stanford Law Review* 52: 1373–1437.

Cohen, J. 2003. DRM and Privacy. *Communications of the ACM* 46(4): 47–49.

Committee on Maintaining Privacy and Security in Health Care Applications of the National Information Infrastructure. 1997. *For the Record: Protecting Electronic Health Information*. Commission on Physical Sciences, Mathematics, and Applications, National Research Council. Washington, DC: National Academies Press.

Computer Matching and Privacy Protection Act of 1988 (CMPPA). 1988. Title 5 United States Code, sec. 552a.

Connecticut Attorney General's Office. 2006. Press Release: Attorney General Investigating MySpace.com for Allowing Minors Easy Access to Pornography, Inappropriate Material. February 2. Accessed March 18, 2006 from http://www.ct.gov/ag/cwp/view.asp?Q=309712&A=2426.

Consumers Against Supermarket Privacy Invasion and Numbering, et al. 2003. *RFID Position Statement of Consumer Privacy and Civil Liberties Organizations*. November 14. Accessed May 6, 2008 from http://www.privacyrights.org/ar/RFID position.htm.

Cranor, L. F. 2003. "I Didn't Buy It for Myself": Privacy and Ecommerce Personalization. In *Proceedings of the 2nd ACM Workshop on Privacy in the Electronic Society*, Washington, DC, October 30. Accessed September 9, 2006 from http://lorrie.cranor.org/pubs/wpes03.html.

Cranor, L. F., Tsai, J., Egelman, S., and Acquisti, A. 2007. The Effect of Online Privacy Information on Purchasing Behavior: An Experimental Study. Paper presented at the Workshop on the Economics of Information Security, Pittsburgh, PA, June 7–8.

Curry, M. R. 2002. Discursive Displacement and the Seminal Ambiguity of Space and Place. In *The Handbook of New Media: Social Shaping and Consequences of ICT*, ed. L. Lievrouw and S. Livingstone. London: Sage Publications, 502–517.

Curry, M. R., Phillips, D. J., and Regan, P. M. 2004. Emergency Response Systems and the Creeping Legibility of People and Places. *The Information Society* 20: 357–369.

Dallaire, G., Shattuck, J., and Kusserow, R. 1984. Computer Matching: Should It Be Banned? *Communications of the Association of Computing Machinery* 27(6): 537–545.

Davis, W. 2008. Blockbuster Sued for Participating in Facebook's Beacon Program. *Online Media Daily*, April 17. Accessed August 9, 2008 from http://www.media post.com/publications/index.cfm?fuseaction=Articles.showArticleHomePage& art_aid=80839.

DeCew, J. 1997. *In Pursuit of Privacy: Law, Ethics, and the Rise of Technology*. Ithaca, NY: Cornell University Press.

Department of Transportation (DOT) and National Highway Traffic Safety Administration (NHTSA). 2004. Notice of Proposed Rulemaking: Event Data Recorders. 49 CFR Part 563, June 9. [Docket No. NHTSA-2004-18029] RIN 2127-AI72. Accessed May 30, 2007 from http://www.nhtsa.dot.gov/cars/rules/rulings/EDRN PRM4–June1/part2.html#A.

Department of Transportation (DOT) and National Highway Traffic Safety Administration (NHTSA). 2007. Event Data Recorders. 49 CFR Part 563, August 2006. [Docket No. NHTSA-2006-25666] RIN 2127-AI72. Accessed July 28, 2008 from http://www.nhtsa.dot.gov/staticfiles/DOT/NHTSA/Rulemaking/Rules/Associated %20Files/EDRFinalRule_Aug2006.pdf.

Direct Marketing Association. 1999. Frequently Asked Questions from Consumers. *DMA Consumers*. Accessed May 6, 2008 from http://www.dmachoice.org/con sumerfaqs.php.

Doe v. Poritz. 1995. 142 N.J. 1, 662 A.2d 367.

Dourish, P., and Anderson, K. 2006. Collective Information Practice: Exploring Privacy and Security as Social and Cultural Phenomena. *Human-Computer Interaction* 21: 319–342.

Drivers Privacy Protection Act (DPPA). 1994. Public Law No. 103-322, codified as amended by Public Law 106-69. Accessed May 6, 2008 from http://www.accessre ports.com/statutes/DPPA1.htm and http://www.law.cornell.edu/uscode/18/2721 .html.

Duong, B. Y. 2005. *Blind Spots: The Social and Cultural Dimensions of Video Surveillance*. PhD diss., New York University.

Dwork, C. 2006. Differential Privacy. *International Colloquium on Automata, Languages and Programming* (Part 2): 1–12.

Dwork, C., McSherry, F., Nissim, K., and Smith, A. 2006. Calibrating Noise to Sensitivity in Private Data Analysis. In *Proceedings of the Theory of Cryptography Conference*. New York: Springer-Verlag, 265–284.

Dworkin, R. 1986. *Law's Empire*. Cambridge, MA: Harvard University Press.

Dworkin, G. 1988. *The Theory and Practice of Autonomy.* Cambridge, MA: Belknap Press of Harvard University Press.

Eagleton Institute of Politics. 2004. Clinton Impeachment. *Eagleton Digital Archive of American Politics.* Eagleton Institute of Politics, Rutgers, the State University of New Jersey. Accessed July 8, 2005 from http://www.eagleton.rutgers.edu/e-gov/e-politicalarchive-Clintonimpeach.htm.

Edwards, L., and Brown, I. 2009. Data Control and Social Networking: Irreconcilable Ideas? In *Harboring Data: Information Security, Law and the Corporation,* ed. A. Matwyshyn. Palo Alto, CA: Stanford University Press.

Electronic Communications Privacy Act of 1986. 1986. Title 18 United States Code, sec. 2510.

Electronic Privacy Information Center (EPIC). 2002. The Video Privacy Protection Act (VPPA). *EPIC.org,* August 6. Accessed July 18, 2007 from http://www.epic.org/privacy/vppa/.

Electronic Privacy Information Center (EPIC). 2003. RFID PR Revealed; Wal-Mart Cancels Major RFID Effort. *EPIC Alert* 10(5), July 22. Accessed July 18, 2007 from http://www.epic.org/alert/EPIC_Alert_10.15.html.

Electronic Privacy Information Center (EPIC). 2004a. Privacy and Consumer Profiling. *EPIC.org,* October 13. Accessed July 18, 2007 from http://www.epic.org/privacy/profiling/default.html.

Electronic Privacy Information Center (EPIC). 2004b. *EPIC.org.* Accessed January 17, 2004 from http://www.epic.org/.

Electronic Privacy Information Center (EPIC). 2005. Carnivore. *EPIC.org,* January 19. Accessed July 18, 2007 from http://www.epic.org/privacy/carnivore/default.html.

Electronic Privacy Information Center (EPIC). 2007a. Public Opinion on Privacy. *EPIC.org,* April 27. Accessed July 18, 2007 from http://www.epic.org/privacy/survey/default.html.

Electronic Privacy Information Center (EPIC). 2007b. Workplace Privacy. *EPIC.org,* May 17. Accessed July 18, 2007 from http://www.epic.org/privacy/workplace/default.html.

Electronic Privacy Information Center (EPIC). 2008. Information Fusion Centers and Privacy. *EPIC.org,* April 18. Accessed July 18, 2007 from http://epic.org/privacy/fusion/.

Electronic Privacy Information Center (EPIC) and Junkbusters.org. 2000. Pretty Poor Privacy: An Assessment of P3P and Internet Privacy. *EPIC.org,* June. Accessed July 18, 2007 from http://www.epic.org/reports/prettypoorprivacy.html.

Ellis-Smith, D. 1980. *Privacy: How to Protect What's Left of It.* New York: Anchor Books/Doubleday.

Estrin, D. 2007. Reflections on Wireless Sensing Systems: From Ecosystems to Human Systems. Paper presented at IEEE Radio and Wireless Symposium, Long Beach, CA, January 9–11.

European Parliament and Council of the European Union. 1995. Directive 95/46/EC of the European Parliament and of the Council of 24 October 1995 on the Protection of Individuals with Regard to the Processing of Personal Data and on the Free Movement of Such Data. *Official Journal of the European Communities*, November 23, L. 281, 31-0050. Accessed July 31, 2008 from http://eur-lex.europa.eu/LexUriServ/LexUriServ.do?uri=CELEX:31995L0046:EN:NOT.

Evans-Pugh, C. 2006. RO4D W4TCH. *Engineering and Technology* 1(4): 36–39.

Fair Credit Reporting Act (FCRA). 1992. Title 15 U.S. Code, sec. 1681.

The Family Educational Rights and Privacy Act (FERPA). 1974. Title 20 United States Code, sec. 1232g; Title 34 Code of Federal Regulations Pt. 99.

Farmer, D., and Mann, C. 2003. Surveillance Nation. *Technology Review* (April): 46–53.

Federal Bureau of Investigation. 2003. *Carnivore / DCS 1000 Report to Congress.* Submitted to the Judiciary Committees of the House of Representatives and the United States Senate, February 24. Accessed July 18, 2007 from http://www.epic.org/privacy/carnivore/2002_report.pdf.

Federal Financial Modernization Act or Gramm-Leach-Bliley Financial Services Modernization Act (GLB). 1999. Pub. L. No. 106-102, 113 Stat. 1338.

Federal Trade Commission. 2000. FTC Final Rule, Privacy of Consumer Information, 65 Fed. Reg. 33, 646, 33, 658.

Federal Trade Commission. 2006. ChoicePoint Settles Data Security Breach Charges; To Pay $10 Million in Civil Penalties, $5 Million for Consumer Redress. Press Release, January 26. Accessed September 18, 2006 from http://www.ftc.gov/opa/2006/01/choicepoint.htm.

Field, A. 1987. Big Brother Inc. May Be Closer Than You Thought. *Business Week,* February 9, 84.

Finder, A. 2006. When a Risqué Online Persona Undermines a Chance for a Job. *New York Times*, June 11, A1.

First Advantage Corporation. 2004. About Us. *First Advantage Corporation.* Accessed September 14, 2006 from http://www.fadv.com/hirecheck/about_us/about_us.html.

Flaherty, D. 1979. *Privacy and Government Data Banks: An International Perspective.* London: Mansell Publishing.

Florida v. Riley. 1989. 488 U.S. 445, 447, 452.

Foucault, M. 1995. *Discipline & Punish: The Birth of the Prison.* New York: Vintage Books.

Fox, S., Rainie, L., Horrigan, J., Lenhart, A., Spooner, T., and Carter, C. 2000. *Trust and Privacy Online: Why Americans Want to Rewrite the Rules.* The Pew Internet and American Life Project, Washington, DC, August 20. Accessed May 8, 2005 from http://www.pewinternet.org/pdfs/PIP_Trust_Privacy_Report.pdf.

Freedom of Information Act. 1966. 5 U.S. Code, sec. 552.

Fried, C. 1968. Privacy: A Moral Analysis. *Yale Law Journal* 77(1): 475–493.

Friedrichs, C. 1971. Secrecy Versus Privacy: The Democratic Dilemma. In *Privacy,* ed. J. R. Pennock and J. W. Chapman. New York: Atherton Press, 105–120.

Froomkin, A. M. 2000. The Death of Privacy? *Stanford Law Review* 52: 1461–1543, http://personal.law.miami.edu/~froomkin/articles/privacy-deathof.pdf.

Froomkin, A. M. 2003. Anonymity in the Balance. In *Digital Anonymity: Tensions and Dimensions*, ed. C. Nicoll, J. E. J. Prins, and M. J. M. van Dellen. The Hague: Asser Press, 4–45.

Furlong, A. 2003. The Questionable Contribution of Psychotherapeutic and Psychoanalytic Records to the Truth-Seeking Process. In *Confidential Relationships: Psychoanalytic, Ethical, and Legal Contexts*, ed. C. M. Koggel, A. Furlong, and C. Levin. Amsterdam: Rodopi, 13–30.

Gal, S. 2002. A Semiotics of the Public/Private Distinction. *Differences: A Journal of Feminist Cultural Studies* 13(1): 77–95.

Gandy, O. 1993. *The Panoptic Sort: A Political Economy of Personal Information*. Boulder, CO: Westview Press.

Gandy, O. 1996. Coming to Terms with the Panoptic Sort. In *Computers, Surveillance, and Privacy*, ed. D. Lyon and E. Zureik. Minneapolis: University of Minnesota Press.

Gandy, O. 2000. Exploring Identity and Identification. *Notre Dame Journal of Law, Ethics & Public Policy* 14(2): 1085–1111.

Gandy, O. 2003. Public Opinion Surveys and the Formation of Privacy Policy. *Journal of Social Issues* 59(2): 283–299.

Garfinkel, S. 2000. *Database Nation*. Sebastopol, CA: O'Reilly Media.

Garfinkel, S. 2002a. An RFID Bill of Rights. *Technology Review* (October). http://www.simson.net/clips/2002/2002.TR.10.RFID_Bill_Of_Rights.htm.

Garfinkel, S. 2002b. Adopting Fair Information Practices to Low Cost RFID Systems. Paper presented at the Privacy in Ubicomp Workshop, Gotenborg, Sweden, September 29.

Garfinkel, S. 2004. RFID Rights. *Technology Review*, November 3. Accessed June 13, 2005 from http://www.technologyreview.com/articles/04/11/wo_garfinkel110304.asp.

Garfinkel, S., Juels, A., and Pappu, R. 2005. RFID Privacy: An Overview of Problems and Proposed Solutions. *IEEE Security and Privacy* 3(3): 34–43. http://www.simson.net/clips/academic/2005.IEEE.RFID.pdf.

Gavison, R. 1980. Privacy and the Limits of the Law. *Yale Law Journal* 89: 421–471. Reprinted in *Philosophical Dimensions of Privacy: An Anthology*, ed. F. D. Schoeman. Cambridge: Cambridge University Press, 1984, 346–402.

Gellman, R. 1995. Public Records: Access, Privacy, and Public Policy. *Center for Democracy and Technology*, May 16. Accessed June 13, 2005 from http://www.cdt.org/privacy/pubrecs/pubrec.html.

Gerety, T. 1997. Redefining Privacy. *Harvard Civil Rights–Civil Liberties Law Review* 12(2): 233–293.

Gerstein, R. 1984. Intimacy and Privacy. In *Philosophical Dimensions of Privacy: An Anthology*. Cambridge: Cambridge University Press, 265–271.

Goffman, E. 1959. *The Presentation of Self in Everyday Life*. New York: Doubleday.

Goldman, J. 1998. Protecting Privacy to Improve Health Care. *Health Care* (November/December): 47–60.

Gomez-Velez, N. M. 2005. Internet Access to Court Records—Balancing Public Access and Privacy. *Loyola Law Review* 51: 365.

Goodman, R. F., and Ben-Ze'ev, A., eds. 1994. *Good Gossip*. Lawrence: University Press of Kansas.

Google. 2007. *Google Maps Street View*. Accessed June 6, 2007 from http://maps .google.com/help/maps/streetview/index.html.

Gottlieb, C. 1996. Privacy: A Concept Whose Time Has Come and Gone. In *Computers, Surveillance, and Privacy*, ed. D. Lyon and E. Zureik. Minneapolis: University of Minnesota Press, 156–171.

Greenhouse, L. 2001. Justices Say Warrant Is Required in High-Tech Searches. *New York Times*, June 12.

Grimmelmann, J. 2008. Accidental Privacy Spills. *Journal of Internet Law* (July): 3–12. Accessed June 4, 2009 from http://works.bepress.com/james_grimmel mann/17.

Grudin, J. 2001. Desituating Action: Digital Representation of Context. *Human-Computer Interaction* 16(1): 269–286.

Gurak, L. 1997. *Persuasion and Privacy in Cyberspace: The Online Protests over Lotus Marketplace and the Clipper Chip*. New Haven, CT: Yale University Press.

Gutmann, A. 1987. *Democratic Education*. Princeton, NJ: Princeton University Press.

Hafner, K. 2006. U.S. Limits Demands on Google. *New York Times*, March 15. Accessed June 11, 2007 from http://www.nytimes.com/2006/03/15/technology/ 15google.html.

Hansell, S. 2006. AOL Removes Search Data on Group of Web Users. *New York Times*, August 8. Accessed June 11, 2007 from http://www.nytimes.com/2006/08/08/ business/media/08aol.html.

Hargittai, E., 2007. The Social, Political, Economic, and Cultural Dimensions of Search Engines: An Introduction. *Journal of Computer-Mediated Communication* 12(3). Accessed June 4, 2009 from http://jcmc.indiana.edu/vol12/issue3/hargittai .html.

Harris Interactive. 2003. Most People Are "Privacy Pragmatists" Who, While Concerned About Privacy, Will Sometimes Trade It Off for Other Benefits. *The Harris Poll #17*, March 19. Accessed August 15, 2005 from http://www.harrisinteractive .com/harris_poll/index.asp?PID=365.

Hart, H. L. A. 1961. *The Concept of Law*. 2nd ed. Reprint, Oxford: Oxford University Press, 1997.

Health Insurance Portability and Accountability Act of 1996. 1996. Title 42 U.S. Code, sec. 1320d–1320d-8; Public Law 104-191, 104th Congress.

Health Privacy Project. 2007. *Health Privacy Project*. Accessed June 20, 2008 from http://www.healthprivacy.org.

Heath, N. 2008. EC Plans Biometric Border Checks. *C|Net News.com*, February 15. Accessed July 28, 2008 from http://news.cnet.com/EC-plans-biometric-border -checks/2100-7348_3-6230775.html?tag=item.

Higg-A-Rella, Inc. v. County of Essex. 1995. 141 N.J. 35.

Hinman, L. 2005. Esse est indicato in Google: Ethical and Political Issues in Search Engines. *International Review of Information Ethics* 3: 19–25.

Hobbes, T. 1660. *Leviathan*. Reprint, ed. C. B. Macpherson, New York: Penguin Books, 1981.

Hoofnagle, C. J. 2004. Big Brother's Little Helpers: How ChoicePoint and Other Commercial Data Brokers Collect, Process, and Package Your Data for Law Enforcement. *University of North Carolina Journal of International Law & Commercial Regulation* 29: 595.

Hoofnagle, C. J. 2005. After the Breach: How Secure and Accurate Is Consumer Information Held by ChoicePoint and Other Data Aggregators? Testimony of Chris Jay Hoofnagle, Director, Electronic Privacy Information Center West Coast Office, Before California Senate Banking, Finance and Insurance Committee, Wednesday, March 30. Accessed June 22, 2007 from http://www.epic.org/privacy/choicepoint/casban3.30.05.html.

Hoven, J. 2004. Privacy and the Varieties of Informational Wrongdoing. In *Readings in Cyber Ethics*, 2nd ed., ed. R. A. Spinello and H. T. Tavani. Boston: Jones and Bartlett Publishers, 488–500.

Howe, D., and Nissenbaum, H. 2009. TrackMeNot: Resisting Surveillance in Web Search. In *On the Identity Trail: Privacy, Anonymity and Identity in a Networked Society*, ed. I. Kerr, C. Lucock, and V. Steeves. Oxford: Oxford University Press, 417–436.

Hunter, L. 1985. Public Image: Privacy in the Information Age. *Whole Earth Review* 44: 32–37. Reprinted in *Computers, Ethics, and Social Values*, ed. D. Johnson and H. Nissenbaum. Englewood Cliffs, NJ: Prentice Hall, 1995.

Individual Reference Services Group, Inc., v. Federal Trade Commission. 2001. No. 00-1828 (D.C. Circuit Court). Accessed July 17, 2005 from http://www.epic.org/privacy/consumer/IRSGvFTC.pdf.

Intel Corporation. 2007. Digital Home Technologies for Aging in Place. *Intel.com*. Accessed June 13, 2007 from http://www.intel.com/research/prohealth/dh_aging_in_place.htm.

Introna, L. 2000. Workplace Surveillance, Privacy and Distributive Justice. *Computers and Society* 30(4): 33–39.

Johnson, D. 2007. Privacy in Public? Technology, Privacy, and Democracy. Presentation for the Association for Practical and Professional Ethics, Poynter Center, Bloomington, IN, September 21.

Jones, C. 2006. Court Records: Online Courthouse. *Daily Business Review*, July 6. Accessed May 10, 2007 from http://www.dailybusinessreview.com/news.html?news_id=39419.

Jones, K. C. 2006. ChoicePoint's Far from Alone in Data Security Dungeon. *InformationWeek*, January 27. Accessed May 10, 2007 from http://www.informationweek.com/news/security/cybercrime/showArticle.jhtml?articleID=177104852.

Joyce, A. 2005. Free Expression Can Be Costly When Bloggers Bad-Mouth Jobs. *Washington Post*, February 11, A01. Accessed October 24, 2006 from http://www.washingtonpost.com/wp-dyn/articles/A15511-2005Feb10.html.

Kafka, J. 2007. Show Us the Money. *Forbes*, February 12. Accessed February 16, 2007 from http://www.forbes.com/free_forbes/2007/0212/086c.html.

Kandra, A., and Brant, A. 2003. Great American Privacy Makeover. *PC World*, October 8. Accessed August 6, 2007 from http:www.pcworld.com/howto/article/0,aid,112468,00.asp.

Kang, J. 1998. Information Privacy in Cyberspace Transactions. *Stanford Law Review* 50(4): 1193–1294.

Katz, J. 2007. RFID Gains Credibility. *Industry Week* (January): 35.

Katz v. United States. 1967. 389 U.S. 347, 361.

Kerr, I. 2001. The Legal Relationship Between Online Service Providers and Users. *Canadian Business Law Journal* 35: 1–40.

Kerr, I. 2005. If Left to Their Own Devices . . . How DRM and Anti-Circumvention Laws Can Be Used to Hack Privacy. In *In the Public Interest: The Future of Canadian Copyright Law*, ed. Michael Geist. Toronto: Irwin Law, 167–210.

Kerr, I., and Bailey, J. 2004. The Implications of Digital Rights Management for Privacy and Freedom of Expression. *Information, Communication and Ethics in Society* 2(1): 87–94.

Kerr, O. S. 2008. Updating the Foreign Intelligence Surveillance Act. *University of Chicago Law Review* 75 (Winter): 225–243.

Kerr, O. S. 2009. The Limits of Fourth Amendment Injunctions. *Journal on Telecommunications and High Technology Law*. Available at Social Science Research Network (SSRN): http://papers.ssrn.com/sol3/papers.cfm?abstract_id=1147798.

Kingsley, S. 1951. *Darkness at Noon*. New York: Random House.

Koestler, A. 1941. *Darkness at Noon*. D. Hardy, trans. New York: The Modern Library.

Krane, D., Light, L., and Gravitch, D. 2002. Privacy On and Off the Internet: What Consumers Want. Harris Interactive, Study No. 15229, February 7. Accessed July 31, 2008 from http://www.aicpa.org/download/webtrust/priv_rpt_21mar02.pdf.

Kubik, J. 2001. Nude Olympics: A Possibly True and Highly Plausible History of the Princeton Nude Olympics. *Princetoniana Committee Home Page*, December 1. Accessed June 15, 2007 from http://tigernet.princeton.edu/~ptoniana/nude.asp.

Kusserow, R. 1983. Fighting Fraud, Waste, and Abuse. *Bureaucrat* 12(3): 19–22.

Kyllo v. United States. 2001. 533 U.S. 27, 34, 40.

LaFave, W. R. 1996. *Search and Seizure: A Treatise on the Fourth Amendment*. St. Paul, MN: West Publishing.

Larson, C. 2007. In Elder Care, Signing on Becomes a Way to Drop By. *New York Times*, February 4. Accessed June 13, 2007 from http://www.nytimes.com/2007/02/04/business/yourmoney/04elder.html.

Latour, B. 1992. Where Are the Missing Masses? Sociology of a Door. In *Shaping Technology/Building Society*, ed. W. E. Bijker and J. Law. Cambridge, MA: MIT Press, 225–259.

Laudon, K. 1986. *Dossier Society: Value Choices in the Design of National Information Systems*. New York: Columbia University Press.

Laudon, K. 1996. Markets and Privacy. *Communications of the ACM* 39(9): 92–104.

Lessig, L. 1999. *Code and Other Laws of Cyberspace*. New York: Basic Books.

Levin, C., and Ury, C. 2003. Welcoming Big Brother: The Malaise of Confidentiality in the Therapeutic Culture. In *Confidential Relationships: Psychoanalytic, Ethical, and Legal Contexts*, ed. C. M. Koggel, A. Furlong, and C. Levin. Amsterdam: Rodopi, 61–79.

LexisNexis. 2007. Home page. *LexisNexis.com*. Accessed May 27, 2007 from http://www.lexisnexis.com/default.asp.

Leyden, J. 2004. Barcelona Nightclub Chips Customers. *The Register*, May 19. Accessed June 13, 2007 from http://www.theregister.co.uk/2004/05/19/veripay/.

Librarica, LLC. 2007. CASSIE–PC Access Control, Patron Authentication, Print Management, Reservations and Waiting Lists, and Statistics. *Librarica.com*. Accessed September 1, 2007 from http://www.librarica.com.

Lichtblau, E. 2008. Senate Approves Bill to Broaden Wiretap Powers. *New York Times*, July 11. Accessed July 28, 2008 from http://www.nytimes.com/2008/07/10/washington/10fisa.html.

Lichtblau, E., and Risen, D. 2005. Spy Agency Mined Vast Data Trove, Officials Report. *New York Times*, December 24. Accessed July 12, 2007 from http://www.nytimes.com/2005/12/24/politics/24spy.html.

Lichtblau, E., and Shane, S. 2006. Report Questions Legal Basis for Bush's Spying Program. *New York Times*, January 6. Accessed July 17, 2007 from http://www.nytimes.com/2006/01/06/politics/06cnd-nsa.html.

Linden, G., Smith, B., and York, J. 2003. Amazon.com Recommendations: Item-to-Item Collaborative Filtering. *Internet Computing, IEEE* 7(1): 76–80.

Litman, J. 2001. *Digital Copyright: Protecting Intellectual Property on the Internet*. Buffalo, NY: Prometheus Books.

Lobron, A. 2006. Googling Your Friday-Night Date May or May Not Be Snooping, but It Won't Let You Peek Inside Any Souls. *Boston Globe Magazine*, February 5, 42.

Locke, J. 1690. *The Second Treatise of Civil Government*. Reprint, ed. T. Peardon, New York: Macmillan, 1986.

Losowsky, A. 2004. I've Got You Under My Skin. *The Guardian*, June 10. Accessed June 13, 2007 from http://technology.guardian.co.uk/online/story/0,3605,1234827,00.html.

Louis Harris & Associates. 1990. *Harris Poll No. 892049*. New York: Louis Harris & Associates.

Louis Harris & Associates and Westin, A. F. 1990. *The Equifax Report on Consumers in the Information Age*. New York: Louis Harris & Associates.

Louis Harris & Associates and Westin, A. F. 1992. *Equifax-Harris Consumer Privacy Survey 1992*. New York: Louis Harris & Associates.

Louis Harris & Associates and Westin, A. F. 1998. *Privacy Concerns & Consumer Choice*. Sponsored by Ameritech and Privacy & American Business. Hackensack, NJ: Privacy and American Business, December.

Lyon, D. 2003. *Surveillance as Social Sorting: Privacy, Risk and Digital Discrimination*. New York: Routledge.

Lyon, D. 2007. *Surveillance Studies: An Overview*. Cambridge: Polity Press.

Mann, S. 2004. Sousveillance: Inverse Surveillance in Multimedia Imaging. In *Proceedings of the 12th Annual ACM International Conference on Multimedia*, New York, October 10–15. New York: ACM Press, 620–627. Accessed March 12, 2006 from http://www.eyetap.org/papers/docs/acmmm2004sousveillance_ p620-mann/.

Markoff, J. 2006. Study Says Chips in ID Tags Are Vulnerable to Viruses. *New York Times*, March 15, C3. Accessed June 13, 2007 from http://www.nytimes.com/2006/ 03/15/technology/15tag.html.

Martin, J. L. 2003. What Is Field Theory? *American Journal of Sociology* 109(1): 1–49.

Marx, G. T. 1988. *Undercover: Police Surveillance in America*. Berkeley: University of California Press.

Mauger, J. 2003. Public, Private. In *Confidential Relationships: Psychoanalytic, Ethical, and Legal Contexts*, ed. C. M. Koggel, A. Furlong, and C. Levin. Amsterdam: Rodopi, 53–60.

Mayer, C. 2005. ChoicePoint Victims Have Work Ahead: Eternal Vigilance Is Price of Credit. *Washington Post*, February 23. Accessed June 13, 2007 from http://www .washingtonpost.com/wp-dyn/articles/A45534-2005Feb22.html.

Megan's Law. 1999. Title 42 U.S. Code, sec. 14071. Amendment to the Jacob Wetterling Crimes Against Children and Sexually Violent Offender Registration Act, 1994.

Mehta, S. 2006. O.C. Boy's Web Threat Could Draw Expulsion. *Los Angeles Times*, March 3.

Meingast, M., King, J., and Mulligan, D. 2007. Embedded RFID and Everyday Things: A Case Study of the Security and Privacy Risks of the U.S. e-Passport. *IEEE International Conference on RFID* (March). Accessed August 26, 2008 from http:// www.truststc.org/pubs/157.html.

Mill, J. S. 1859. *On Liberty*. Reprint, Indianapolis, IN: Hackett Publishing Company, 1978.

Millar v. Taylor. 1769. 4 Burr. 2303, 98 Eng. Rep. 201.

Miller, A. 1972. *The Assault on Privacy*. New York: Signet Books.

Miller, S. 2001. *Social Action: A Teleological Account*. Cambridge: Cambridge University Press.

Mills, E. 2005. Google Balances Privacy, Reach. *CnET News.com*, August 3. Accessed January 7, 2007 from http://news.com.com/Google+balances+privacy,+reach/ 2100-1032_3-5787483.html.

Moore, J. 2005. RFID's Positive Identification: Wireless ID Apps Gaining Foothold Beyond the Military. *Federal Computer Week.com*, April 18. Accessed March 12, 2006 from http://www.fcw.com/article88603-04-18-05-Print.

Mulligan, D., Han, J., and Burstein, A. 2003. How DRM-Based Content Delivery Systems Disrupt Expectations of "Personal Use." In *Proceedings of the 2003 ACM Workshop on Digital Rights Management*, Washington, DC, October 27. New York: ACM Press, 77–89.

Murphy, D. 2008. Technology that Exposes Your Dirty Linen. *Sydney Morning Herald*, January 7, 1.

Nagel, T. 1979. The Fragmentation of Value. In *Mortal Questions*. Cambridge: Cambridge University Press, 128–141.

Naone, E. 2008. Maintaining Multiple Personas Online: A New Site Lets Users Create Profiles for the Different Sides of Their Personality. *Technology Review*, February 11. Accessed May 7, 2008 from http://www.technologyreview.com/Infotech/20183/page1/?a=f.

National Association of State Chief Information Officers (NASCIO). 2004. Think Before You Dig: The Privacy Implications of Data Mining & Aggregation. *NASCIO .org* (September). Accessed May 10, 2008 from http://www.nascio.org/publications/documents/NASCIO-dataMining.pdf.

Nehf, J. P. 2003. Recognizing the Societal Value in Information Privacy. *Washington Law Review* 78: 1–91.

Nissenbaum, H. 1997. Toward an Approach to Privacy in Public: The Challenges of Information Technology. *Ethics and Behavior* 7(3): 207–219.

Nissenbaum, H. 1998. Protecting Privacy in an Information Age: The Problem of Privacy in Public. *Law and Philosophy* 17: 559–596. http://www.nyu.edu/projects/nissenbaum/papers/privacy.pdf.

Norman, D. A. 2002. *The Design of Everyday Things*. New York: Basic Books.

O'Connor, M. C. 2007. One Year Later, US E-passport Architect Says System Is a Success. *RFID Journal*, August 16. Accessed July 28, 2008 from http://www.rfidjournal .com/article/articleview/3567/1/1/.

Odlyzko, A. M. 2003. Privacy, Economics, and Price Discrimination on the Internet. In *ICEC2003: Fifth International Conference on Electronic Commerce*, ed. N. Sadeh. New York: ACM Press, 355–366. Accessed February 15, 2008 from http://www.dtc .umn.edu/~odlyzko/doc/privacy.economics.pdf.

Olmstead v. United States. 1928. 277 U.S. 438.

Olsen, S. 2007. At Rapleaf, Your Personals Are Public. *CNET News.com*, August 31. Accessed February 28, 2008 from http://www.news.com/At-Rapleaf,-your -personals-are-public/2100-1038_3-6205716.html.

Olson, J. S., Grudin, J., and Horvitz, E. 2004. Toward Understanding Preferences for Sharing and Privacy. *MSR Technical Report 2004-138*. ftp://ftp.research.microsoft .com/pub/tr/TR-2004-138.pdf.

Olson, J. S., Grudin, J., and Horvitz, E. 2005. A Study of Preferences for Sharing and Privacy. Paper presented at the CHI'05 Extended Abstracts on ACM SIGCHI Conference on Human Factors in Computing Systems, Portland, OR, April 2–7. New York: ACM Press.

Organization for Economic Cooperation and Development (OECD). 1980. Guidelines on the Protection of Privacy and Transborder Flows of Personal Data. September 23. Accessed July 31, 2008 from http://www.oecd.org/document/18/0,3343,en_2649 _34255_1815186_1_1_1_1,00.html.

Orwell, G. 1949. *Nineteen Eighty-Four*. Reprint, London: Penguin Books, 1990.

Parent, W. 1983. Privacy, Morality, and the Law. *Philosophy and Public Affairs* 12(5): 269–288.

Parfit, D. 1986. *Reasons and Persons*. Oxford: Oxford University Press.

Pepper, S. 1958. *The Sources of Value*. Berkeley: University of California Press.

Pet-ID. 2006. About Pet-ID. *Pet-ID.net*. Accessed March 12, 2006 from http://www.pet-id.net/whatispetid.htm.

Phillips, D. J. 2003. Beyond Privacy: Confronting Locational Surveillance in Wireless Communication. *Communication Law and Policy* 8(1): 1–23.

Pierce, D., and Ackerman, L. 2005. Data Aggregators: A Study of Data Quality and Responsiveness. *PrivacyActivism.org*. http://www.privacyactivism.org/Item/222.

Posner, R. A. 1978a. An Economic Theory of Privacy. *Regulation* (May/June): 19–26.

Posner, R. A. 1978b. The Right of Privacy. *Georgia Law Review* 12(3): 393–422.

Post, R. C. 1989. The Social Foundations of Privacy: Community and Self in the Common Law Tort. *California Law Review* 77(5): 957–1010.

Powers, M. 1996. A Cognitive Access Definition of Privacy. *Law and Philosophy* 15: 369–386.

Priest, L. 2008. A Security Blanket for Babies—And Parents; Computerized Identification Tags Worn by Mother and Child Help Prevent the Abduction of Infants from Hospitals. *The Globe and Mail*, January 24, A10.

The Privacy Act of 1974. 1974. 5 U.S. Code, sec. 552a.

Privacy Rights Clearinghouse/UCAN. 2006. Online Data Vendors and Information Brokers: How to Opt Out. *Privacy Rights Clearinghouse*, November. Accessed June 22, 2007 from http://www.privacyrights.org/ar/infobrokers-no-optout.htm.

Privacy Rights Clearinghouse/UCAN. 2007a. A Chronology of Data Breaches. *Privacy Rights Clearinghouse*, June 21. Accessed June 22, 2007 from http://www.privacyrights.org/ar/ChronDataBreaches.htm.

Privacy Rights Clearinghouse/UCAN. 2007b. How Many Identity Theft Victims Are There? *Privacy Rights Clearinghouse*, June. Accessed July 9, 2007 from http://www.privacyrights.org/ar/idtheftsurveys.htm.

Prosser, W. 1960. Privacy. *California Law Review* 48(3): 383–423. Reprinted in *Philosophical Dimensions of Privacy: An Anthology*, ed. F. Schoeman. Cambridge: Cambridge University Press, 1984, 104–155.

Public Welfare and Human Services. 2003. 45 Code of Federal Regulations 164.102–535. http://www.access.gpo.gov/nara/cfr/waisidx_02/45cfr164_02.html.

Rachels, J. 1975. Why Privacy Is Important. *Philosophy & Public Affairs* 4(4): 323–333.

Radin, M. J., Chander, A., and Gellman, L. 2007. *Securing Privacy in the Internet Age*. Stanford, CA: Stanford University Press.

Radio Silence. 2007. *The Economist* (Technology Quarterly), June 9.

Radwanski, G. 2003. PIPED Act Case Summary #15: Privacy Commissioner Releases His Finding on the Prescribing Patterns of Doctors. *Office of the Privacy Commission of Canada*, November 6. Accessed August 7, 2008 from http://www.privcom.gc.ca/media/an/wn_011002_e.asp.

Ramasastry, A. 2005. Tracking Every Move You Make: Can Car Rental Companies Use Technology to Monitor Our Driving? A Connecticut Court's Ruling

Highlights an Important Question. *Findlaw News*, August 23. Accessed October 3, 2006 from http://writ.news.findlaw.com/ramasastry/20050823.html.

Raz, J. 1975. *Practical Reason and Norms*. Oxford: Oxford University Press.

Regan, P. 1995. *Legislating Privacy*. Chapel Hill: University of North Carolina Press.

Reidenberg, J. R. 2003. Privacy Wrongs in Search of Remedies. *Hastings Law Journal* 54(4): 877–898.

Reiman, J. 1976. Privacy, Intimacy and Personhood. *Philosophy and Public Affairs* 6(1): 26–44.

Reiman, J. 1995. Driving to the Panopticon: A Philosophical Exploration of the Risks to Privacy Posed by the Highway Technology of the Future. *Santa Clara Computer and High Technology Law Journal* 11(1): 27–44.

Reno v. American Civil Liberties Union. 1997. 521 U.S. 844.

Resnicow, H. 1983. *The Gold Solution*. New York: St. Martin's Press.

Richardson, H. 1990. Specifying Norms as a Way to Resolve Concrete Ethical Problems. *Philosophy & Public Affairs* 19: 279–310.

Right to Financial Privacy Act of 1978. 1978. Title 12 United States Code, Chapter 35, secs. 3401–3422.

Rosen, J. 2000. *The Unwanted Gaze: The Destruction of Privacy in America*. New York: Random House.

Rosen, J. 2004. *The Naked Crowd: Reclaiming Security and Freedom in an Anxious Age*. New York: Random House.

Rotenberg, M. 1992. Protecting Privacy. *Communications of the ACM* 35(4): 164.

Rotenberg, M. 1998. Testimony and Statement for the Record of Marc Rotenberg. Director, Electronic Privacy Information Center Adjunct Professor, Georgetown University Law Center on the European Union Data Directive and Privacy Before the Committee on International Relations, U.S. House of Representatives, May 7, 1998. *Epic.org*. Accessed August 20, 2008 from http://epic.org/privacy/intl/rotenberg-eu-testimony-598.html.

Rotenberg, M., ed. 2004. *The Privacy Law Sourcebook 2004: United States Law, International Law, and Recent Developments*. Washington, DC: Electronic Privacy Information Center.

Rousseau, J.-J. 1762. *The Social Contract*. Reprint, ed. M. Cranston, Harmondsworth, UK: Penguin Books, 1968.

Rubin, A. D. 2006. *Brave New Ballot: The Battle to Safeguard Democracy in the Age of Electronic Voting*. New York: Broadway.

Rubinstein, I., Lee, R. D., and Schwartz, P. M. 2008. Data Mining and Internet Profiling: Emerging Regulatory and Technological Approaches. *University of Chicago Law Review* 75: 261–285.

Rule, J. 1973. *Private Lives and Public Surveillance*. New York: Random House.

Rule, J. 1980. Preserving Individual Autonomy in an Information-Oriented Society. In *Computer Privacy in the Next Decade*, ed. L. Hoffman. New York: Atheneum, 65–87.

Rule, J., McAdam, D., Stearns, L., and Uglow, D. 1983. Documentary Identification and Mass Surveillance in the United States. *Social Problems* 31(2): 222–234.

Sanger, D. E. 2006. Restoring a Constitutional Balance. *New York Times*, July 14, A15.

Schank, R. C., and Abelson, R. P. 1977. *Scripts, Plans, Goals and Understanding: An Inquiry into Human Knowledge Structures.* Hillsdale, NJ: Lawrence Erlbaum.

Schatzki, T. 2001. Practice Mind-ed Orders. In *The Practice Turn in Contemporary Theory,* ed. T. R. Schatzki, K. K. Cetina, and E. von Savingny. London: Routledge, 42–55.

Schmidt, T. S. 2006. Inside the Backlash Against Facebook. *Time.com*, September 6. Accessed November 4, 2006 from http://www.time.com/time/nation/article/ 0,8599,1532225,00.htm.

Schneier, B. 2006. The ID Chip You Don't Want in Your Passport. *Washington Post,* September 16, A21. Accessed June 13, 2007 from http://www.washingtonpost.com/ wp-dyn/content/article/2006/09/15/AR2006091500923.html.

Schoeman, F. 1984. Privacy and Intimate Information. In *Philosophical Dimensions of Privacy: An Anthology,* ed. F. Schoeman. Cambridge: Cambridge University Press, 403–418.

Schroeder, S. 2007. Top 15 Google Street View Sightings. *Mashable.com,* May 31. Accessed June 14, 2007 from http://mashable.com/2007/05/31/top-15-google-street -view-sightings/.

Schwartz, J. 2001. Giving the Web a Memory Cost Its Users Privacy. *New York Times,* September 4. Accessed June 13, 2007 from http://query.nytimes.com/gst/ fullpage.html?sec=technology&res=9B0DE1D61639F937A3575AC0A9679 C8B63.

Schwartz, P. 1999. Privacy and Democracy in Cyberspace. *Vanderbilt Law Review* 52: 1609–1701.

Schwartz, P. 2000. Free Speech vs. Information Privacy: Eugene Volokh's First Amendment Jurisprudence. *Stanford Law Review* 52: 1559–1572. http://ssrn.com/ abstract=248415.

Schwartz, P. 2004. Property, Privacy, and Personal Data. *Harvard Law Review* 117(7): 2055–2128.

Schweitzer, S. 2005. When Students Open Up—A Little Too Much. *Boston Globe,* September 26. Accessed June 15, 2007 from http://www.boston.com/news/local/ articles/2005/09/26/when_students_open_up____a_little_too_much/.

Searle, J. 1995. *The Construction of Social Reality.* New York: The Free Press.

Sharma, M. 2007. Social Networking God: 350+ Social Networking Sites. *Mashable .com: Social Networking News,* October 23. Accessed May 7, 2008 from http:// mashable.com/2007/10/23/social-networking-god/.

Shattuck, J. 1984. In the Shadow of 1984: National Computer Identification Systems, Computer-Matching, and Privacy in the United States. *Hastings Law Journal* 35: 991–1005.

Singel, R. 2007. Which ISPs Are Spying on You? *Wired News*, May 30. Accessed June 4, 2007 from http://www.wired.com/politics/onlinerights/news/2007/05/isp_privacy.

Slevin, P. 2001. Police Video Cameras Taped Football Fans. *Washington Post*, February 1, A01.

Smith, E. 2008. Experiencing Surveillance in the Airport: The Globalization of Personal Data Survey and Traveler Perspectives on Visibility. Paper presented at Hixon Riggs Forum on Science and Society, Harvey Mudd College, Claremont, CA, March 27–28.

Smith, L., and Benko, M. 2007. Electronic Toll Collection. *Intelligent Transportation Systems Decision*. The Institute of Transportation Studies at the University of California at Berkeley and Caltrans, June 20. Accessed July 28, 2008 from http://www.calccit.org/itsdecision/serv_and_tech/Electronic_toll_collection/electron_toll_collection_report.html.

The Smoking Gun. 2008. Google: "Complete Privacy Does Not Exist." *The Smoking Gun*, July 30. Accessed July 30, 2008 from http://www.thesmokinggun.com/archive/years/2008/0730081google1.html.

Software Personalizes Advertising to Web Surfer. 2007. *ThomasNet Industrial News Room*, January 5. Accessed February 1, 2007 from http://news.thomasnet.com/fullstory/503824.

Solove, D. 2002a. Access and Aggregation: Privacy, Public Records, and the Constitution. *Minnesota Law Review* 86(6): 1137–1209.

Solove, D. 2002b. Digital Dossiers and the Dissipation of Fourth Amendment Privacy. *Southern California Law Review* 75: 1083–1167.

Solove, D. 2004. *The Digital Person: Technology and Privacy in the Information Age*. New York: New York University Press.

Solove, D. 2006. A Taxonomy of Privacy. *University of Pennsylvania Law Review* 154(3): 477–564.

Solove, D., and Rotenberg, M. 2003. *Information Privacy Law*. New York: Aspen Publishers.

Spying on Americans. 2007. Editorial, *New York Times*, May 2. Accessed July 16, 2007 from http://www.nytimes.com/2007/05/02/opinion/02wed1.html.

Stephen, J. F. 1873. *Liberty, Equality, Fraternity*. London: Smith & Elder.

Stone, M. A. 1999. Princeton Students Grin and Bear It. *Packet OnLine*, January 9. Accessed June 15, 2007 from http://www.pacpubserver.com/new/news/1-9-99/nude.html.

Strahilevitz, L. J. 2007. *Reputation Nation: Law in an Era of Ubiquitous Personal Information*. University of Chicago, John M. Olin Law & Economics Working Paper No. 371, Public Law and Legal Theory Working Paper No. 190, November.

Strandburg, K. J. 2005. Privacy, Rationality, and Temptation: A Theory of Willpower Norms. *Rutgers Law Review* 57: 1237.

Stross, R. 2005. Google Anything, So Long as It's Not Google. *New York Times*, August 28. Accessed January 7, 2007 from http://www.nytimes.com/2005/08/28/technology/28digi.html.

Sullivan, L. 2006. RFID World Still Reacting Strongly to Virus Research. *Information Week*, March 16. Accessed June 13, 2007 from http://www.informationweek.com/security/showArticle.jhtml?articleID=183700423&subSection=Cybercrime.

Swidey, N. 2003. A Nation of Voyeurs: How the Internet Search Engine Google Is Changing What We Can Find Out About One Another—And Raising Questions About Whether We Should. *Boston Globe Sunday Magazine*, February 2, 10.

Swire, P. 2002. The Surprising Virtues of the New Financial Privacy Law. *Minnesota Law Review* 86: 1263–1323.

Swire, P. 2003. Trustwrap: The Importance of Legal Rules for E-Commerce and Internet Privacy. *Hastings Law Journal* 54: 847, 859–871.

Taipale, K. A. 2006. Whispering Wires and Warrantless Wiretaps: Data Mining and Foreign Intelligence Surveillance. *NYU Review of Law & Security*, no. 7, Supplemental Bulletin on Law and Security: *The NSA and the War on Terror* (Spring). Accessed June 22, 2007 from http://whisperingwires.info.

Taurek, J. 1977. Should the Numbers Count? *Philosophy and Public Affairs* 6: 293–316.

Tavani, H. T. 1999. Informational Privacy, Data Mining, and the Internet. *Ethics and Information Technology* 1(2): 137–145.

Tavani, H. T. 2005. Search Engines, Personal Information, and the Problem of Protecting Privacy in Public. *International Review of Information Ethics* 3: 40–45.

Tavani, H. T., and Moor, J. 2001. Privacy Protection, Control of Information, and Privacy-Enhancing Technologies. *Computers and Society* 31(1): 6–11.

Texas Instruments, Inc. 2007. Animal Tracking. *T-RFID & Contactless Commerce, Technology for Innovators*. Accessed June 11, 2007 from http://www.ti.com/rfid/shtml/apps-anim-tracking.shtml.

TexasOnline. 2007. *TexasOnline: Texas at Your Fingertips*. Accessed October 19, 2006 from http://www.state.tx.us/.

Trans Union v. Federal Trade Commission. 2001. No. 00-1141 (D.C. Circuit Court). http://pacer.cadc.uscourts.gov/common/opinions/200104/00-1141a.txt.

Troshynski, E., Lee, C., and Dourish, P. 2008. Accountabilities of Presence: Reframing Location-Based Systems. In *Proceedings of the ACM Conference on Human Factors in Computing Systems, CHI 2008*, Florence, Italy. New York: ACM Press, 487–496.

TRUSTe and TNS. 2006. Consumers Have False Sense of Security About Online Privacy—Actions Inconsistent with Attitudes. *TRUSTe/TNS Online Privacy Survey*, December 6, San Francisco, CA. Accessed August 6, 2007 from http://www.truste.org/about/press_release/12_06_06.php.

Tsai, J., Egelman, S., Cranor, L., and Acquisti, A. 2007. The Effect of Online Privacy Information on Purchasing Behavior: An Experimental Study. Paper presented at The 6th Workshop on the Economics of Information Security (WEIS), Carnegie Mellon University, Pittsburgh, PA.

Turkington, R., and Allen, A. 2002. *Privacy Law: Cases and Materials*. St. Paul, MN: West Group Publishing.

Turow, J. 2003. *Americans and Online Privacy: The System Is Broken*. Annenberg Public Policy Center of the University of Pennsylvania, June. http://www.asc.upenn.edu/usr/jturow/internet-privacy-report/36-page-turow-version-9.pdf.

Turow, J., Feldman, L., and Meltzer, K. 2005. *Open to Exploitation: American Shoppers Online and Offline*. Annenberg Public Policy Center of the University of Pennsylvania, June 1. http://www.annenbergpublicpolicycenter.org/Downloads/Information_And_Society/Turow_APPC_Report_WEB_FINAL.pdf.

Uniting and Strengthening America by Providing Appropriate Tools Required to Intercept and Obstruct Terrorism Act of 2001 (USA PATRIOT Act). 2001. Pub. L. No. 107-56, 115 Stat. 272.

U.S. Bill of Rights. 1789. General Records of the U.S. Government; Record Group 11; National Archives, September 25.

U.S. Department of Defense v. Fair Labor Relations Authority. 1994. 510 U.S. 487.

U.S. Department of Health, Education, & Welfare. 1973. *Records, Computers, and the Rights of Citizens*. Report of the Secretary's Advisory Committee on Automated Personal Data Systems, July. http://aspe.hhs.gov/datacncl/1973privacy/tocprefacemembers.htm.

U.S. Food and Drug Administration. 2004. Radiofrequency Identification Feasibility Studies and Pilot Programs for Drugs. *Report of the U.S. Food and Drug Administration*, November, Sec. 400.210.

Van den Hoven, J. 2001. Privacy and the Varieties of Informational Wrongdoing. In *Readings in CyberEthics*, ed. R. A. Spinello and H. T. Tavani. Sudbury, MA: Jones and Bartlett Publishers, 488–500.

Vara, V. 2006. MySpace and Facebook Rivals Are Growing. *Wall Street Journal*, October 2.

Verichip Corporation. 2006. Verichip: RFID for People. *Verichipcorp.com*. Accessed June 11, 2007 from http://www.verichipcorp.com/.

Video Privacy Protection Act of 1988. 2002. Title 18 U.S. Code, sec. 2710.

Volokh, E. 2000a. Freedom of Speech and Information Privacy: The Troubling Implications of a Right to Stop People from Speaking About You. *Stanford Law Review* 52: 1049–1124.

Volokh, E. 2000b. Personalization and Privacy. *Communications of the ACM* 43(8): 84–88.

Von Staden, H. 1996. In a Pure and Holy Way: Personal and Professional Conduct in the Hippocratic Oath. *Journal of the History of Medicine and Allied Sciences* 51(4): 404–437.

Von Wright, G. H. 1963. *Norm and Action*. New York: Humanities Press.

Vora, P., Reynolds, D., Dickinson, I., Erickson, J., and Banks, D. 2001. Privacy and Digital Rights Management. Paper presented at W3C Workshop on Digital Rights Management, January 22–23. Accessed June 11, 2007 from http://www.w3.org/2000/12/drm-ws/pp/hp-poorvi2.html.

Wacks, R. 1989. *Personal Information: Privacy and the Law*. Oxford: Clarendon Press.

Waldo, J., Lin, H. S., and Millett, L. I., eds. 2007. *Engaging Privacy and Information Technology in a Digital Age*. Committee on Privacy in the Information Age, National Research Council. Washington, DC: National Academies Press.

Walzer, M. 1984. *Spheres of Justice: A Defense of Pluralism and Equality*. New York: Basic Books.

Warren, S., and Brandeis, L. 1890. The Right to Privacy (The Implicit Made Explicit). In *Philosophical Dimensions of Privacy: An Anthology*, ed. F. D. Schoeman. Cambridge, MA: Harvard Law Review, 193–220.

Weber, M. 1946. Religious Rejections of the World and Their Directions. In *Max Weber: Essays in Sociology*, ed. H. H. Gerth and C. W. Mills. New York: Oxford University Press.

Weckert, J., ed. 2004. *Electronic Monitoring in the Workplace: Controversies and Solutions*. Hershey, PA: IGI Global.

Weier, M. H. 2007. RFID Tags Are on the Menu: Tracking Technology Will Improve Food Safety and Lower Costs. *InformationWeek*, February 5, 49.

Weiss, P. 2006. What a Tangled Web We Weave: Being Googled Can Jeopardize Your Job Search. *New York Daily News*, March 19.

Westin, A. 1967. *Privacy and Freedom*. New York: Atheneum.

Westin, A. 2003. Social and Political Dimensions of Privacy. *Journal of Social Issues* 59(2): 439–451.

Wikipedia Contributors. 2006a. List of Social Networking Websites. In *Wikipedia, The Free Encyclopedia*. Accessed October 20, 2006 from http://en.wikipedia.org/wiki/List_of_social networking_websites.

Wikipedia Contributors. 2006b. Jennicam. In *Wikipedia, The Free Encyclopedia*. Accessed June 23, 2006 from http://en.wikipedia.org/w/index.php?title=Jenni Cam.

Wikipedia Contributors. 2007a. Electronic Toll Collection. In *Wikipedia, The Free Encyclopedia*. Accessed June 10, 2007 from http://en.wikipedia.org/w/index.php?title=Electronic_toll_collection&oldid=130665055.

Wikipedia Contributors. 2007b. Caller ID. In *Wikipedia, The Free Encyclopedia*. Accessed October 10, 2007 from http://en.wikipedia.org/w/index.php?title=Caller_ID&oldid=163254952.

Wilkinson, A. 2007. Remember This? A Project to Record Everything We Do in Life. *The New Yorker*, May 28, 38–44.

Winn, P. 2004. Online Court Records: Balancing Judicial Accountability and Privacy in an Age of Electronic Information. *Washington Law Review* 79: 307–330.

Winn, P. 2008. On-Line Access to Court Records. Paper presented at Privacy Law Scholars Conference, George Washington University Law School, Washington, DC, June 12–13.

Winner, L. 1986. Do Artifacts Have Politics? In *The Whale and the Reactor*, ed. L. Winner. Chicago: University of Chicago Press, 19–39.

Wolfe, D. 2003. Nanotech on the Front Lines. *Forbes*, March 19. Accessed June 10, 2005 from http://www.forbes.com/2003/03/19/cz_jw_0319soapbox.html.

Wong, K. L. 2006. The NSA Terrorist Surveillance Program. *Harvard Journal on Legislation* 43(2): 517–534.

Wright, R. 2008. Privacy in a Networked World. In *Frontiers of Engineering: Reports on Leading-Edge Engineering from the 2007 Symposium*, National Academy of Engineering of the National Academies. Washington, DC: National Academies Press.

Wright, R., Yang, Z., and Zhong, S. 2005. Distributed Data Mining Protocols for Privacy: A Review of Some Recent Results. In *Proceedings of the Secure Mobile Ad-hoc Networks and Sensors Workshop* (MADNES'05). New York: Springer. Accessed June 4, 2009 from http://www.cs.rutgers.edu/~rebecca.wright/Publications/madnes05.pdf.

Zarsky, T. Z. 2002. "Mine Your Own Business!" Making the Case for the Implications of the Data Mining of Personal Information in the Forum of Public Opinion. *Yale Journal of Law and Technology* 5: 1–56. Accessed June 4, 2009 from http://research.yale.edu/lawmeme/yjolt/modules.php?name=News&file=categories&op=newindex&catid=7.

Zarsky, T. Z. 2004. Desperately Seeking Solutions: Using Implementation-Based Solutions for the Troubles of Information Privacy in the Age of Data Mining and the Internet Society. *Maine Law Review* 56(1): 13–59.

Zeller, T. 2006. Your Life as an Open Book. *New York Times*, August 12. Accessed June 11, 2007 from http://www.nytimes.com/2006/08/12/technology/12privacy.html.

Zetter, K. 2005. Driving Big Brother. *Wired News*, June 21. Accessed May 30, 2007 from http://www.wired.com/news/privacy/0,1848,67952,00.html.

Zimmer, M. 2005. Surveillance, Privacy and the Ethics of Vehicle Safety Communication Technologies. *Ethics and Information Technology* 7: 201–210.

Zimmer, M. 2007. *The Quest for the Perfect Search Engine: Values, Technical Design, and the Flow of Personal Information in Spheres of Mobility*. Unpublished PhD diss., New York University.

Zimmer, M. 2008a. Privacy on Planet Google: Using the Theory of "Contextual Integrity" to Expose the Privacy Threats of Google's Quest for the Perfect Search Engine. *Journal of Business & Technology Law* 3(2): 109–126.

Zimmer, M. 2008b. Privacy on the Roads: Mobility, Vehicle Safety Communication Technologies, and the Contextual Integrity of Personal Information Flows. In *Contours of Privacy*, ed. David Matheson, Newcastle, UK: Cambridge Scholars Publishing.

Zimmer, M. 2008c. Moli: Maintaining Multiple Personas Online, Sharing More Personal Information. *MichaelZimmer.org Blog*, February 11. Accessed May 7, 2008 from http://michaelzimmer.org/2008/02/11/moli-maintaining-multiple-personas-online-sharing-more-personal-information/.

Zimmer, M. 2008d. More on Moli, and Designing for Privacy. *MichaelZimmer.org Blog*, February 15. Accessed May 7, 2008 from http://michaelzimmer.org/2008/02/15/more-on-moli-and-designing-for-privacy/.

Zureik, E. 2006. International Surveillance and Privacy Opinion Research. *The Surveillance Project*, November 13. Accessed August 8, 2008 from http://www.surveil lanceproject.org/research/intl_survey.

Zureik, E., Stalker, L. L. H., Smith, E., Lyon, D., and Chan, Y. E., eds. 2008. *Privacy, Surveillance and the Globalization of Personal Information: International Comparisons*. Kingston: McGill–Queen's University Press.

Index